SO-AAZ-894

Patricia Smith's

DOLL VALUES

Antique to Modern

Tenth Edition

COLLECTOR BOOKS

A Division of Schroeder Publishing Co., Inc.

The current values in this book should be used only as a guide. They are not intended to set prices, which vary from one section of the country to another. Auction prices as well as dealer prices vary greatly and are affected by condition and demand. Neither the Author nor the Publisher assumes responsibility for any losses which might be incurred as a result of consulting this guide.

Searching For A Publisher?

We are always looking for knowledgeable people considered experts within their fields. If you feel that there is a real need for a book on your collectible subject and have a large comprehensive collection, contact us.

COLLECTOR BOOKS
P.O. Box 3009
Paducah, Kentucky 42002-3009

Additional copies of this book may be ordered from:

COLLECTOR BOOKS
P.O. Box 3009
Paducah, KY 42002-3009

@ $12.95 add $2.00 for postage and handling.

Copyright: Patricia Smith, 1994

This book or any part thereof may not be reproduced without the written consent of the Author and Publisher.

Printed by IMAGE GRAPHICS, INC., Paducah, Kentucky

CREDITS

Thanks to the following for helping to make this a much better book!

Gloria Anderson, Jan Aufiero, Sandy Johnson-Barts, Shirley Bertrand (Shirley's Doll House, P.O. Box 99, Wheeling, IL 60090), Margaret Bigger, Barbara Earnshaw-Cain, Jane Carlisle, Belinda Morse-Carpenter, Remie Culp, Marie Ernst, Ellen Dodge, Frasher Doll Auction (Rt. 1, Box 72, Oak Grove, MO 64075), Maureen Fukushima, Susan Girardot, Amanda Hash, Sharon Hamilton, Mike Head, Marcie Jarmush, Chris Johnson, Phyllis Houston-Kates, Ivy A. Koehn, Charlene Lopez, Kris Lundquist, Jeannie Mauldin, Claudia Meeker (Claudia's Collectibles, Box 52, Hollister, MO 65672), Don Meeker, Sandy McDowell, Ellen McCorkell, Marla McKesh, Arthur Michnevitz, Peggy Millhouse, June Murkins, Christine Perisho, Leslie Robinson, Nanette Ringer, Charmaine Shields, Ricki Small, Linda Smith (Lawton Doll Co., 548 North First Street, Turlock, CA 95380), Barbara Spears, Paul Spencer (1414 Cloverleaf, Waco, TX 76705), David Spurgeon, Pat Timmons, Betty Todd, Kathy and Don Tvrdik, Turn of Century Antiques (1421 Broadway, Denver, CO 80210), Marjorie Uhl, Greta Williams, Jane Walker, Chris McWilliams, Glorya Woods, Patricia Woods.

COVER PHOTO CREDIT

14" "Rapunzel" is one of the heroines from the "Fairy Tale Forest" sets. Very round open mouth and glass eyes. Original. Designed by Diana Effner for Knowles. $165.00.

8" "Yellow Bon Bon Ginny" made by Vogue in 1955. Excellent condition. $450.00. *Courtesy Peggy Millhouse.*

19" Limoges "Cherie" with set glass eyes and open mouth. On fully jointed French body. Incised "A.L. & C." $775.00. *Courtesy Turn of Century Antiques.*

PRICES

This book is divided into "Antique" and "Modern" sections, with the older dolls in the first section and the newer dolls in the second section. To make a quick reference, each section alphabetically lists the dollmaker, type of material or name of doll. (Example: Bye-Lo or Kewpie.) An index is provided for locating a specific doll.

In antique dolls, the uppermost concern is the condition of the head and body. It is also important for the body to be correct to the doll. An antique doll must be clean, nicely dressed and ready to place into a collection. It must have no need of any repair for it to bring book price. An all original doll with original clothes, marked shoes and original wig will bring a lot more than list price. Boxes are very rare and also will bring a higher price for the doll.

In modern dolls, the condition of the doll is the uppermost concern in pricing. An all original modern doll in excellent condition will bring a much higher price than listed in this price guide. A doll that is damaged, without original clothes, soiled and dirty, will bring far less than the top price listed. The cost of doll repairs and cleanup has soared, so it is wise to judge the damage and estimate the cost of repairs before you attempt to sell or buy a damaged doll. An excellent reference concerning storing and restoring is *Dolls – Preserve and Restore Your Collection* by Kathy Tvrdik (6415 S.W. 27th Street, Topeka, KS 66614).

For insurance reasons, it is very important to show the "retail" price of dolls in a price guide and to try to be as accurate as possible. The "retail" price can be referred to as "replacement cost" so that insurance companies or postal services can appraise a damaged or stolen doll for the insured, and the collectors can judge their own collections and purchase adequate amounts of insurance.

No one knows your collection better than yourself and in the end, when you consider a purchase, you must ask yourself if the doll is affordable to you and whether you want it enough to pay the price. You will buy the doll, or pass it up — it is as simple as that!

Prices shown are for dolls that are clean, undamaged, well-dressed and in overall excellent condition. Many prices are also listed for soiled, dirty, and redressed dolls.

ANTIQUE AND OLDER DOLLS

22" early turned head doll, $1,150.00; 23" glass eyed Parian, $2,500.00; 15½" Heubach "Baby Stewart" with intaglio eyes, $950.00; 14" C/M turned head doll with solid dome. Marked "151." $895.00; 20" unusual Parian with flowers in hair, $695.00; Bahr & Proschild boy, $595.00. *Courtesy Turn of Century Antiques.*

Henri Alexandre dolls were made from 1889 to 1891 only. The dolls have closed mouths with a white space between the lips, fat cheeks, and early French bodies with straight wrists. (Also see under "Phenix" section.)

18" - $6,800.00; 22" - $7,500.00; 25" - $7,900.00.

Mark:

H ⋈ A

ALL BISQUE – FRENCH

French all bisque dolls are jointed at the necks, shoulders and hips. They have slender arms and legs, glass eyes and most have kid-lined joints. Most of the heads have sliced pates with tiny cork inserts. French all-bisque dolls have finely painted features with outlined lips, well-tinted bisque, and feathered eyebrows. They can have molded-on shoes, high-top boots with painted toes, high-top buttoned boots with four or more painted straps. They can also be barefooted or just have stockings painted on the legs.

Any French bisque should be in very good condition, not have any chips, breaks, or hairline cracks to bring the following prices. Allow more for original clothes; less for damage or repairs.

Swivel Neck: (Socket head) Molded shoes or boots. 7" - $1,400.00; 7" repaired - $650.00; 8" - $2,200.00; 8" repaired - $975.00.

Bare Feet: 5" - $985.00; 8" - $1,600.00; 10" - $2,500.00.

With Jointed Elbows: 5½" - $2,200.00; 8½"" - $3,100.00.

With Jointed Elbows and Knees: 6" - $3,200.00; 8" - $3,950.00.

S.F.B.J., UNIS: Or other late French all bisques. Painted eyes. 5" - $465.00; 7" - $725.00.

Marked E.D., F.G.: Or other French makers. Glass eyes, bare feet. Allow more for original clothes. 7–8" - $2,400.00–2,600.00.

5" French all-bisque dolls with slim bodies and limbs. Kid-lined swivel necks, glass eyes, and closed mouths. Stockings to knees and two strap shoes. Original clothes. Each - $1,000.00 up. *Courtesy Shirley Bertrand.*

German-made all bisque dolls run from excellent to moderate quality. Prices are for excellent quality and condition with no chips, cracks, breaks or hairlines. Dolls should be nicely dressed and can have molded hair or wig. They generally have painted-on shoes and socks. Ca. 1880s–1930s.

French types: Slender dolls, socket head or one-piece body and head. Usually peg or wire jointed hips and shoulders, glass eyes, closed mouth. Molded boots or shoes; 1880s on. 4–5" - $285.00–365.00; 6–7" - $475.00–525.00.

Swivel neck, glass eyes: 1880–1910. Open or closed mouth, good wig, nicely dressed, painted-on shoes and socks. Allow more for unusual boot colors (orange, gold or yellow). 4½–5" - $325.00; 6" - $475.00; 7½" - $525.00; 9" - $750.00 up. **Jointed knees or elbows:** 6" - $1,850.00; 8" - $2,500.00. **Jointed knees or elbows, swivel waist:** 6" - $3,000.00. **Swivel waist only:** 6" - $2,000.00.

Swivel neck, painted eyes: Open or closed mouth, one-strap shoes and painted socks. Nice clothes and wig. 2" - $125.00; 4" - $185.00; 6" - $300.00; 8" - $425.00; 10" - $650.00 up.

One-piece body and head (sometimes also legs), glass eyes: 1880–1913. Excellent bisque, open or closed mouth with good wig and nicely dressed. Allow $50.00–75.00 more for unusual footwear such as yellow boots, multi-strap boots. 3" - $200.00; 5" - $300.00; 7" - $425.00; 9" - $675.00; 11" - $865.00. **Bent at knees:** 8" - $575.00; 11" - $750.00.

One-piece body and head (sometimes also legs), painted eyes: 1880–1913; 1921–1932. Open or closed mouth with good wig or molded hair and nicely dressed. 2½" - $85.00; 5" - $165.00; 6" - $200.00; 8" - $300.00; 10" - $600.00.

Pin-jointed boys with molded-on clothes. One-piece bodies and heads. All have pouty look. Marked "Made in Germany." 8" - $475.00; 5¾" - $350.00; 4½" - $200.00. *Courtesy Shirley Bertrand.*

Marked: 155, 156, 158, 162: Smiling, closed or open/closed mouth, glass eyes and swivel head. 5½" - $600.00; 7" - $800.00. Same, with one-piece body and head: 6" - $400.00; 7" - $500.00.

Molded-on Clothes or Underwear: Ca. 1890s. Jointed at shoulders only or at shoulders and hips. Molded hair, painted eyes, molded shoes or bare feet. **Excellent artist workmanship:** No cracks, chips or breaks. 4½" - $185.00; 6" - $350.00. (See photo in Series 5, pg. 11.) **Glass eyes:** 5" - $385.00; 7" - $475.00. **Medium to poor quality:** 3" - $75.00; 4" - $90.00; 6" - $140.00. **Molded Bonnet:** See listing in this section.

Marked: 100, 125, 161, 225: (Made by Alt, Beck and Gottschalck.) Closed mouth or open/closed, sleep or inset glass eyes, chubby body and limbs and molded-on one-strap shoes with painted socks. No chips, cracks or breaks. Has one-piece body and head: 5" - $200.00; 6½" - $285.00; 8" - $425.00; 10" - $625.00.

Marked 130, 150, 257, 602 with glass eyes: (Made by Kestner or Bonn.) One-piece body and head, painted-on one strap shoes with painted socks. Not damaged and nicely dressed. 4" - $225.00; 6" - $300.00; 7" - $375.00; 8" - $450.00; 9" - $625.00; 10" - $800.00; 11" - $1,100.00; 12" - $1,300.00.

Marked 130, 150, 160, 208, 602 with painted eyes: Kestner with jointed shoulders and hips. Open mouth, wigged, painted blue or pink stockings, black strap shoes. No damage and very good quality. 5" - $185.00; 6" - $265.00; 7" - $350.00; 9" - $600.00; 11" - $925.00; 12" - $1,100.00.

Marked 130, 150, 160, 208, 602: With swivel neck and glass eyes. 4" - $325.00; 6" - $400.00; 8" - $625.00; 9½" - $850.00.

Marked 184: Kestner, swivel neck, sweet face, glass eyes. Outlined, solid colored boots. 5" - $450.00; 8" - $700.00.

Molded Hair: One-piece body and head, painted eyes, painted-on shoes and socks. Excellent quality bisque and artist workmanship. No chips, cracks, and nicely dressed. 5½" - $145.00 up; 7" - $265.00 up.

Marked: 881, 886, 890: (Simon and Halbig or any all bisque marked S&H. Swivel neck, painted-on high-top boots with four or five straps. No damage and nicely dressed. 6 – 7" - $1,000.00; 8 – 9" - $1,450.00. **Painted stockings:** Above knees. 5½" - $700.00; 7½" - $1,000.00; 8½" - $1,200.00 up.

Black or Brown All Bisque: See Black Section.

Molded-on Hat or Bonnet: All in perfect condition. 5 – 6½" - $365.00 up; 8 – 9" - $500.00 up. **Stone (Porous) Bisque:** 4 – 5" - $135.00; 6 – 7" - $165.00.

With Long Stockings: To above the knees. Glass eyes, open or closed mouth. Jointed at neck. Stockings will be black, blue or green. Perfect condition. 4 – 5½" - $565.00; 6½ – 7" - $785.00.

Hertel, Schwab: See that section.

Flapper: One-piece body and head, thin limbs. Fired-in tinted bisque. Wig, painted eyes, painted-on long stockings, one-strap painted shoes. 6" - $400.00; 8" - $500.00. **Molded hair:** 6" - $350.00; 8" - $450.00. **Medium quality bisque/artist workmanship:** 5" - $150.00; 7 – 8" - $250.00.

Marked with maker: (S&H, JDK, A.B.G., mold #369. See photo in Series #9, pg. 9.) Closed mouth, early fine quality face. 8" - $1,100.00; 10" - $1,600.00 up. **Same, with open mouth:** Later quality bisque: 6" - $485.00; 8" - $750.00; 10" - $1,000.00. **K★R:** 8" - $1,250.00 up.

Pink Bisque: 1920s and 1930s. Jointed shoulders and hips with painted features, can have molded hair or wig. All in excellent condition: 2 – 3" - $35.00; 4 – 5½" - $50.00. **Bow loop in hair:** 3" - $40.00; 7" - $75.00.

Bathing Dolls: See that section.

Mold 415: Aviator with molded-on goggles and cap. 3½" - $225.00; 5" - $400.00; 7" - $525.00.

Immobilies: Figurines with no joints. **Child:** 3" - $30.00 up. **Adults:** 5" - $50.00 up. **Bride/groom cake top:** 6" - $365.00. **Santa:** 3½" - $165.00. **Child with animal on string:** 3½" - $125.00.

Wrestler: (So called.) Considered French. Fat thighs, bent arm at elbow, open mouth (can have two rows of teeth) or closed mouth, stocky body. Glass eyes, socket head, individual fingers or molded fists. **Painted boots:** (Multi-strapped, various colors) 6" - $1,000.00 up; 8" - $1,300.00 up; 9" - $1,800.00. **Bare feet:** 6" - $1,500.00; 9" - $2,300.00; 11" - $3,200.00. **Long painted stockings:** Above knees. 7" - $1,600.00; 9" - $1,900.00. **Jointed elbows and/or knees:** 6" - $1,750.00; 8" - $2,600.00 up.

All bisque babies were made in both Germany and Japan, and dolls from either country can be excellent quality or poor quality. Prices are for excellent painting and quality of bisque. There should be no chips, cracks, or breaks. Dressed or nude - 1900; bent limbs - after 1906.

Germany (Jointed necks, shoulders and hips): Wigs or painted hair. **Glass eyes:** 4" - $225.00; 5" - $285.00; 7" - $475.00; 9" - $725.00. **Painted eyes:** 3½" - $150.00; 5" - $175.00; 6½" - $300.00; 8½" - $475.00.

Germany (Jointed at shoulders and hips only): Well-painted features, free-formed thumbs and many have molded bottle in hand. Some have molded-on clothes. 3½" - $75.00; 5" - $125.00.

Germany (Character Baby): Jointed shoulders and hips, molded hair, painted eyes with character face. 4" - $175.00; 6" - $250.00. **Glass eyes:** 4" - $350.00; 6" - $450.00. **Mold #830, 833, and others:** 8" - $650.00 up; 11" - $1,200.00 up. **Swivel neck, glass eyes:** 6" - $675.00; 10" - $1,100.00 up.

Germany (Toddler): #369, 372. Jointed neck, glass eyes, perfect condition. 7" - $800.00; 9" - $1,200.00; 11" - $1,500.00 up.

"Candy Babies": (Can be either German or Japanese.) Ca. 1920s. Generally poorly painted with high bisque color. Were given away at candy counter with purchase. 4" - $35.00; 6" - $50.00.

Pink Bisque Baby: Ca. 1920s. Jointed at shoulders and hips, painted features and hair, bent baby legs. 2" - $20.00; 4" - $35.00; 8" - $95.00.

Mold #231: (A.M.) Toddler with open mouth, glass eyes. 9" - $1,600.00 up.

Standing: 7½" Kestner girl with one-piece body and head. Label on front. Glass sleep eyes, open mouth, original wig. Baby: 8" all bisque baby with Kestner label. Painted eyes, open/closed mouth. Delicate detail to modeling. In box: All original German all bisque with wardrobe. Swivel neck, painted eyes. 7½" $495.00; 8" - $800.00; In box - $395.00. *Courtesy Turn of Century Antiques.*

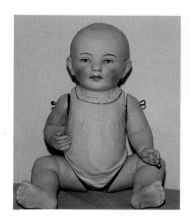

7" German baby with one-piece body and head. Pin-jointed hips and shoulders. Very unusual modeled-on clothes. Painted features. $475.00 up. *Courtesy Barbara Spears.*

All bisque dolls with character faces or stances were made both in Germany and Japan. The German dolls have finer bisque and workmanship of the painted features. Most bisque character dolls have jointed shoulders only, with some having joints at the hips. A very few have swivel heads. They can have molded-on shoes or be barefooted. Prices are for dolls with no chips, cracks, hairlines or breaks.

Annie Rooney, Little: See All Bisque – Comic Characters.

Baby Bo Kaye: Made by Alt, Beck & Gottschalck. Marked with mold number **1394**. 5" - $1,400.00; 7" - $1,800.00.

Baby Bud: Glass eyes, wig: 6 – 7" - $700.00 up.

Baby Darling: Mold #497; Kestner #178. (Allow more for toddler body.) **Swivel neck, glass eyes:** 5" - $500.00; 9" - $900.00. **One-piece body, painted eyes:** 7" - $485.00; 9" - $675.00; 11" - $975.00 up.

Baby Peggy Montgomery: Made by Louis Amberg and marked with paper label. 4" - $400.00; 6" - $685.00.

4½" **"Happifats"** with molded-on underwear. Boy on left has straighter molded curl than the girls. All made in Germany. Rare with molded undies. **Each - $525.00 up.** *Courtesy Shirley Bertrand.*

Bonnie Babe: Made by Georgene Averill. Has paper label. 5" - $700.00; 7" - $900.00. **Molded-on clothes:** 6" - $1,100.00.

Bye-Lo: Made by J.D. Kestner. Has paper label. Jointed neck, glass eyes, solid dome. 4" - $485.00; 6" - $585.00. **Jointed neck, wig, glass eyes:** 5" - $600.00; 8" - $1,000.00. **Painted eyes, molded hair and one-piece body and head:** 5" - $325.00; 7" - $525.00. **Immobilies:** "Salt" and "Pepper" on back or stomach. 3-3½" - $350.00. **One piece:** Various poses. 3" - $325.00.

Campbell Kids: Molded-on clothes, "Dutch" hairstyle. 5" - $235.00.

Chi Chi: Made by Orsini. 5–6" - $1,200.00. **Painted eyes:** $675.00.

Chin-Chin: Made by Heubach. 4½" - $325.00. **Poor quality:** 4½" - $175.00.

Didi: Made by Orsini. 5–6" - $1,200.00. **Painted eyes:** $675.00.

Fefe: Orsini. 5–6" - $1,200.00. **Painted eyes:** $675.00.

Googly: 1911 on. **Glass eyes:** 4" - $385.00, 6" - $600.00. **Painted eyes:** 4" - $265.00; 6" - $400.00. **Glass eyes, swivel neck:** 6" - $650.00; 8" - $1,000.00. **Jointed elbow and/or knees:** 6" - $2,600.00; 7–7½" -$3,200.00. **Marked with maker:** Example K*R. 6½" - $2,600.00 up.

Grumpy Boy: Marked "Germany." 4" - $135.00. Marked "Japan": 4" - $50.00.

Happifats: Boy or girl. 5" - $325.00 each and up.

Hebee or Shebee: 5" - $425.00. (See photo in Series 5, pg. 11; Series 7, pg. 9.)

Heubach: Molded hair, side glance eyes. Molded ribbon or bows: 7" - $700.00; 9" - $900.00. Wigged: 7" - $925.00.

Bunny Boy or Girl figurine: By Heubach. 5" - $365.00; 8½" - $575.00.

Little Imp: Has hooved feet. 6½" - $650.00.

Kestner: Marked mold number **257, 262,** etc. **Baby:** Glass eyes, swivel head. 9–10" - $1,000.00. **One piece body and head:** 5½–6½" - $300.00.

Max and Moritz: Kestner. See All Bisque – Comic Character (See photo in Series 7, pg. 12.)

Medic: One piece, molded-on uniform, carries case. 3½–4" - $230.00. (See photo in Series 7, pg. 9.)

Mibs: Made by Louis Amberg. May be marked "1921" on back and have paper label with name. 3½" - $250.00; 5" - $425.00.

Mimi: Made by Orsini. 6" - $1,500.00. Painted eyes: $985.00.

Orsini: Head tilted to side, made in one piece and hands hold out dress. 4" - $500.00; 6" - $750.00.

Our Fairy: Molded hair and painted eyes. 9–10" - $1,700.00. **Wig and glass eyes:** 9–10" - $2,000.00.

Our Mary: Has paper label. 5" - $525.00.

Peek-a-boo: By Drayton. 5" - $365.00.

Peterkin: 9" - $525.00.

Peterkin, Tommy: Horsman. 4" - $250.00.

Prize Baby (Mildred) #880: 7" - $1,850.00; 8½" - $2,250.00.

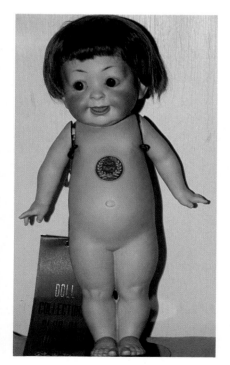

12" "Our Fairy" is an all bisque googly. Excellent modeling with open/closed mouth and glass eyes. Detailed fingers and toes. Jointed shoulders only. In this condition - $2,000.00. *Courtesy Barbara Spears.*

5½" all bisque "Scootles" that is jointed at shoulder only. Shown in original box. Made in Germany. Mint in box - $1,200.00; Doll only - $900.00. *Courtesy Shirley Bertrand.*

ALL BISQUE CHARACTERS

Queue San Baby: Various poses. **Germany:** 5½" - $265.00. **Japan:** 4" - $70.00–90.00.

Scootles: Made by Cameo. 6" - $750.00 up.

Sonny: One piece body and head; made by Averill. 5" - $675.00 up. **Glass eyes, swivel neck:** 6–7" - $1,800.00.

Teenie Weenie: Made by Donahey. Painted one-piece eyebrows and features. 4½" - $225.00.

Tynie Baby: Made by Horsman. **Glass eyes:** 6" - $1,000.00; 9" - $1,700.00. **Painted eyes:** 6" - $565.00.

Wide Awake Doll: Germany: 7½" - $425.00. **Japan:** 7½" - $145.00.

Veve: Made by Orsini. 6" - $1,500.00. **Painted eyes:** $985.00.

ALL BISQUE – NODDERS

"Knotters" are called "Nodders" since when their heads are touched, they "nod." The reason they should correctly be called "knotters" is due to the method of stringing. The string passed through a hole in the head and knotted. They can also be made with cutouts on the bodies to take a tiny rod that comes out of the side of the neck. Both styles were made in Germany and Japan. Ca. 1920s.

Santa Claus or Indian: 6" - $145.00–175.00

Teddy Bear: 5" - $150.00.

Other Animals: (rabbit, dog, cat, etc.) 3½–5" - $35.00–75.00. **Molded-on clothes:** 4" - $125.00 up.

Comic Characters: 3½–5" - $65.00–135.00 up.

Children/Adults: Made in Germany. 4½–5½" - $35.00–145.00.

Japan/Nippon: 3½" - $15.00; 4½" - $35.00.

Sitting Position: 5" - $150.00 up; 9" - $245.00 up.

ALL BISQUE – JAPAN

All bisque dolls from Japan vary a great deal in quality. They are jointed at shoulders and may have other joints. Good quality bisque is well painted with no chips or breaks. (Also see all bisque characters and nodder sections.)

Marked Nippon: The mark "Nippon" ceased in 1923. 4" - $40.00; 6" - $65.00.

"Betty Boop": Style with bobbed hair, large painted eyes to side and one-piece body and head. 4" - $25.00; 6–7" - $45.00.

Child: With molded clothes. 4½" - $40.00; 6" - $60.00.

Child: 1920s and 1930s. Pink or painted bisque with painted features. Jointed at shoulders and hips. Has molded hair or wig. Excellent condition. 3" - $15.00; 4–5" - $27.50; 7" - $45.00 up. **Bow loop in hair:** 4" - $20.00; 7" - $45.00.

Comic Characters: See "All bisque – Comic Characters" section.

Occupied Japan: 3½" - $20.00; 5" - $30.00; 7" - $45.00.

Immobilies: Figurines with no joints. **Bride & groom cake top:** 6–6½" - $110.00. **Children:** 3–4" - $10.00–20.00, 6–7" - $25.00–45.00. **Teddy Bears:** 3" - $60.00. **Indians, Dutch, etc:** 2½" - $25.00. **Santa Claus:** 3½" - $75.00. **Adults:** 5" - $65.00. **Child with animal on string:** 3½" - $75.00.

Bent Leg Baby: May or may not be jointed at hips and shoulders. Very nice quality: 3½–5" - $25.00-60.00.

Bye-Lo Copy: (See photo in Series 6, pg. 12.) 3½" - $95.00, 5" - $145.00. **Medium to poor quality:** 3½–5" - $6.00–45.00.

4" Dutch immobilies. This type of figurines was popular in the 1910s–1930s. Made in Japan. Each - $50.00.
Courtesy Gloria Anderson.

ALL BISQUE – COMIC CHARACTERS

Annie Rooney, Little: Made in Germany. 4" - $350.00; 7" - $475.00.

Betty Boop: With musical instrument. Made in Japan. 3½" - $60.00 up.

Betty Boop: Fleisher Studios. Made in Japan. 3½" - $40.00 up.

Dick Tracy: Made in Germany. 5" - $245.00.

Gasoline Alley: Uncle Walt, Auntie Blossom (black), Corky, Rachel. 2–3½", each - $90.00 up.

Made in Japan: Paint washes off easily. 3–4½" - $25.00 up.

Jackie Coogan: Japan. 6½" - $135.00.

Johnny: "Call for Phillip Morris." Made in Germany. 5" - $100.00.

Katzenjammer: Mama: 4" - $50.00; 8" - $100.00. **Uncle Ben:** 4" - $60.00, 8" - $125.00. **Kids:** 4" - $60.00 each ; 6" - $145.00 each. **Papa:** 4" - $65.00; 8" - $165.00.

Max or Moritz: (K*R): 5–5½", each - $2,200.00 up.

Mickey Mouse: Walt Disney. 5", each - $250.00 up.

Mickey Mouse: With musical instrument. $250.00 up.

Minnie Mouse: Walt Disney. $250.00 up.

Moon Mullins and Kayo: Mushmouth (black), Uncle Willie, Aunt Mamie, Little Egypt, Emmy, and Lord Plushbottom. 4" - $70.00 up.

Orphan Annie: 3½" - $60.00. Nodder - $70.00 up.

Mr. Peanut: Made in Japan. 4" - $35.00.

Our Gang: Boys: 3½" - $70.00. Girls: 3½" - $80.00.

Popeye: 3" - $125.00 up.

Seven Dwarfs: Walt Disney. 3½", each - $75.00 up.

Skeezix: 3½" - $75.00.

ALL BISQUE – COMIC CHARACTERS

Skippy: 5" - $110.00. (See photo in Series 6, pg. 13.)

Snow White: Japan. 5½" - $90.00. **Boxed with Dwarfs:** $550.00 up. (See photo in Series 6, pg. 13.) **Germany:** $800.00.

Three Bears/Goldilocks: Japan, boxed set: $300.00 up. **Germany:** $600.00.

Winnie Winkle: Mr. Bibb, Pa & Ma Winkle, Perry Winkle, Patsy. **Germany:** 3-4½", each - $95.00 up.

ALL BISQUE – PAINTED BISQUE

Painted bisque has a layer of paint over the bisque which has not been fired. The color can be washed off or can come off with the glue of a wig. These dolls have molded hair, painted features, painted-on shoes and socks, and are jointed at shoulder and hips.

All should be in good condition with no paint chips.

Boy or Girl: German: 3" - $30.00; 4½-5" - $55.00-60.00. Japan: 3" - $15.00; 5" - $30.00.

Baby: Germany: 3½" - $45.00; 5" - $60.00. Japan: 3" - $10.00; 5" - $30.00.

ALT, BECK & GOTTSCHALCK

Alt, Beck & Gottschalck was located at Nauendorf, Germany, near Ohrdruf, as a porcelain factory from 1854. It is not known when they started making dolls. The firm was the maker of both the **"Bye-lo"** baby and **"Bonnie Babe"** for the distributor, George Borgfeldt. The leading authorities in Germany, and now the United States, have assigned nearly all the turned-head dolls as being made by Alt, Beck & Gottschalck, with the bodies being made by **Wagner & Zetzsche.** It is claimed that this firm produced dolls with tinted bisque and molded hair (see that section of this book), as well as wigged turned head and shoulder head dolls and also dolls made of china. There is a vast variation to the eyebrows among these dolls. Prices are given for just one eyebrow style. (Also see All Bisque section.)

Babies: After 1909. Open mouth, some have pierced nostrils, bent leg

Marks:

baby body and are wigged. Prices will be higher if on toddler body or has flirty eyes. Allow more for toddler body. Clean, nicely dressed and with no cracks, chips or hairlines. 7–8" - $375.00; 14" - $445.00; 18" - $625.00; 22" - $800.00; 26" - $1,450.00.

Child, #1361, 1362, 1367, etc.: Socket head on jointed composition body, sleep or set eyes. No crack, chips or hairlines. Clean and nicely dressed. 12–13" - $435.00; 18" - $545.00; 23" - $675.00; 26" - $775.00; 32" - $1,200.00; 36" - $1,500.00; 40–42" - $2,500.00.

Character Child or Baby: Ca. 1910 on. Socket head on jointed composition body, sleep or set eyes, open mouth. Nicely dressed with good wig or molded hair with no hairlines, cracks or chips. **#630:** 22" - $2,300.00. **#911:** Closed mouth. 20" - $2,500.00. **#1322:** 12" - $325.00; 16" - $550.00; 21" - $750.00. **#1352:** 14" - $475.00; 18" - $600.00; 22" - $850.00. **#1357:** 16" - $675.00; 20" - $975.00. **#1358, 1359:** 15" - $1,900.00; 20" - $3,200.00. **#1361:** 12–13" - $375.00; 17" - $500.00; 23" - $675.00. **#1367:** 15" - $450.00; 19" - $700.00.

Turned Shoulder Head: 1880s. Bald head or plaster pate, closed mouth, glass eyes, kid body with bisque lower arms. All in good condition with no chips, hairline and nicely dressed. Dolls marked "DEP" or "Germany" date after 1888. Some have the Wagner & Zetzsche mark on head or paper label inside top of body. Some mold numbers include: **639, 698, 870, 890, 911, 912, 916, 990, 1000, 1008, 1028, 1032, 1044, 1064, 1123, 1127, 1142, 1234, 1235, 1254, 1288, 1304. Glass eyes:** 12–13" - $800.00; 16" - $1,525.00; 18" - $1,800.00; 22" - $2,200.00; 26" - $2,600.00. (Allow more for molded bonnet or elaborate hairdo.)

Turned Shoulder Head: Same as above, but with open mouth. 16–17" - $465.00; 21" - $675.00; 25" - $785.00.

Excellent example of a 17" German turned shoulder head doll with solid dome head. Kid body with bisque lower arms. Glass eyes, closed mouth. **$1,600.00.** *Courtesy Turn of Century Antiques.*

16" with solid dome turned shoulder head with set glass eyes and closed mouth. Kid body with bisque lower arms. **$1,500.00.** *Courtesy Turn of Century Antiques.*

Bisque Shoulder Head: 1880s. Molded hair, glass or painted eyes, closed mouth. Cloth or kid body, bisque lower limbs. No damage and nicely dressed. (Allow much more for molded bonnet or hat.) **Painted eyes:** 15" - $375.00; 18" - $500.00; 22" - $600.00. **Glass eyes:** 15" - $500.00; 18" - $625.00; 22" - $900.00.

China Shoulder Head: 1880s. Blonde or black hair, china limbs (or leather), cloth body and nicely dressed with no damage. **Mold #784, 786, 1000, 1003, 1008, 1028, 1032, 1046, 1142, 1144, 1210.** May also have mark X or N⁄B. 15" - $400.00; 19" - $525.00; 23" - $950.00.

AMBERG, LOUIS & SONS

Louis Amberg & Sons were in business from 1878 to 1930 in New York City and Cincinnati, Ohio.

Prices are for dolls in perfect condition, with no cracks, chips or breaks, clean and nicely dressed. (Allow more for original clothes and wig.)

21" "Baby Peggy" by Louis Amberg. Shoulder head with pin-jointed kid body and bisque lower arms. Sleep eyes. Marked "1924 L.A. & S. N.Y./Germany 50/982." $2,200.00. *Courtesy Frasher Doll Auctions.*

Marks:

L.A. & S. 1926

AMBERG DOLLS
THE WORLD
STANDARD
MADE
IN
U.S.A.

AMBERG
L.A. & S. 1928

Baby Peggy (Montgomery): 1923 and 1924. Closed mouth, socket head. **Mold # 973 or 972:** 17" - $2,300.00; 22" - $2,700.00.

Baby Peggy: Shoulder head. **Mold #983 or 982:** 17" - $2,500.00; 23" - $2,900.00.

Baby Peggy: All bisque. See "All Bisque" section.

Baby Peggy: Composition head and limbs with cloth body, painted eyes, closed mouth, molded brown short bobbed hairdo. 1923. 14" - $350.00; 17" - $525.00; 21" - $725.00.

Baby, Mold #88678: Cloth body. 16–17" - $1,200.00; 25" - $1,600.00.

Charlie Chaplin: Marked "Amberg. Essamay Film Co." 1915–1920s. Portrait head of composition with painted features, composition hands, cloth body and legs. Black suit and white shirt.

Cloth tag on sleeve or inside seam of coat. 13–14" - $550.00; 20" - $800.00.

Newborn Babe: Bisque head with cloth body and can have celluloid, composition or rubber hands. Lightly painted hair, sleep eyes, closed mouth with protruding upper lip. 1914 and reissued in 1924. Marks: "L.A.&S. 1914/**G45520** Germany." Some will be marked "L. Amberg and Son/**886**" and some will be marked "Copyright by Louis Amberg." (See photo in Series 7, pg. 15.) 8" - $285.00; 11" - $365.00; 14" - $575.00; 18" - $975.00.

Newborn Babe: Open mouth version. Marked "L.A.&S. **371**." 10" - $400.00; 15" - $675.00.

Mibs: Marked "L.A.&S. 1921/ Germany" and can have two different paper labels with one "Amberg Dolls/ Please Love Me/I'm Mibs," and some with the same label, but does not carry the name of Amberg. Molded hair with long strand down center of forehead. Composition head and limbs with cloth body, painted eyes. All in good condition. (See photo in Series 6, pg. 17.) 12" - $550.00; 16–17" - $850.00.

Mibs: All bisque. See All Bisque section.

Sue (Edwina or Peggy): All composition with painted features, molded hair and with a waist that swivels on a large ball attached to the torso. Jointed shoulders, neck and hips. Molded hair has side part and swirl bangs across forehead. Marked "Amberg/Pat. Pen./ L.A.&S." 1928. (See photo in Series 6, pg. 17.) 14" - $485.00

14" "Peggy" dolls by Louis Amberg. Painted hair, jointed waists. Marked "Amberg Pat. Pend. L.A. & S. 1928." Dress tagged "Peggy." Both dolls are original. In this condition, each - $485.00. *Courtesy Frasher Doll Auctions.*

Twist Bodies: (Tiny Tots) 1926, 1928. All composition with swivel waist made from large ball attached to torso. Boy or girl with molded hair and painted features. Tag attached to clothes: "An Amberg Doll/Body Twist/Pat. Pend. #32018." 7½–8½" - $200.00.

Vanta Baby: Marked "Vanta Baby-Amberg (or L.A.&S.)" Composition head and limbs with fat legs. Cloth body, spring strung, sleep eyes, open/closed mouth with two teeth. Made to advertise Vanta baby garments. 1927. 18" - $265.00; 23" - $375.00.

Vanta Baby: Same as above, but with bisque head. (See photo in Series 6, pg. 17.) **Glass eyes, open mouth:** 18" - $1,100.00; 24" - $1,700.00. **Glass eyes, closed mouth:** 18" - $1,400.00; 24" - $2,000.00.

AMERICAN DOLL CO.

Composition shoulder head with cloth body and composition limbs. Painted-on shoes and socks. Painted eyes and hair. Can also have wig. Original clothes. Ca. 1918. Marked "American Doll Co." In this condition: 16" - $165.00; 20" - $250.00; 24" - $375.00. Not original: Some craze and flaking. 16" - $90.00; 20" - $145.00; $24: - $200.00.
Courtesy David Spurgeon.

Prices are for perfect dolls with no chips, cracks, breaks or hairline cracks. Dolls need to be clean and nicely dressed.

Armand Marseille made the majority of their dolls after the 1880s and into the 1920s, so they are some of the most often found dolls today. The factory was at Koppelsdorf, Germany. A.M. marked dolls can be of excellent to very poor quality. The finer the bisque and artist workmanship, the higher the price. This company also made a great many heads for other companies, such as George Borgfeldt, Amberg (Baby Peggy), Hitz, Jacobs & Kassler, Otto Gans, Cuno & Otto Dressel, etc. They were marked with "A.M." or full name "Armand Marseille."

Mold #370, 326, 309, 273, 270, 375, 376, 920, 957: Kid or kidaleen bodies, open mouths. 12" - $165.00; 16" - $185.00; 20" - $265.00; 22" - $385.00; 25" - $475.00.

Mold #390, 266, 300, 310, (not "Googly"), 384, 390N, 391, 395: Socket head, jointed body and open mouth. 14" - $185.00; 17" - $265.00; 19" - $325.00; 23" - $465.00; 26" - $565.00; 29" - $695.00; 32" - $850.00; 36" - $975.00; 42" - $1,800.00. **Closed mouth:** 6" - $185.00; 8" - $265.00. **Crude body:** 8" - $125.00; 10" - $185.00. **Jointed body:** 8" - $245.00; 10" - $300.00. **Flapper:** 5-piece body with long painted stockings. 9" - $175.00.

Large Sizes Marked Just A.M.: Jointed bodies, socket head and open mouths. 32"- $1,300.00; 35" - $1,500.00; 40" - $2,000.00.

Mold Number 1776, 1890, 1892, 1893, 1894, 1896, 1897 (which can be a shoulder head or have a socket head); **1898, 1899, 1901, 1902, 1903, 1908, 1909, 3200:** Kid or kidaleen body, open mouth. (See below for prices if on composition bodies.) 10" - $145.00; 14" -

$185.00; 17" - $285.00; 20" - $350.00; 24" - $425.00; 27–28" - $700.00.

Same as previously listed, on composition jointed bodies: 10" - $265.00; 14" - $325.00; 17" - $495.00; 20" - $575.00; 24" - $685.00; 28" - $775.00; 32" - $900.00; 36" - $1,300.00.

Alma, Floradora, Mabel, Lily, Lissy, Darling, My Dearie, My Playmate, Sunshine, Duchess, #2000, 3700, 14008: 1890s. Kid or kidaleen body. 12" - $165.00; 15" - $250.00; 18" - $325.00; 22" - $400.00; 26" - $485.00; 30" - $900.00.

Same as above, on composition body: 15" - $365.00; 19" - $565.00; 24" - $650.00; 27" - $750.00; 32" - $995.00.

Queen Louise, Beauty, Columbia, Jubilee, Majestic, My Companion, Princess, Rosebud, Sadie: Kid or kidaleen body. 14" - $325.00; 17" - $495.00; 22" - $550.00; 25" - $645.00; 28" - $765.00; 32" - $900.00.

23" marked "Queen Louise" with sleep eyes, hair lashes, open mouth, and original wig. Excellent bisque. On fully jointed body. $575.00. *Courtesy Turn of Century Antiques.*

Same as above, on composition body: 12" - $285.00; 15" - $345.00; 18" - $525.00; 22" - $600.00; 26" - $700.00; 29" - $825.00; 30" - $975.00; 34" - $1,000.00.

Babies (infant style): Some from 1910; others from 1924. Can be on composition bodies, or have cloth bodies with curved or straight cloth legs. (Add $100.00–150.00 more for toddler babies.)

Mold #340, 341: With closed mouth (**My Dream Baby,** also called **Rock-A-Bye Baby.**) Made for the Arranbee Doll Co. **Composition body:** 6–7" - $200.00; 9" - $250.00; 12" - $300.00; 14" - $450.00; 16" - $550.00; 20" - $700.00; 24" - $950.00; 28" - $1,300.00. **Toddler:** 20" - $800.00; 25" - $1,100.00.

Mold #345, 351: With open mouth. Same as above, but some will

16½" with five-piece bent limb baby body. Sleep eyes, open mouth with two upper teeth. Marked "Germany AM 990 A 6 M."$450.00. *Courtesy Frasher Doll Auctions.*

also be marked **"Kiddiejoy"** or **"Our Pet."** 7–8" - $225.00; 10" - $275.00; 14" - $550.00; 20" - $725.00; 28" - $1,300.00.

Mold #340, 341 or 345, 347, 351: Twin puppets in basket - $650.00 up. Hand puppet, single doll - $350.00 up.

Mold #341, 345, 351 ("Kiddiejoy" or **"Our Pet"):** With fired-on black or brown color. See Black section.

Babies: 1910 on. (Add $100.00-150.00 for toddler bodies.) **Mold #256, 259, 326, 327, 328, 329, 360, 750, 790, 900, 927, 971, 975, 980, 984, 985, 990, 991, 992, 995, 996, 1321, 1330, 1330A, 1333:** 9" - $225.00; 12" - $300.00; 14" - $385.00; 17" - $425.00; 20" - $575.00; 23" - $685.00. **Same mold numbers as above, but painted bisque:** 13–14" - $200.00; 17" - $325.00; 20" - $425.00; 23" - $585.00

Character Babies: 1910 on. (Add $100.00–150.00 for toddler body.) Composition jointed body. Can have open mouth or open/closed mouth.

Mold # 225: Baby, toddler. (Also see child.) 1916. Glass eyes, upper and lower teeth. 16" - $3,600.00; 19" - $4,200.00.

Mold #233: 9" - $300.00; 13" - $565.00; 16" - $700.00; 19" - $850.00.

Mold #248: Open/closed mouth: 15" - $1,800.00. **Open mouth:** 15" - $900.00.

Mold #251: Open/closed mouth: 16" - $1,700.00; 19" - $1,900.00. **Open mouth:** 16" - $900.00.

Mold #327, 328: 9" - $250.00; 13" - $400.00; 17" - $575.00; 21" - $750.00.

Mold #346: 17" - $685.00; 22" - $750.00; 25" - $875.00.

Mold #347: 16" - $585.00.

Mold #352: (See photo in Series 7, pg. 18.) 9" - $250.00; 14" - $425.00; 17" - $575.00; 25" - $1,000.00.

Mold #355: A. Eller/3K. Closed mouth, sweet face. 11–12" - $650.00; 16" - $875.00.

Mold #362: 10" - $265.00; 16" - $600.00; 20" - $800.00.

Mold #410: Two rows of teeth, some are retractable. 15" - $1,000.00; 17" - $1,300.00; 22" - $1,600.00.

Mold #518: 15" - $550.00; 21" - $650.00.

Mold #506A, 560A: 12" - $400.00; 14" - $550.00; 19" - $850.00.

Mold #560, 570: Open/closed mouth. 6½" - $300.00; 12" - $525.00; 16" - $1,600.00; 20" - $2,000.00.

Mold #550, 580: Has open/closed mouth. 12–13" - $1,200.00; 16" - $1,600.00; 20" - $2,000.00.

Mold #590: Has open/closed mouth. (See photo in Series 7, pg. 19.) 16" - $1,600.00; 22" - $2,100.00. **Open mouth:** 14" - $650.00; 17" - $900.00.

Mold #920: Cloth body, shoulder head. 21" - $985.00 up.

Mold #970: 18" - $600.00; 22" - $875.00; 26" - $1,050.00.

Baby Gloria: Mold #240: (See photo in Series 5, pg. 18.) 10" - $400.00; 15" - $600.00; 17" - $1,000.00; 22" - $1,400.00.

15" with lightly molded hair, sleep eyes, and closed pouty mouth. Very character face. On fully jointed toddler body. Marked "Fany 230/A 4 M." Shown with 7" googly on five-piece composition body that is marked "AM 323." Googly sleep eyes, closed smile mouth, painted-on shoes and socks. All original. Also shown are two Steiff animals. 15" - $4,500.00; 7" - $600.00; Animals, pair - $200.00.
Courtesy Frasher Doll Auctions.

15" painted bisque head baby on five-piece bent limb baby body. Open mouth with two upper teeth. May be original dress and bonnet. Marked "995/A 7 M." $400.00. *Courtesy Kathy Tvrdik.*

ARMAND MARSEILLE

Baby Phyllis: Heads by Armand Marseille. Painted hair, closed mouth. 12" - $450.00; 17" - $700.00; 21" - $1,200.00.

Baby Florence: 12" - $500.00; 16" - $825.00; 19" - $1,300.00.

Baby Betty: 1890s. Jointed composition child body, but few heads found on bent limb baby body. 13" - $465.00; 17" - $600.00; 20" - $700.00. **Kid body:** 15" - $285.00; 18" - $450.00.

Fany Baby: Mold #231 along with incised "Fany." Can be baby, toddler or child. With wig: 16" - $4,500.00; 20" - $6,000.00.

Fany Baby: Mold #230 along with incised "Fany." Molded hair. 16" - $4,500.00; 19"- $5,900.00; 24" - $7,800.00.

24½" doll with painted bisque head with molded hair. On five-piece papier maché toddler body. Sleep eyes, open mouth with two teeth. Marked "A.M. 66/10." **$850.00.** *Courtesy Jeannie Mauldin.*

Just Me: Mold #310. See Googly section.

Melitta: (See photo in Series 8, pg. 20.) **Baby:** 16" - $550.00; 19" - $700.00. **Toddler:** 20" - $1,000.00; 25" - $1,500.00.

Character Child: 1910 on. May have wig, molded hair, glass or intaglio painted eyes and some will have fully closed mouths while others have open/closed mouth. For these prices, doll must be in excellent condition and have no damage.

Mold #225: Little Mary. (See photo in Pat Smith's *Armand Marseille 1865–1925* book, pg. 133.) Open mouth with two rows of teeth. Glass eyes. 15" - $3,500.00; 18" - $4,000.00.

Mold #250: 16" - $950.00; 19" - $1,400.00.

Mold #340: 15" - $2,850.00.

Mold #345: (See photo in Series 5, pg. 17.) 11–12" - $1,100.00; 16" - $1,850.00.

Mold #350: Socket head, glass eyes, closed mouth. 9" - $1,200.00; 16" - $2,300.00; 24" - $3,900.00.

Mold #360: 14" - $465.00; 18" - $850.00.

Mold #372 "Kiddiejoy": Kid body, molded hair, glass eyes. (See photo in Series 5, pg. 18.) 12" - $465.00; 16" - $600.00; 18" - $850.00; 22" - $1,200.00.

Mold #400: Glass eyes, socket head and closed mouth. (See photo in Series 8, pg. 21 and Series 9, pg. 22.) 12" - $2,000.00; 14" - $2,600.00; 17" - $2,950.00.

Mold #449: Painted eyes, socket head and closed mouth. 9" - $450.00; 16" - $1,200.00; 19" - $1,550.00.

Mold #450: Socket head, glass eyes and closed mouth. 20–21" - $2,100.00 up.

Mold #500, 520: Molded hair, intaglio eyes, open/closed mouth. 9" - $500.00; 17" - $1,200.00; 22" - $1,800.00.

Mold #500, 520, 620, 640: Wigged, glass eyes and open/closed mouth. **Composition, jointed body:** 9" - $700.00; 16" - $1,400.00; 20" - $2,300.00. **Same, with kid body:** 16" - $875.00; 20" - $1,300.00.

Mold #550, 600, 640: (See photo in Series 7, pg. 19 and Series 8, pg. 21.) **Molded hair, painted eyes:** 10–11" - $1,100.00; 16" - $2,200.00. **Glass eyes:** 12" - $1,750.00; 16" - $3,400.00; 21" - $4,000.00. **Closed mouth, dimples:** 15" - $1,750.00.

Mold #570, 590: Open mouth: 10" - $485.00; 16" - $900.00. Open/closed mouth: 17" - $2,000.00.

Mold #700: (See photo in Series 8, pg. 21 and Series 9, pg. 23.) **Glass eyes:** 12" - $2,000.00; 14–15" - $2,800.00; 17" - $3,600.00. **Painted eyes:** 15" - $2,500.00.

Mold #701, 709, 711: Glass eyes, closed mouth, sweet expression. 9" - $1,200.00; 16" - $2,900.00.

Mold #800, 820: Glass eyes, open/closed mouth. (See photo in Series 6, pg. 21 and Series 8, pg. 21.) 13" - $1,600.00; 16" - $2,400.00; 20" - $3,000.00.

Mold #950: Painted hair and eyes, open mouth. 12" - $600.00; 16" - $1,000.00.

Character marked only "A.M.": Closed mouth. **Intaglio eyes:** 17" - $4,600.00. **Glass eyes:** 18" - $5,200.00.

Googly: See Googly section.

9" doll on five-piece body with molded high heels. Beautiful quality bisque. Glass eyes, closed mouth, and painted-on gold shoes. All original, never played with. Marked "A.M. 800." $975.00 up. *Courtesy Ricki Small.*

Black/Brown Dolls: See that section.

Adult Lady Dolls: 1910–1920s. Adult face with long, thin jointed limbs. Knee joint is above knee area.

Mold #300: 10" - $1,200.00; 14" - $1,650.00.

Mold #400, 401: Closed mouth. 10" - $1,400.00; 15" - $2,300.00; 18" - $2,600.00.

Mold #400, 401: Open mouth. 10" - $750.00; 15" - $1,100.00; 18" - $1,400.00.

Painted Bisque: Mold #400, 401: 15" - $800.00; 18" - $1,000.00.

Painted Bisque: Mold #242, 244, 246, etc. 15" - $400.00; 19" - $650.00; 26" - $850.00.

Biscoloid: Like painted bisque but material under paint more plastic type.

Mold #378, 966, etc. 16" - $565.00; 18" - $765.00.

Max Arnold made dolls from 1876 into the 1920s in Germany.

Mark:

M.O.A.

(for Max Oscar Arnold)

Child: Excellent bisque: 15" - $300.00; 20" - $425.00; 24" - $575.00. Poor to medium bisque: 15" - $185.00; 20" - $285.00; 24" - $315.00.

Baby: 12" - $145.00; 16" - $225.00; 19" - $425.00.

Left: 12" girl with jointed body, sleep eyes, and open mouth. Original. Marked "France S.F.B.J. 60 Paris 8/0." Right: 11" boy made by Max Arnold. Sleep eyes, open mouth, jointed body. Original. Marked "M.O.A. 200/Made in Germany/9/0." 12" - **$600.00**; 11" - **$200.00**. *Courtesy Frasher Doll Auctions.*

A.T.

A. Thuillier made dolls in Paris from 1875 to 1893 and may be the maker of the dolls marked with "A.T." A.T. marked dolls can be found on wooden, jointed composition or kid bodies and can range in sizes from 14" to 30". The dolls can have closed mouths or open mouths with two rows of teeth. The following prices are for marked A.T. dolls on correct body, clean, beautiful face, dressed nicely and with no damage, such as a hairline cracks, chips or breaks. (See photos in Series 7, pgs. 21–22.)

Marks:

A.T. N°3

A N°6 T

A. 8 T.

Closed Mouth: (See photo in Series 8, pg. 23.) Jointed composition body. 14" - $45,000.00; 16" - $49,000.00; 19" - $56,000.00; 24" - $60,000.00; 27" - $67,000.00.

Kid Body, Closed Mouth: Bisque lower arms. 16" - $49,000.00; 19" - $56,000.00; 23" - $60,000.00.

Open Mouth: Jointed composition body. 15" - $15,000.00; 18" - $20,000.00; 22" - $24,000.00; 26" - $30,000.00.

22½" doll with excellent pale bisque and large expressive eyes. Open mouth and two rows of tiny teeth. Jointed body. $24,000.00. *Courtesy Frasher Doll Auctions.*

AVERILL, GEORGENE (MADAME HENDRON)

Georgene Averill used the business names of Madame Georgene Dolls, Averill Mfg. Co., Georgene Novelties and Madame Hendron. Averill began making dolls in 1913 and designed several for George Borgfeldt.

First prices are for extra clean dolls. Second prices for dolls with chips, craze lines, dirt, or missing some or all of the original clothes.

Baby Georgene or Baby Hendron: 1918 on. Composition/cloth and marked with name on head. (Add more if tagged and mint in box.) Original. 16" - $300.00, $80.00; 22" - $350.00, $95.00; 26" - $485.00 up, $125.00.

Baby Yawn: Composition with closed eyes and yawn mouth. 15" - $500.00, $165.00; 18" - $600.00, $225.00.

Body Twist Dolls: 1927. Composition with large ball joint at waist, painted hair and features. 13–14" - $425.00, $90.00.

Bonnie Babe: Mold #1368-140 or 1402. 1926. Bisque head, cloth body, open mouth/two lower teeth, molded hair and composition arms/or hands. 15" - $1,000.00; 18" - $1,300.00; 24" - $1,900.00 up. **Celluloid head:** 15–16" - $725.00 up. **Composition body, bisque head:** 10" - $985.00; 15" - $1,500.00.

Bonnie Babe: All bisque. See "All Bisque" section.

Cloth Dolls: 1930s. Mask face with painted features, yarn hair, cloth body. First price for clean dolls; second for soiled dolls.

Characters: Such as Becassine, etc. 1950s. Must be mint. (See photo in Series 7, pg. 24; Series 8, pg. 24.) 13–14" - $400.00 up.

International: 12" - $95.00, $20.00; 15" - $165.00, $60.00; 20" - $265.00.

Children: (Add more if mint in box.) 12" - $100.00; $35.00; 15" - $185.00, $80.00; 20" - $275.00, $80.00; 22" - $300.00, $100.00. **Musical:** 14" - $250.00, $70.00. **Brownies:** 14" - $200.00, $70.00. **Scout:** 14" - $250.00, $80.00.

Tear Drop Baby: One tear painted on cheek. 15" - $250.00, $60.00.

Animals: 1930s on. Must be mint. B'rer Rabbit, Fuzzy Wuzzy, Nurse Jane, Uncle Wiggley, etc. (See photos in Series 7, pg. 25; Series 8, pg. 25; Series 9, pg. 27.) 18" - $500.00 up.

Children: Composition, cloth body. Perfect and original. 14–15" -

$285.00, 18" - $425.00; less than mint - $165.00. **Scout, Pirate, Brownie, Storybook:** 14" - $350.00, $100.00; 18" - $600.00, $225.00. **Patsy type:** 14" - $245.00, $95.00.

Comic Characters: 1944–1951. All cloth with mask faces and painted features. Includes **Alvin, Little Lulu (round face, fat cheeks), Nancy, Sluggo, Tubby Tom.** 14" - $500.00. **Little Lulu:** In rare cowgirl outfit. 14" - $585.00.

Dolly Dingle (for Grace Drayton): All cloth. 12" - $425.00, $100.00.

Dolly Record: 1922. Composition with record player in back. 26" - $600.00, $250.00.

26" "Dolly Record" by Madame Hendron. Tin sleep eyes, open mouth. Cloth body with composition shoulder head and limbs. Original wig. Has phonograph in torso that plays records and recites nursery rhymes, etc. **$600.00 up.**
Courtesy Turn of Century Antiques.

Googly: Composition/cloth. 12" - $250.00, $70.00; 14" - $325.00, $100.00; 16" - $465.00, $150.00.

Indian, Cowboy, Sailor, Soldier, Scout, Pirate: Composition/cloth, molded hair or wig, sometimes yarn hair, painted features. 14" - $450.00, $150.00.

Krazy Kat: Felt, unjointed, 1916. (See photo in Series 6, pg. 27.) 14" - $350.00, $85.00. 18" - $500.00, $125.00.

Snookums: 1927. Composition/cloth. Smile face, character from George McManus's "The Newlyweds." 14" - $400.00, $150.00.

Vinyl Head, Laughing Child: With oil cloth body. 26" - $185.00, $70.00.

Whistling Dan: Sailor, cowboy, policeman, child, etc. 1925–1929. (See photo in Series 6, pg. 26.) 14" - $225.00, $85.00; 16" - $285.00, $100.00.

Whistling Rufus/Nell: Black doll. Whistles well. 14" - $425.00, $125.00.

Whistling Dolly Dingle: 14" - $450.00, $125.00.

Babies, Infant Types: 1920s. Composition/cloth, painted hair, sleep eyes. 15" - $200.00, $80.00; 20" - $285.00, $100.00; 24" - $365.00, $145.00.

14" Madame Hendron "Whistling Nell" doll from 1929. Mouth is open in whistling position. When doll is pushed down on legs, it forces air out of mouth, causing whistle. Cloth body and composition head and limbs. Painted eyes, molded hair with three tufts of hair through holes in head. All original. **$425.00.** *Courtesy Marcia Jarmush.*

BABY BO-KAYE

Bisque heads for Baby Bo-Kaye were made by Alt, Beck & Gottschalck in 1925. Celluloid heads were made in Germany, and composition heads were made in the U.S. by Cameo Doll Company. Designer of the doll was Joseph L. Kallus, owner of Cameo Doll Co. (See photo in Series 8, pg. 26; Series 9, pg. 28.)

Bisque Head: Molded hair, open mouth, glass eyes, cloth body, composition limbs. **Mold #1307-124,** **1394-30.** In overall good condition with no damage. 17" - $2,700.00; 20" - $3,000.00.

Celluloid Head: Same as "Bisque Head" description. 13" - $400.00; 16" - $750.00.

Composition Head: Same as above description. 14" - $700.00. Light craze: 16" - $425.00. Cracks and/or chips: 16" - $125.00.

All Bisque: 4½" - $1,300.00; 6½" - $1,700.00.

17" "Baby Bo-Kaye" has cloth body with composition head and limbs. Molded, painted hair. Sleep eyes, closed mouth with downward corners, and very full cheeks. Marked "Copr. by Jos. Kallus/ Germany 17." $2,700.00. *Courtesy Frasher Doll Auctions.*

BAHR & PROSCHILD

Bahr & Proschild operated at Ohrdruf, Germany from 1871 into the late 1920s. They also made celluloid dolls (1910).

Marks:

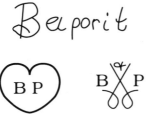

Character Baby: 1909 on. Bent limbs, sleep eyes, wigged and open mouths. Allow $100.00–150.00 more for toddler body. Clean, nicely dressed and no damage.

Mold #592: Baby: 12" - $675.00. **Toddler:** 12" - $850.00.

Mold #585, 586, 587, 604, 620, 624, 630, 678, 619, 641: 14" - $465.00; 17" - $600.00; 20" - $725.00; 24" - $1,000.00. **Toddler:** 9–10" - $575.00; 16" - $865.00; 19" - $1,100.00.

Mold #169: 12" - $450.00; 18" - $725.00; 22" - $925.00.

Character Child: Can be on fully jointed composition body or toddler body. Ca 1910. Nicely dressed, clean and no damage. Can have molded hair or be wigged.

Mold #526, 2072, or marked B.P baby body: 1910. Open/closed mouth. 14" - $3,000.00; 18" - $4,000.00.

Mold # in 200 and 300 Series: Now attributed to Bahr & Proschild. Can be on French bodies. Open mouth, jointed composition bodies. Ca. 1880s. Prior to recent findings, these dolls were attributed to Kestner.

Mold #204, 224, 239, 246, 273, 274, 275, 277, 281, 286, 289, 293, 297, 309, 325, 332, 340, 379, 394, etc.: 1880s. As described in previous listing. 8", five-piece body - $400.00; 10" - $550.00; 14" - $650.00; 17" - $800.00; 20" - $875.00; 23" - $1,100.00.

Same as above, on kid bodies: Open mouth. 16" - $375.00; 18" - $500.00; 24" - $675.00.

Same as above, closed mouth: Dome head or "Belton type," socket head on composition or kid body with bisque shoulder plate. 12" - $1,650.00; 16" - $1,800.00; 21" - $2,300.00; 24" - $3,000.00.

Mold #2025: Painted eyes, closed mouth: 16" - $1,500.00. **Glass eyes:** 19" - $4,000.00.

Mold #2072: Child: Closed mouth, glass eyes. 18" - $4,000.00. **Toddler:** 22" - $4,350.00.

Left: 23" with closed mouth, molded tongue, and original mohair wig. On chunky fully jointed body. Marked "2072 by Bahr & Proschild." Right: 17" doll made by Swaine & Co. Sleep eyes, open/closed mouth. On toddler body. Marked "DIP (green stamp) Germany/S&C." Holding 8" all celluloid baby that is jointed at shoulders and hips. Made by Minerva. Dolls shown with French toy wash set, ca. 1920. 23" - $4,500.00; 17" - $1,800.00; 8" - $75.00; Wash stand - $375.00. *Courtesy Frasher Doll Auctions.*

BATHING DOLLS

Bathing dolls of the 1920s can be in any position, including standing on a base. They are all bisque and will have painted-on bathing costumes or be nude. They were made in Germany and some in the United States. Prices are for dolls with no damage, chips or breaks. Must be clean.

Excellent quality bisque and artist workmanship, painted eyes: 3" - $285.00; 6" - $450.00; 9" - $600.00 up. **With animal:** 5½" - $1,500.00 up. **Two modeled together:** 4½-5½" - $1,600.00 up. **Glass eyes:** 5" - $450.00; 6" - $650.00. **Swivel neck:** 5" - $675.00; 6" - $725.00.

Marked Japan: Fair quality of bisque and workmanship. Some pebbling worn off. 3" - $95.00; 5-6" - $145.00; 9" - $225.00. **Unusual or with animal:** 4" - $250.00; 6" - $350.00.

Ederle, Gertrude: In diving pose. (See photo in Series 7, pg. 26.) 8" - $700.00; 13" - $1,450.00; 18" - $1,850.00.

All of these bathing dolls were made in Germany. Left center doll in blue is marked "5727." Left front doll in yellow is marked "6874." The yellow doll with ring is marked "4457." The doll dressed in gold suit, right of center, and the large center figure have the same "5684" number but have different poses. $165.00–485.00. *Courtesy Glorya Woods.*

BELTON-TYPE

"Belton-type" dolls are not marked or will just have a number on the head. They have a concave top to a solid uncut head with one to three holes for stringing and/or plugging in wig. The German dome heads have a full round solid uncut head, but some of these may even have one or two holes in them. (See photo in Series 7, pg. 28.) This style doll was made from 1875 on, and most likely a vast amount of these dolls were actually German made, although they must be on a French body to qualify as a "Belton-type." Since these dolls are found on French bodies, it can be assumed the German heads were made for French firms.

Prices are for nicely dressed dolls with excellent quality bisque with closed or open/closed mouths. Bodies are French with straight wrists and no damage.

French Style Face: #124, 136, 137, 191, 204, etc. 8" on five-piece body - $800.00; 8" on jointed body - $1,200.00; 12" - $1,600.00; 14" - $2,350.00; 17" - $2,700.00; 20" - $3,200.00; 23" - $3,500.00; 26" - $4,000.00.

Bru Look: 16" - $2,600.00; 20" - $3,000.00. (*See Bahr & Proschild #200 series for open mouth dolls.)

German Style Face: 10" - $1,250.00; 12" - $1,350.00; 14" - $1,550.00; 16" - $1,750.00; 21" - $2,100.00; 25" - $2,450.00.

13" Belton-type fashion doll. Shoulder head on kid adult style body with bisque lower arms. Large paperweight eyes, open/closed mouth. $975.00. *Courtesy Turn of Century Antiques.*

21" Belton-type with stringing holes in concave top of head. Paperweight eyes, closed mouth. Excellent bisque with a "long face" look. On jointed French body. $3,200.00. *Courtesy Turn of Century Antiques.*

BERGMANN, C.M.

Charles M. Bergmann made dolls from 1889 at both Waltershausen and Friedrichroda, Germany. Many of the Bergmann heads were made for him by other companies, such as Simon & Halbig, Kestner, Armand Marseille and others.

Marks:

C.M. BERGMANN

S. & H
C.M. BERGMANN
*Waltershausen
Germany*

Child: 1880s into early 1900s. On fully jointed composition bodies and open mouth. (Add $100.00 more for heads by Simon & Halbig.) 10" - $400.00; 15" - $425.00; 19" - $500.00; 24" - $725.00; 28" - $900.00; 34" - $1,400.00; 42" - $2,000.00.

Character Baby: 1909 and after. Socket head on five-piece bent limb baby body. Open mouth. 10" - $365.00; 14" - $485.00; 18" - $550.00; 21" - $685.00.

Mold #612 Baby: Open/closed mouth. 14" - $1,400.00; 18" - $2,000.00.

Lady Doll: Adult-style body with long thin arms and legs. "Flapper-style" doll. 12" - $700.00; 15" - $900.00; 19"- $1,700.00.

BERGMANN, C.M.

22" doll on fully jointed body. Has sleep eyes and open mouth. Marked "C.M.B./Simon & Halbig/10" on head. **$665.00.** *Courtesy Jeanie Mauldin.*

B.F.

The French dolls marked "B.F." were made by Ferte (Bébé Ferte), and some collectors refer to them as Bébé Française by Jumeau. They are now being attributed to Danel & Cie who also used the Bébé Française trademark. They have closed mouths and are on jointed French bodies with most having straight wrists.

Marks:

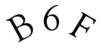

Child: 12" - $2,500.00; 14" - $2,800.00; 16" - $4,000.00; 19" - $4,600.00; 25" - $5,500.00; 28" - $5,900.00.

22" doll on French jointed body. Closed mouth, glass eyes. Marked "B. 9 F." **$4,850.00.** *Courtesy Frasher Doll Auctions.*

Dolls marked "B.L." are referred to as "Bébé Louvre," but they most likely were made by Alexandre Lefebvre, who made dolls from 1890 and by 1922 was part of S.F.B.J. (See photo in Series 7, pg. 30; Series 8, pg. 31; Series 9, pg. 34) Allow more if all original. 12" - $2,500.00; 18" - $4,600.00; 21" - $4,800.00; 25" - $5,500.00; 27" - $5,900.00.

22" "Bébé Louvre" on French jointed body. Closed mouth. Feathered eyebrows come close together. Marked "B. 10 L." **$4,800.00.** *Courtesy Frasher Doll Auctions.*

BLACK OR BROWN DOLLS

Black or brown dolls can have fired-in color or be painted bisque, composition, cloth, papier maché and other materials. They can range from very black to a light tan and also be a "dolly" face or have Negroid features.

The quality of these dolls varies greatly and prices are based on this quality. Both the French and Germans made these dolls. Prices are for un-damaged, nicely dressed and clean dolls.

Alabama: See Cloth Doll section.

All Bisque: Glass eyes, one-piece body and head. 4-5" - $450.00 up.

All Bisque: Glass eyes, swivel head. 5–6" - $650.00 up.

All Bisque: Painted eyes, one-piece body and head. 5" - $265.00. Swivel head: 5" - $525.00. **French type:** 4" - $400.00 up.

All Bisque marked with maker: (S&H, JDK, etc.): 6½–7" - $1,400.00 up.

A.M. 341 or 351: 9–10" - $375.00; 13" - $550.00; 16" - $800.00; 20" - $1,100.00.

A.M. 362: 16" - $775.00.

A.M. 390: (See photo in Series 6, pg. 39.) 16" - $575.00, 19" - $800.00; 23" - $925.00; 28–29" - $1,000.00.

A.M. 390n: 16" - $600.00; 20" - $975.00.

A.M. 518, 362, 396, 513: 15"- $700.00; 21" - $900.00.

A.M. 451, 458 (Indians): 9" - $350.00; 12" - $485.00.

A.M. 970, 971, 992, 995 Baby or Toddler: 9–10" - $300.00; 14" - $600.00; 18" - $975.00.

A.M 1894, 1897, 1912, 1914: 12" - $400.00; 14" - $485.00.

Baby Grumpy: Made by Effanbee. 10" - $265.00; 16" - $475.00. Craze, dirty: 10" - $95.00; 16" - $125.00.

Bahr & Proschild #277: Open mouth. 12" - $700.00; 16" - $1,650.00.

Bruckner: See Cloth Section.

Bru Jne: 18" - $30,000.00 up; 23" - $42,000.00 up.

Bru, Circle Dot or Brevette: 16" - $26,000.00 up; 19" - $31,000.00 up.

Bubbles: Made by Effanbee. 17" - $425.00; 22" - $650.00. Craze, dirty: 17" - $100.00; 22" - $200.00.

Bye-Lo: 14–15" - $2,800.00 up.

Candy Kid: 12" - $350.00. Craze, dirty: 12" - $145.00.

Celluloid: All celluloid (more for glass eyes.) 10–12" - $235.00 up; 15" - $325.00; 18" - $600.00. **Celluloid shoulder head, kid body:** (Add more for glass eyes.) 17" - $300.00; 21" - $425.00.

12" with sleep eyes and open mouth with four teeth. Original mohair wig. On fully jointed body. Marked "34-21." 17" with full lips, open mouth, glass eyes. On fully jointed body. 12" - **$12,000.00; 17"** - **$4,600.00.** *Courtesy Frasher Doll Auctions.*

Chase: 24" - $7,900.00; 28" - $9,500.00.

Cloth: See cloth section.

Composition: Made in Germany. Glass eyes, sometimes flirty. 15" - $565.00; 19" - $750.00; 24" - $950.00 up.

E.D.: Open mouth: 16" - $2,200.00; 22" - $2,800.00.

F.G.: Open/closed mouth. 17–18" - $3,900.00. **Fashion:** Kid body, swivel neck. 17" - $3,800.00.

Fashion: Swivel neck. **Original:** 16" - $14,600.00. **Redressed:** 16" - $9,200.00. **Shoulder Head: Original:** 16" - $6,000.00. **Redressed:** 16" - $4,200.00.

French, Unmarked or Marked "DEP": Closed mouth, bisque head: 11–12" - $1,800.00 up; 15" - $3,200.00; 20" - $4,300.00. **Painted bisque:** 15" - $975.00; 20" - $1,200.00.

French, Unmarked or Marked "DEP": Open mouth, bisque head: 10" - $500.00; 15" - $1,200.00; 22" - $1,900.00. **Painted bisque:** 15" - $500.00; 20" - $800.00. **Negroid features:** 18" - $4,400.00 up.

French marked "SNF": Celluloid. 14" - $300.00; 18" - $550.00.

Frozen Charlotte/Charlie: 3" - $165.00; 6" - $285.00; 8–9" - $365.00. **Jointed shoulder:** 3" - $200.00; 6" - $350.00.

German, Unmarked: Closed mouth, bisque head: 10" - $525.00; 13" - $785.00; 15" - $925.00. **Painted bisque:** 14" - $325.00; 18" - $550.00.

German, Unmarked: Open mouth, bisque head. 10–11" - $300.00; 14" - $400.00; 17" - $525.00; 21" - $800.00. **Painted bisque:** 16" - $350.00; 19" - $500.00. **Negroid features:** 15" - $3,000.00; 18" - $3,800.00.

Heinrich Handwerck: Open mouth. 18" - $700.00; 22" - $800.00; 25" - $1,200.00.

Hanna: Made by Schoenau & Hoffmeister. 8" - $300.00; 10–12" - $450.00; 15" - $600.00; 18" - $800.00.

Heubach, Gebruder Mold #7657, 7658, 7668, 7671: 9" - $1,400.00; 12–13" - $2,000.00.

Heubach, Gebruder: (Sunburst mark) Boy, eyes to side. 12" - $2,600.00.

Heubach, Gebruder Mold #7661, 7686: 10" - $1,300.00; 14" - $2,800.00; 17" - $4,000.00.

Heubach Koppelsdorf Mold #320, 339 350: 10" - $400.00; 13" - $550.00; 18" - $750.00; 21" - $950.00 up.

Heubach Koppelsdorf Mold #399: Allow more for toddler. 9–10" - $450.00; 14" - $650.00; 17" - $850.00. **Celluloid:** 14" - $325.00; 17" - $625.00.

Heubach Koppelsdorf Mold #414: 9" - $285.00; 14" - $650.00; 17" - $1,100.00.

Heubach Koppelsdorf Mold #418: (Grin) 9" - $675.00; 14" - $900.00.

Heubach Koppelsdorf Mold #463: 12" - $625.00; 16" - $975.00.

Heubach Koppelsdorf Mold #444, 451: 8–9" - $400.00; 14" - $725.00.

Heubach Koppelsdorf Mold #452: Brown. Can be Spanish, gypsy, Moor, etc. 10" - $550.00; 14" - $625.00.

Heubach Koppelsdorf Mold #458: 12" - $500.00; 16" - $750.00.

Heubach Koppelsdorf Mold #1900: 14" - $475.00; 17" - $675.00.

Kestner #134: 12" - $685.00; 15" - $985.00.

Kestner #245, 237: Hilda. 13-14" - $3,450.00; 17" - $5,800.00; 20" - $7,200.00.

Kestner: Child, no mold number. **Open mouth:** 12" - $450.00; 16" - $650.00. **Closed mouth:** 14" - $625.00; 17" - $825.00 up. **Five-piece body:** 12" - $325.00.

Jumeau (Tete): Open mouth. 15" - $2,700.00; 18" - $2,900.00; 23" - $3,400.00.

Jumeau (Tete): Closed mouth. 15" - $4,900.00; 18" - $5,100.00; 22" - $6,200.00.

Jumeau Type: Unmarked/number only. (See photo in Series 7, pg. 33.) 12" - $2,600.00; 15" - $3,400.00; 19" - $4,200.00.

Jumeau: Marked "E.J." 15" - $7,200.00; 18" - $9,000.00.

K Star R: Child, no mold number. 14" - $700.00; 17" - $900.00.

K Star R #100: (See photo in Series 6, pg. 38.) 10" - $750.00; 14" - $1,100.00; 17" - $1,600.00; 19" - $1,900.00.

K Star R #101: Painted eyes: 15" - $2,300.00. **Glass eyes:** 17" - $5,000.00.

K Star R #114: (See photo in Series 7, pg. 35.) 13" - $4,600.00

K Star R #116, 116a: 15" - $3,400.00; 19" - $4,000.00.

K Star R #126: (See photo in Series 5, pg. 28.) Baby. 10" - $625.00; 17" - $1,100.00.

Kewpie ("Hottentot"): Bisque. 4" - $400.00; 5" - $565.00; 9" - $985.00. **Papier maché:** 8" - $265.00.

Kewpie: Composition. 12" - $400.00. **Toddler:** 12" - $650.00; 16" - $875.00.

KW/G (Konig & Wernicke) 17" - $785.00.

Kühnlenz, Gebruder: Mold #34-17, 44-16, etc. Open mouth. 10" - $500.00; 15" - $625.00.

Moss, Leo: Papier maché head and lower limbs. Molded hair or wig. Inset glass eyes. Closed mouth, full lips, brown twill body. Excelsior filled. With or without tear on cheek. 1920s. 21" - $7,400.00; 27" - $8,800.00.

Papier Maché: Negroid features. 8" - $275.00; 13" - $525.00; 17" - $825.00. **Others:** 15" - $325.00; 22" - $685.00.

Paris Bébé: 16" - $4,600.00; 19" - $5,500.00.

Parson-Jackson: Baby: 13" - $500.00. **Toddler:** 14" - $625.00.

Recknagel: Marked "R.A." May have mold **#138.** 16" - $950.00; 22" - $1,900.00.

13" doll with closed mouth and on French body. Original sparce human hair wig and original clothes. Boots have been replaced. Marked "3 Paris Bébé. By Danel & Cie." **$4,200.00.** *Courtesy Frasher Doll Auctions.*

Schoenau & Hoffmeister #1909: (See photo in Series 5, pg. 29.) 15–16" - $585.00; 18" - $775.00.

Scowling Indian: (See photo in Series 6, pg. 41.) 10" - $350.00; 13" - $450.00.

Scootles: Composition: 15" - $750.00 up. **Vinyl:** 14" - $285.00; 19" - $475.00; 27" - $600.00.

Simon & Halbig #639: 14" - $6,800.00; 17" - $10,000.00.

Simon & Halbig #729: Open mouth and smiling. 16–18" - $3,900.00-4,100.00

Simon & Halbig #739: (See photo in Series 6, pg. 38.) Closed mouth: 18" - $3,000.00; 23" - $4,100.00.

Simon & Halbig #939: Closed mouth: 18" - $3,500.00; 21" - $4,500.00. **Open mouth:** (See photo in Series 7, pg. 34.): 16" - $1,450.00; 20" - $1,900.00.

Simon & Halbig #949: Closed mouth: 18" - $3,200.00; 21" - $4,000.00. **Open mouth:** 18" - $1,700.00.

Simon & Halbig #969: Open mouth, puffed cheeks. 18" - $1,400.00.

Simon & Halbig #1039, 1079: (See photo in Series 8, pg. 35.) **Open mouth:** 16" - $1,600.00; 19" - $1,900.00. **Pull string, sleep eyes:** 19" - $2,400.00.

Simon & Halbig #1248: Open mouth. 15" - $850.00; 18" - $1,100.00.

Simon & Halbig #1302: Closed mouth, glass eyes, very character face. **Black:** 18" - $6,800.00. **Indian:** 18" - $7,700.00.

Simon & Halbig #1303 Indian: 16" - $6,000.00; 21" - $7,600.00.

Simon & Halbig #1339, 1358, 1368: 16" - $5,900.00; 20" - $7,400.00.

Simon & Halbig #1368: (See photo in Series 6, pg. 37.) 15" - $5,700.00; 18" - $6,600.00.

S.F.B.J. #301 or 60: Open mouth. 10" - $465.00; 14" - $650.00.

S.F.B.J. #235: Open/closed mouth. 16" - $2,800.00; 18" - $3,100.00.

S.F.B.J. 34-29: Open mouth. 17" - $4,600.00 up; 23" - $5,400.00.

Sarg, Tony: Mammy doll. Composition/cloth. (See photo in Series 8, pg. 36.) 18" - $575.00 up.

S.P. mark: Toddler, glass eyes, open mouth: 16" - $650.00.

Steiner, Jules: Open mouth. "A" series: 16" - $4,600.00; 19" - $5,200.00.

Steiner, Jules: Closed mouth. "A" series: 18" - $5,900.00; 22" - $6,500.00. "C" series: 18" - $5,400.00; 21" - $6,200.00.

Stockinette: Oil-painted features. 16" - $2,350.00; 22" - $2,700.00.

S & Q #251: 9" - $600.00; 15" - $2,000.00. **#252:** 14" - $1,700.00.

UNIS #301 or 60: Open mouth. 13" - $425.00; 16" - $750.00.

18" with high cheeks, slightly open smiling mouth, and square cut teeth. On jointed body. Marked "S. 12 H. 969 DEP." $10,000.00 up. *Courtesy Frasher Doll Auctions.*

17" with character face. Glass eyes with lashes, open mouth. On fully jointed body. Marked "Simon & Halbig 1039 DEP." Holds 8" child by Kühnlenz with glass eyes and open mouth. On fully jointed body. 17" - $1,700.00; 8" - $900.00 up. *Courtesy Turn of Century Antiques.*

Bonnet dolls date from the 1880s to the 1920s. They can be all bisque or have cloth or kid bodies. The lower limbs can be china, leather, or stone bisque. Most were made in Germany, but some were made in Japan. Also see under Goebel, Googly, and Recknagel sections.

All Bisque: One-piece body and head, painted or glass eyes. Germany. 4-5" - $95.00; 7" - $135.00; 7" - $175.00; 10" - $225.00.

All Bisque: Swivel neck, glass eyes. Germany. 4½-5" - $375.00; 7" - $500.00 up.

Bisque Head: Excellent bisque. Glass eyes, hat or bonnet, molded hair. Five-piece papier maché, kid, or cloth body. 7" - $185.00; 9" - $300.00; 12" - $425.00; 15" - $650.00; 18" - $1,000.00; 21" - $1,250.00.

Bisque Head: Excellent bisque. Glass eyes, hat or bonnet, molded hair. Fully jointed composition or kid body with bisque lower arms. 7" - $225.00; 9" - $365.00; 12" - $485.00; 15" - $725.00; 21" - $1,200.00.

Stone Bisque: 8-9" - $165.00; 12" - $225.00; 15" - $385.00; 18" - $600.00; 21" - $850.00.

Googly: See that section.

Japan: 8-9" - $95.00; 12" - $145.00.

Left: 11" hatted doll with stone bisque shoulder head and applied necklace. Painted features and hair. Stone bisque lower limbs. Right: 11" Mason-Taylor wooden doll with painted features and hair. Pewter hands on multi-jointed body. (See Joel Ellis section.) 11" - $285.00; Mason-Taylor - $575.00.

Courtesy Turn of Century Antiques.

The "Bonnie Babe" was designed by Georgene Averill in 1926 with the bisque heads being made by Alt, Beck & Gottschalck and the cloth bodies made by the K & K Toy Co. (NY). The dolls were distributed by George Borgfeldt. The doll can have cloth body and legs or composition arms and legs with cloth body.

Marks: "Copr. by Georgene Averill/Germany/1005/3652" and sometimes "1368."

All Bisque: See the All Bisque section.

Bisque head: Crooked smile, open mouth. 9–10" - $465.00; 14" - $950.00; 17" - $1,100.00; 21" - $1,500.00; 23" - $1,700.00; 25" - $1,950.00.

Celluloid head: 10" - $425.00; 16" - $725.00.

Composition Body: Bisque socket head. 10" - $985.00; 15" - $1,500.00.

Large 21" "Bonnie Babe" with 15" head circumference. Cloth body with composition arms. Sleep eyes, crooked smile, open mouth with lower teeth, and tremble tongue. $1,500.00. *Courtesy Turn of Century Antiques.*

BORGFELDT, GEORGE

George Borgfeldt imported, assembled, and distributed dolls in New York. The dolls that he carried or had made ranged from bisque to composition. Many dolls were made for him in Germany. Many heads were made for this firm by Armand Marseille.

Marks:

G.B.

Child: Mold #325, 327, 329, or marked "G.B.": 1910–1922. Fully jointed composition body, open mouth. No damage and nicely dressed. 10" - $265.00; 13" - $285.00; 15" - $365.00; 17" - $525.00; 20" - $600.00; 22" - $675.00; 25" - $850.00 up.

Baby: 1910. Five-piece bent limb baby body, open mouth. 10" - $265.00; 14" - $500.00; 17" - $625.00; 22" - $850.00; 27" - $1,300.00 up.

Babykins: Made for G. Borgfeldt by Grace S. Putnam. Round face, glass eyes, and pursed lips. 1931. 14" - $950.00; 17" - $1,200.00.

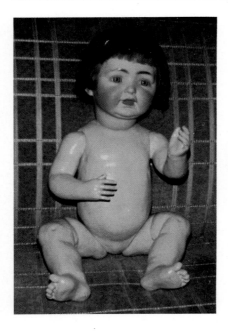

Large 26" baby on beautifully detailed five-piece bent limb body. Sleep eyes, open mouth. Marked "G.B." and made for George Borgfeldt. $1,200.00. *Courtesy Jeannie Mauldin.*

BOUDOIR DOLLS

Boudoir dolls are also called "Flapper" dolls and were most popular during the 1920s and early 1930s, although they were made through the 1940s. Very rarely is one of these dolls marked with the maker or country of origin, but the majority were made in the United States, France and Italy.

The most desirable boudoir dolls are the ones from France and Italy (Lenci, especially. See that section.) These dolls will have a silk or cloth painted face mask, an elaborate costume, and be of excellent quality.

The least expensive ones have a full or half-composition head, some with glass eyes, and the clothes will be stapled or glued to the body.

Boudoir Dolls: Finely painted features, excellent clothes. **Excellent quality:** 16" - $300.00 up; 28" - $475.00 up; 32" - $500.00 up. **Average quality:** 16" - $125.00; 28" - $185.00; 32" - $245.00. **Undressed:** 28–32" - $85.00. **Glass eyes:** 28–32" - $585.00 up.

Boudoir Dolls: With composition head, stapled or glued-on clothes. No damage, and original clothes. 15" - $95.00; 28" - $165.00; 32" - $185.00.

Lenci: See that section.

Smoking Doll: Cloth: 16–17" - $285.00 up; 25" - $465.00 up. **Composition:** 25" - $245.00 up; 28" - $375.00 up.

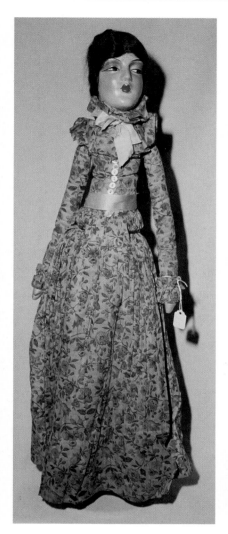

15" French "Miniature Boudoir" with stockinette face with oil-painted features, long lashes, floss rolled hair, and original side saddle riding costume. All yellow satin legs simulate boots. Tagged "Souvenir de Paris/Promenade en Bois de Boulogne. 'AMAZONE' #7." $325.00.

28" boudoir doll with composition head, blue eyeliner, and painted features. Long limbed cloth body. Mohair wig. Skirt flares out to full circle. All original. $165.00 up. *Courtesy Kathy Tvrdik.*

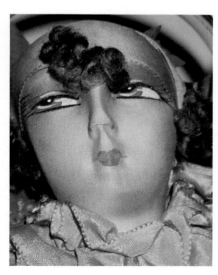

Right: Close-up of mask faced boudoir doll. Back of head made of cloth. Cloth body with long limbs. Painted features and sewn-on hair tufts. $300.00. *Courtesy Marla McKesh.*

Bru dolls will be marked with the name Bru or Bru Jne, Bru Jne R. Some will have a circle and dot (⊙) or a half circle and dot (◡). Some have paper labels – see marks. Prices are for dolls with no damage at all, very clean, and beautifully dressed. Add $2,000.00 up for all original clothes and marked shoes.

Marks:

14" with gusset-jointed kid body with bisque lower arms and kid over wood upper arms and legs. Has modeled tongue, original wig, factory dress, newer hat and marked Bru shoes. Marked "Bru Jne 3" on head and shoulder plate. Doll holding metal 4" Victorian baby rattle and whistle. Doll - $19,000.00; rattle/whistle - $275.00. *Courtesy Frasher Doll Auctions.*

Closed mouth, all kid body: Bisque lower arms. 15" - $9,500.00; 17" - $12,000.00; 23" - $22,000.00; 25" - $26,000.00.

Bru Jne: Ca. 1880s. Kid over wood, wood legs, bisque lower arms. 12–13" - $18,000.00; 15" - $15,000.00; 18" - $20,000.00; 21" - $24,000.00; 24" - $28,000.00; 27" - $34,000.00; 29–30" - $38,000.00.

Bru Jne: All wood body. 17" - $14,000.00; 20" - $20,000.00.

Circle Dot or Half Circle: Ca. 1870s. 15" - $20,000.00; 19" - $22,000.00; 24" - $27,000.00; 27" - $30,000.00; 30" - $35,000.00.

Brevette: Ca. 1870s. 13" - $17,000.00; 18" - $21,000.00; 22" - $26,000.00.

Beautiful 19" doll with large glass eyes and closed mouth with space between lips. On fully jointed wooden body. Marked "Bru Jne R 8" on head; "Bebe Bru No. 8" on torso. $9,300.00. *Courtesy Frasher Doll Auctions.*

Bru Jne R., Closed Mouth: 18" - $9,300.00; 22" - $9,850.00. **Rubber/Gutta Percha heads:** 18" - $8,200.00; 22" - $9,000.00.

Bru Jne R., Open Mouth: 1890s. Jointed composition body. First price for excellent quality bisque and second for poor quality bisque. 14" - $7,000.00, $4,500.00; 16" - $7,600.00, $5,200.00; 19" - $8,500.00, $6,400.00; 23" - $12,000.00, $7,600.00.

Walker Body: Throws kiss. 17" - $7,600.00; 21" - $8,300.00; 25" - $9,400.00.

Nursing Bru: 1878–1899. Operates by turning key in back of head. **Early, excellent quality:** 14" - $5,400.00 up; 17" - $8,200.00; 20" - $9,800.00. **Not as good quality:** 15" - $5,400.00; 18" - $6,200.00. **High color, late S.F.B.J. type:** 12" - $2,600.00; 15" - $3,200.00.

Breathing, Crying, Kissing: (See photo in Series 7, pg. 41.) 19" - $18,000.00; 23–24" - $20,000.00.

17" fourth generation face of a Bru Jne R. She is completely original and a very rare example in that the head is made of rubber and marked "Gomme Durée" (*durée* is French for *wears well, endures*) and with number "6." All original - $9,700.00; redressed - $8,200.00. *Courtesy Ellen Dodge.*

Left: 15" Brevette Bru is made of very pale bisque. Has kid body and bisque lower arms, closed mouth, and lamb's wool wig. $18,000.00. *Courtesy Ellen Dodge.*

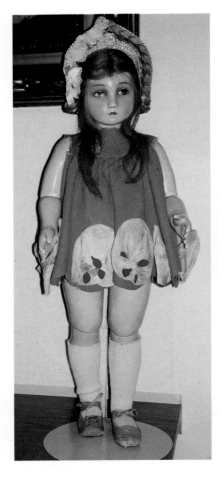

This 22" Burgarella character girl is all original. (Hat added.) She has painted features and extra French joints at knees and elbows. Head is made of unknown material that is like biscoloid or a composition over heavy cardboard papier maché. 15" - $450.00; 22" - $900.00; 25" - $1,300.00. *Courtesy Ricki Small.*

BYE-LO

The Bye-Lo baby was designed by Grace Storey Putnam, distributed by George Borgfeldt, and the cloth bodies were made by K & K Toy Co. of New York. The bisque heads were made by Kestner, Alt, Beck & Gottschalck and others. The all bisque dolls were made by Kestner. The dolls date from 1922. Most dolls have celluloid or composition hands. Prices are for undamaged, clean and nicely dressed dolls.

Marks:

1923 by
Grace S. Putnam
Made in Germany
7372145

Copy. By
Grace S. Putnam

Bye-Lo Baby
Pat. Appl'd For

Bisque Head: 8" - $475.00; 10" - $500.00; 12"- $600.00; 15" - $950.00; 17–18" - $1,400.00. **Black:** 14–15" - $2,700.00 up.

Mold #1415, Smiling Mouth: Very rare bisque with painted eyes. 14–15" - $5,200.00 up. **Composition head:** 14–15" - $900.00 up.

Socket Head: Bisque head on five-piece bent limb baby body. 14–15" - $1,400.00; 17" - $1,800.00.

Composition Head: 1924. 10–11" - $345.00; 13–14" - $450.00; 16–17" - $650.00.

Painted Bisque: With cloth body, composition hands. 10" - $275.00; 14" - $425.00; 16" - $575.00.

Schoenhut, wood: 1925. Cloth body, wooden hands. 14–15" - $1,900.00 up.

All Celluloid: 6" - $200.00. **Celluloid head/cloth body:** 10–11" - $350.00; 13-14" - $465.00.

All Bisque: See All Bisque section, Characters.

Vinyl Heads: Early 1950s. Cloth/ stuffed limbs. Marked "Grace Storey Putnam" on head. 16" - $300.00.

Honey Child: Bye-Lo look-alike made by Bayless Bros. & Co. in 1926. 16" - $365.00; 20" - $485.00.

Wax Bye-lo: Cloth or sateen body. 15-16" - $3,800.00 up.

Basket with blanket and extra clothes: Five babies in basket, bisque heads: 12" - $4,400.00 up. Composition heads: 12" - $2,700.00 up.

Mold #1418, Fly-Lo Baby (Baby Aero): Bisque head, cloth body, celluloid hands, glass eyes. Closed mouth, deeply molded hair. Very rare. 10" - $3,400.00; 13" - $4,600.00; 16" - $5,300.00.

This Bye-Lo doll has cloth "frog" body with celluloid hands. 10" long with 8½" head circumference. Head and body fully marked. Brown sleep eyes. **$500.00.** *Courtesy Turn of Century Antiques.*

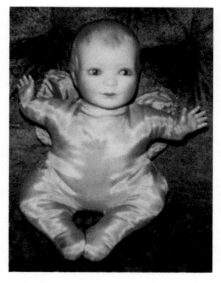

Extremely rare "Fly-Lo Baby." Also called "Baby Aero." Bisque head, glass eyes. Closed, slightly smiling mouth. Cloth body with celluloid hands. Original non-removable outfit with wings. 10" - $3,400.00; 13" - $4,600.00; 15" - $5,300.00. *Courtesy Jan Aufiero.*

Catterfelder Puppenfabrik of Germany made dolls from 1902 until the late 1930s. The heads for their dolls were made by various German firms, including Kestner.

Marks:

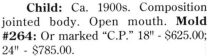

Child: Ca. 1900s. Composition jointed body. Open mouth. **Mold #264:** Or marked "C.P." 18" - $625.00; 24" - $785.00.

Character Child: 1910 or after. Composition jointed body, closed mouth and can be boy or girl, with character face. **Mold #207:** 15–16" - $6,200.00. **Mold #215:** 16" - $4,800.00; 20" - $5,200.00 **Mold #219:** 16" - $3,850.00; 20" - $4,600.00.

Babies: 1909 or after. Wig or molded hair, five-piece bent limb baby body, glass or painted eyes. Add more for toddler body.

Mold #262, 263, 264: 10–11" - $325.00; 14" - $500.00; 20" - $685.00; 25" - $1,000.00.

Mold #200, 201: 17" - $650.00.

Mold #207, 208, 209, etc.: 15" - $475.00; 17" - $625.00; 21" - $850.00; 24" - $1,000.00.

24" toddler with bisque head, sleep eyes, and open mouth with teeth and tongue. Five-piece body with toddler legs. Marked "262 Made in Germany. Made by Catterfelder Puppenfabrik." $1,450.00.
Courtesy Jeannie Mauldin.

Celluloid dolls date from the 1880s into the 1940s when they were made illegal in the United States because they burned or exploded if placed near an open flame or heat. Some of the makers were:

United States: Marks Bros., Irwin, Horsman, Averill, Parsons-Jackson, Celluloid Novelty Co.

France: Societe Industrielle de Celluloid (Sisoine), Petitcolin (eagle symbol), Societe Nobel Française (SNF in diamond), Jumeau/Unis (1950s), Neumann & Marx (dragon symbol).

Germany: Rheinische Gummi und Celluloid Fabrik Co. (turtle mark), Minerva (Buschow & Beck) (helmet symbol), E. Maar & Sohn (3 M's mark), Adelheid Nogler Innsbruck Doll Co. (animal with spread wings and a fish tail, in square), Cellba (mermaid symbol).

Poland: P.R. Zask ("ASK" in triangle).

England: Cascelloid Ltd. (Palitoy).

Prices for perfect, undamaged dolls.

All Celluloid Baby: 1910 on. **Painted eyes:** 8" - $75.00; 12" - $100.00; 14" - $145.00; 16" - $175.00; 19–20" - $265.00; 24" - $350.00; 26" - $450.00. **Glass inset eyes:** 14" - $200.00; 16" - $265.00; 20" - $425.00; 24" - $485.00.

Bye-Lo: See that section.

12" all celluloid character girl with "turtle mark." Sleep eyes, original clothes. Made in Germany during mid-1930s or late 1940s. $185.00 up. *Courtesy Kathy Tvrdik.*

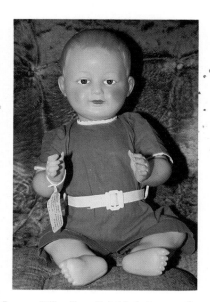

Large 22" all celluloid baby on five-piece bent limb body. Set glass eyes, molded hair. Marked ⊕. Made by Societe Nobel Française of France. $350.00 up. *Courtesy Jeannie Mauldin.*

All Celluloid Child Dolls: Made in Germany. Jointed at neck, shoulders and hips. **Painted eyes:** 6" - $45.00; 8" - $75.00; 12" - $125.00; 15" - $185.00; 18" - $350.00. **Jointed at neck and shoulders only:** 5" - $25.00; 7" - $40.00; 9–10" - $60.00.

All Celluloid Child Dolls: Same as previous listing. **Glass eyes:** 13" - $225.00; 15" - $350.00; 17–18" - $500.00. **Jointed at neck and shoulders only:** 12" - $175.00; 16" - $250.00.

All Celluloid Child Dolls: Same as above, but marked "France": 8" - $185.00; 10" - $245.00; 16" - $350.00; 19" - $550.00.

All Celluloid with molded-on clothes: Jointed at shoulders only. 4" - $55.00; 6" - $75.00; 8" - $125.00.

6" all celluloid boy with wire ladder and coil of rope. Possibly lamp lighter or fireman. Painted features. One-piece body and head. **$45.00.**

3½" all celluloid cowboy with modeled gun on hand. Other hand has hole for rope. Removable hat. **$35.00.** *Courtesy Kathy Tvrdik.*

Immobilies: No joints. 4" - $25.00; 6" - $40.00.

All Celluloid Black Dolls: See Black Doll section.

Celluloid Shoulder Head: 1900–1912. Germany. Molded hair or wigged, painted eyes, open or closed mouth, kid, kidaleen, or cloth bodies. Can have any material for arms. 13–14" - $185.00; 16" - $250.00; 19" - $400.00.

Celluloid Shoulder Head: Same as previous listing. **Glass eyes:** 13–14" - $225.00; 16" - $325.00; 19" - $450.00; 23" - $500.00.

11" teddy bear with short beige mohair fur and celluloid half face with painted features. Jointed, felt paws, and squeeker in body. Shown with 22" pouty made by Kammer & Reinhardt. Closed mouth, sleep eyes. Jointed toddler body. Marked "K*R S&H 115A." Bear - **$650.00; Doll - $4,900.00.** *Courtesy Frasher Doll Auctions.*

Celluloid Socket Heads: Made in Germany. Glass eyes. (Allow more for flirty eyes). Ball-jointed body or five-piece bodies. Open or closed mouths. 14" - $265.00; 18" - $400.00; 20" - $500.00; 25" - $700.00.

Celluloid/Plush: Teddy bear body. Can have half or full celluloid body with hood half head. 12" - $650.00; 14" - $785.00; 17" - $925.00.

Bye-Lo: 4–4½" - $135.00; 6" - $200.00.

Jumeau: Marked on head, jointed body. 12" - $425.00; 15" - $575.00.

Heubach Koppelsdorf Mold #399: Brown or Black. See Black section.

Kruse, Käthe: All original. 14" - $550.00; 17" - $875.00.

Kammer & Reinhardt: (K star R) Mold #406, 700: Child or baby. 14"- $450.00. **Mold #701:** 15" - $750.00. **Mold #714 or 715:** 16" - $750.00. **Mold #717:** 16" - $465.00; 20" - $800.00. **Mold #728, 828:** 16" - $550.00; 20" - $800.00. **Mold #826, 828, 406, 321, 255, 225: Baby:** 12" - $225.00; 14" - $465.00; 17" - $600.00; 20" - $750.00. **Child:** 14" - $385.00; 16" - $625.00; 20" - $750.00; 23" - $875.00.

Kewpie: See that section.

Konig & Wernicke (K&W): Toddler: 15" - $450.00; 19" - $625.00.

Japan: 4" - $25.00; 7" - $40.00; 10–11" - $65.00; 14" - $125.00; 17" - $225.00; 19" - $300.00; 22" - $375.00.

Parsons-Jackson: Baby: 13–14" - $285.00. **Toddler:** 14–15" - $385.00. **Black:** 13–14" - $485.00.

12" all celluloid Parsons-Jackson baby with open/closed mouth and painted eyes. Marked with stork. $185.00. *Courtesy Gloria Anderson.*

Chad Valley dolls usually will have a felt face and all velvet body that is jointed at the neck, shoulders and hips. They can have painted or glass eyes and will have a mohair wig. First prices are for those in mint condition. Second prices are for dolls that are dirty, worn or soiled and/or do not have original clothes.

Marks: "Hygienic Toys/Made in England by/Chad Valley Co. Ltd."

"The Chad Valley Hygienic Textile/Toys/Made in England."

Child with painted eyes: 9–10" - $165.00, $50.00; 12" - $350.00, $100.00; 15" - $500.00, $185.00; 18" - $650.00, $250.00.

Child with glass eyes: 14" - $550.00, $165.00; 16" - $700.00, $200.00; 18" - $725.00, $300.00.

Child representing Royal Family: Four in set: Princess Elizabeth, Princess Margaret Rose, Prince Edward, Princess Alexandria. All four have glass eyes. (See photos in Series 5, pgs. 39–40.) 16" - $1,600.00 up; 18" - $1,900.00 up. **Prince Edward as Duke of Kent:** 15" - $1,500.00, $600.00; 18" - $1,800.00, $700.00. **As Duke of Windsor:** 15" - $1,500.00, $600.00; 18" - $1,800.00, $700.00. **Others:** 15" - $1,300.00 up, $500.00; 18" - $1,500.00 up, $500.00.

Long John Silver, Captain Bly, Policeman, Train Conductor, Pirates, Fisherman, etc.: (See photo in Series 6, pg. 56.) 18" - $985.00 up, $325.00; 20" - $1,050.00 up.

Ghandi/India: 13" - $675.00 up, $200.00. **Rahma-Jah:** (See photo in Series 9, pg. 53.) 26" - $875.00.

Animals: Cat: 12" plush - $165.00 up; 6" cloth - $95.00 up. **Dog:** 12" plush - $200.00 up. **Bonzo:** Cloth dog with painted eyes almost closed and smile. 4" - $225.00; 13" - $500.00. Eyes open: 5½" - $265.00; 14" - $565.00.

18" Chad Valley "Princess Elizabeth" of Royal Children Series. Felt face with glass eyes, velvet body. Tagged blue/white print dress; felt coat, hat, and shoes. Original. 16" "Princess Margaret Rose." Same construction and markings as other. 18" - $1,900.00 up; 16" - $1,600.00 up.
Courtesy Frasher Doll Auctions.

13" golliwog is an early Chad Valley doll. Made of velvet corduroy and plain velvet. Rare red hair model. Felt eyes and mouth. Has felt spots on buttons down front. $500.00.

CHASE, MARTHA

Martha Jenks Chase of Pawtucket, Rhode Island began making dolls in 1893, and they are still being made by members of the family. They all have oil painted features and are made of stockinette and cloth. They will be marked "Chase Stockinette" on left leg or under the left arm. There is a paper label (often gone) on the backs with a drawn head, shown here. The words "Stockinette Doll" may also appear on brim of hat.

Mark:

The older Chase dolls are jointed at the shoulders, hips, knees and elbows; the newer dolls are jointed at the shoulders and hips with straight arms and legs. Prices are for very clean dolls with only minor wear.

Older Dolls:

Babies: 15" - $600.00; 18" - $775.00; 23" - $850.00. **Hospital used:** 23" - $485.00; 28" - $650.00.

Child: Molded bobbed hair. 12–13" - $1,250.00; 15" - $1,500.00; 23" - $2,000.00. **Solid dome, painted hair:** 14" - $465.00; 17" - $600.00; 20" - $700.00; 24" - $800.00.

Lady: 15" - $1,900.00; 18" - $2,200.00; 22" - $2,500.00. **Life size, hospital used:** $1,800.00.

Man: 16" - $2,200.00; 23" - $2,600.00. **Life size:** $2,000.00.

Black: 23" - $7,900.00; 27" - $9,500.00.

Alice In Wonderland: 16" - $1,800.00.

Frog Footman: 16" - $2,000.00 up.

Mad Hatter: 16" - $2,100.00 up.

Duchess: 16" - $1,900.00 up.

Tweedledum: 16" - $2,200.00 up.

George Washington: 26" - $3,000.00 up.

Newer Dolls:

Babies: 14" - $200.00; 16" - $275.00; 20" - $425.00.

Child, boy or girl: 14" - $265.00; 16" - $365.00.

Chase Type: Child. 14" - $950.00 up; 19" - $1,200.00 up.

26" "George Washington" is stuffed with cotton and oil painted by hand. All original and in unplayed with condition. Marked "Chase Stockinette." Mint condition - $4,800.00 up; played with condition - $3,000.00. *Courtesy Frasher Doll Auctions.*

Left: 17½" Chase stockinette with trademark on left leg. Oil-painted finish with bobbed Dutch hairstyle of 1920s. Thick painted upper lashes, stitched toes and fingers with free-standing thumbs. $1,600.00. *Courtesy Frasher Doll Auctions.*

Chelsea Art is known for their doll commemorating the 1953 coronation of Queen Elizabeth. This doll was made by Major Puslowski under the supervision of the Council of Industrial Design and Board of Trade. The doll's head was sculptured by Bruckner and painted and fired at Staffordshire. The body was made by Miss Tearle of Leicester. Norman Hartwell designed her famous coronation robe. The metal crown, orb, and sceptre were made in Spain and feature semi-precious stones. Beadwork and other decorations were also made in Spain. The doll cost $100.00 in 1953. Other royal dolls made by Chelsea Art were Prince Phillip, Princess Anne, and Prince Charles.

The company also made character dolls from *Alice In Wonderland* and a Danny Kaye figure portraying his role from the motion picture *Hans Christian Andersen*.

Chelsea Art made dolls from 1953 to 1956.

15" "Queen Elizabeth" and "Prince Phillip" made by Chelsea Art of England. Bisque shoulder heads with painted hair and features. Unjointed ceramic body on queen; cloth body on prince. Bisque hands and shoes. The costumes and decorations are of extremely fine quality. Each - $800.00. *Courtesy Frasher Doll Auctions.*

CHINA DOLLS

Almost all china heads were made in Germany between 1840 and the 1900s. Most have black hair, but blondes became popular by the 1880s. By 1900, one out of every three dolls was blonde. China dolls can be on a cloth or kid body with leather or china limbs. Generally, these heads are un-marked, but a few will have a number and/or "Germany" on the back shoulder plate. Prices are for clean dolls with no cracks, chips, or repairs on a nice body and nicely dressed. Also see Huret/Rohmer under "Fashions" and Alt, Beck & Gottschalck.

Alice In Wonderland: Snood, head band. 16" - $450.00; 20" - $785.00.

With flange neck: Motschmann style body. 9" - $1,600.00; 14" - $2,200.00.

Alice In Wonderland

Adelina Patti: 1860s. Center part, roll curl from forehead to back on each side of head and "spit" curls at temples and above exposed ears. 14" - $250.00; 18" - $400.00; 22" - $485.00.

Adelina Patti

Bald Head/Biedermeir: Ca. 1840. Has bald head, some with top of head glazed black, takes wigs. **Excellent quality:** 12" - $600.00; 14" - $875.00; 18" - $1,200.00. **Medium quality:** 10–12" - $250.00; 14" - $400.00; 18" - $675.00. **Glass eyes:** 16" - $2,100.00; 21" - $2,700.00.

Bald Head/Biedermeir

Bangs: Full across forehead, 1870s. **Black hair:** 14" - $225.00; 17" - $400.00; 20" - $500.00. **Blondes:** 15" - $250.00; 20" - $525.00; 23" - $625.00.

Brown eyes: (See photo in Series 8, pg. 51.) Painted eyes, can be any hairstyle and date, but usually has short, "flat top" Civil War hairdo. 11" - $500.00; 15" - $625.00; 18" - $1,000.00; 22" - $1,200.00.

Brown hair: Early hairdo with flat top or long sausage curls around head. Center part and smooth around face. 16" - $2,700.00; 20" - $3,600.00. **With bun:** 16-17" - $3,650.00 up.

Bun: 1830s–1840s. China with bun, braided or rolled and pulled to back of head. Usually has pink luster tint. Cloth body, nicely dressed, undamaged. Prices depend upon rarity of hairdo and can run from $700.00 – 3,800.00.

Bun Hairdo

Early Hairdo: Also see "Wood Body." 7" - $1,300.00 up; 14" - $1,700.00 up; 17" - $2,400.00 up; 23" - $3,200.00 up.

Common Hairdo: Called "Low-brow" or "Butterfly." Made from 1890, with most being made after 1900. Black or blonde hair. Wavy hairdo, center part with hair that comes down low on forehead. Also see "Pet Names." 8" - $80.00; 12" - $145.00; 14" - $165.00; 17" - $200.00; 21" - $265.00; 25" - $345.00. **Jewel Necklace:** 14" - $225.00; 20" - $325.00. **Molded-on Poke Bonnet:** 8" - $165.00; 13" - $225.00.

Common Hairdo

Child: Swivel neck, china shoulder plate and may have lower torso and limbs made of china. 12" - $2,400.00.

Child or Boy: Short black or blonde hairdo, curly with partly exposed ears. 14" - $285.00; 20" - $500.00.

18" china doll with hair pulled back into bun. Cloth body with china lower limbs. Long neck and deep shoulder plate. Unusual for this early doll to have brown eyes. **$2,600.00.** *Courtesy Ricki Small.*

16½" china glazed man, ca. 1840s. Shoulder head, molded eyelids, brown painted eyes. Excellent modeling to hair with deep brush strokes. Double chin, cloth body, beautiful china lower limbs. **$2,600.00.** *Courtesy Frasher Doll Auctions.*

Currier & Ives: 14" - $450.00; 19" - $625.00.

Currier & Ives

Covered Wagon: 1840s. Hair parted in middle with flat hairstyle and has sausage-shaped curls around head. 8" - $185.00; 12" - $285.00; 15" - $525.00; 18" - $625.00; 22" - $800.00; 35–36" - $975.00 up.

Covered Wagon

Countess Dagmar: Pierced ears. 16" - $625.00; 19" - $900.00.

Countess Dagmar

Curly Top: 1845–1860s. Ringlet curls that are loose and over entire head. 16" - $500.00; 20" - $700.00.

Curly Top

Dolly Madison

Dolly Madison: 1870–1880s. Loose curly hairdo with modeled ribbon and bow in center of the top of the head. Few curls on forehead. 14" - $285.00; 18" - $500.00; 21" - $585.00; 24" - $600.00; 28" - $725.00.

Early Marked China (Nurenburg, Rudustat, etc.): 16" - $2,600.00 up; 18" - $3,000.00 up.

Fancy Hairstyles: Flared sides, rolls of hair over top of head, long hair cascading down back, ringlet curls around face and full exposed ears. 14" - $500.00 up; 17" - $600.00 up; 21" - $750.00 up.

Flat Top, Civil War: Also called **"High Brow."** 1850–1870s. Black hair parted in middle, smooth on top with short curls around head. 12" - $165.00; 14" - $225.00; 17" - $300.00; 20" - $350.00; 24" - $400.00; 26" - $485.00; 30" - $575.00; 35" - $800.00. **Swivel neck:** 14" - $800.00 up; 21" - $1,500.00 up.

15" china lady with slim face, deep shoulder plate and modeled bosom. Light brown hair fashioned into rolled curls on top and sides cascade into longer curls with very long curls in back. Molded eyelids and headband. Cloth body with delicate china lower limbs. Most likely Meissen, ca. 1840s. $2,950.00. *Courtesy Frasher Doll Auctions.*

Flat Top, Civil War, High Brow

French: China shoulder head, painted eyes, cut pate with cork, wigged, fashion kid body. (See Fashions, Huret type.) 16" - $3,500.00; 19" - $4,400.00.

Glass eyes: Can have a variety of hairdos. 1840–1870s. 14" - $1,400.00; 18" - $2,400.00; 23" - $2,900.00.

Hat or Bonnet: Molded on. 13" - $3,500.00; 16" - $4,200.00.

High Brow: Like Covered Wagon, but has very high forehead, smooth on top with a center part, curls over ears and around base of neck, and has a very round face. 1860–1870s. 14" - $425.00; 20" - $625.00; 24" - $725.00.

Highland Mary: 16" - $365.00; 19" - $465.00; 23" - $585.00.

Highland Mary

Japanese: 1910–1920s. Can be marked or unmarked. Black or blonde and can have a "common" hairdo, or have much more adult face and hairdo. 12" - $125.00; 14" - $185.00.

Jenny Lind: Hair pulled back in bun. 16" - $1,200.00.

Jenny Lind

Kling: Number and bell. 13" - $350.00; 16" - $450.00; 20" - $750.00.

Man or Boy: Excellent quality, early date, side part hairdo. Brown hair. 14" - $1,900.00; 17" - $2,600.00; 21" - $3,100.00 up.

Man hairdo with side part

Man or Boy, glass eyes: 15" - $2,300.00; 17" - $3000.00; 21" - $3,800.00.

Man: Coiled, graduated size curl hairdo. 16" - $1,500.00; 20" - $2,000.00.

Man hairdo with curls

Mary Todd Lincoln: Has snood. 15" - $550.00; 19" - $850.00.

Mary Todd Lincoln

Open Mouth: Common hairdo. 14" - $450.00; 18" - $800.00.

Pet Names: 1905, same as "Common" hairdo with molded shirtwaist with the name on front: **Agnes, Bertha, Daisy, Dorothy, Edith, Esther, Ethel, Florence, Helen, Mabel, Marion, Pauline.** 8–9" - $125.00; 14" -

$200.00; 16" - $225.00; 19" - $265.00; 22" - $300.00; 25" - $425.00.

Pierced Ears: Can have a variety of hairstyles (ordinary hairstyle, flat top, curly, covered wagon, etc.) 14" - $465.00 up; 18" - $700.00 up.

Pierced Ears: Rare hairstyles. 14" - $1,200.00 up; 18" - $1,800.00 up.

Snood, Combs: Applied hair decoration. 14" - $650.00; 17" - $800.00.

Grapes in hairdo: 18" - $1,850.00 up.

Sophia Smith: Straight sausage curls ending in a ridge around head rather than curved to head. 14" - $2,300.00; 18" - $3,200.00.

Spill Curls

Sophia Smith

Spill Curls: With or without headband. Many individual curls across forehead and over shoulders. Forehead curls continued to above ears. 14" - $425.00; 18" - $775.00; 27" - $900.00.

Swivel Flange Neck: 8–9" - $1,800.00 up; 12" - $2,600.00 up.

Whistle: Has whistle holes in head. 14" - $575.00; 18" - $750.00.

Young Queen Victoria: 16" - $1,600.00; 21" - $2,000.00; 25" - $3,200.00.

Wood Body: Articulated with slim hips, china lower arms. 1840-1850s. Hair pulled back in bun or coiled braids. 6" - $1,200.00; 8" - $1,400.00; 12" - $1,500.00 up; 15" - $1,800.00 up; 18" - $3,600.00 up. **Same with Covered Wagon hairdo:** 8" - $775.00; 12" - $985.00; 16" - $1,400.00.

CLOTH DOLLS

Alabama Indestructible Doll: All cloth with head molded and painted in oils, painted hair, shoes and stockings. Marked on torso or leg "Pat. Nov. 9, 1912. Ella Smith Doll Co." or "Mrs. S.S. Smith/Manufacturer and dealer/ The Alabama Indestructible Doll/ Roanoke, Ala./Patented Sept. 26, 1905 (or 1907)." Prices are for clean dolls with only minor scuffs or soil. Allow more for mint dolls. **Child:** 16" - $1,800.00; 22" - $2,500.00. **Baby:** 14" - $1,600.00; 21" - $2,200.00. **Barefoot baby:** Rare. 22" - $2,800.00. **Black child:** 18" - $6,500.00; 23" - $7,000.00. **Black baby:** 20" - $6,200.00.

Art Fabric Mills: See Printed Cloth Dolls.

Babyland: Made by E.I. Horsman from 1904 to 1920. Marked on torso or bottom of foot. Oil-painted features, photographic features or printed features. With or without wig. All cloth, jointed at shoulders and hips. First price for extra clean, original dolls; second price for dolls in fair condition that show wear and have slight soil. Allow more for mint dolls. **Oil-painted features:** 13" - $800.00, $325.00; 15" - $895.00, $400.00; 18" - $1,000.00, $500.00; 22" - $1,400.00, $650.00; 28" - $1,800.00, $900.00. **Black oil-painted features:** 14" - $875.00, $350.00; 17" - $1,100.00, $550.00; 26" - $1,800.00, $850.00; 29" - $2,200.00; $950.00. **Photographic face:** 14–15" - $465.00, $200.00; 19" - $875.00, $400.00. **Black photographic face:** 14–15" - $650.00, $275.00; 19" - $1,000.00; $450.00.

The printed face on this all cloth doll is of a real child. Body construction and clothes could be from the 1930s or 1940s, but magazine ads featured "...have your child's own face on her doll" as late as the 1960s. **$250.00.**

Photographic face: 1930s–1960s. Mint and original. 15" - $250.00. Played with, little soil. 15" - $100.00. **Printed:** 16" - $285.00, $95.00; 20" - $575.00, $125.00; 23" - $785.00, $250.00. **Black printed:** 16" - $400.00, $150.00; 20" - $700.00, $200.00; 23" - $925.00, $325.00.

Topsy-Turvy: Two-headed doll. One black, other white. Oil painted: $700.00. Printed: $500.00.

Beecher: 1893–1910. Stuffed stockinette, painted eyes, needle sculptured features. Originated by Julia Jones Beecher of Elmira, N.Y., wife of Congregational Church pastor. Dolls made by sewing circle of church and

All cloth doll with oil-painted features and hair from 1920s or 1930s. Patterned body and limbs. Mask face with back of head being same material as body. May have been designed by Grace Drayton for Georgene Averill. 15" - **$500.00.** *Courtesy Kathy Tvrdik.*

all proceeds used for missionary work, so dolls can also be referred to as **"Missionary Babies."** Have looped wool hair. Extra clean: 15" - $2,700.00; 21" - $6,100.00. Slight soil and wear: 15" - $1,300.00; 21" - $2,400.00. **Black:** Extra clean: 15" - $3,300.00; 21" - $7,000.00 up. Soil and wear: 16" - $1,500.00; 23" - $3,500.00.

Bing Art: By Bing Werke of Germany, 1921–1932. All cloth, all felt, or composition head with cloth body. Molded face mask, oil-painted feature, wig or painted hair, can have pin joints on cloth body, seams down front of legs, mitt hands with free formed thumbs. **Painted hair, cloth or felt:** Unmarked or "Bing" on sole of foot. 10" - $625.00; 15" - $785.00. **Wig:** 10" - $300.00; 15" - $500.00. **Composition head:** 7–8" - $125.00; 12" - $165.00, 15" - $200.00.

Bruckner: Made for Horsman from 1901–on. Cloth with mask face stiffened and printed. Marked on shoulder "Pat'd July 8, 1901." Clean: 13–15" - $300.00 up. Soil and wear: 13–15" - $100.00. **Black:** Clean: 13–15" - $400.00 up. Soil and wear: 13–15" - $180.00.

Chad Valley: See that section.

Columbian Doll: Ca. 1890s. Sizes 15–29". Stamped "Columbian Doll/ Manufactured by/Emma E. Adams/ Oswego Centre/N.Y." After 1905–1906, the mark was "The Columbian Doll/ Manufactured by/Marietta Adams Ruttan/Oswego, NY." All cloth with painted features and flesh-painted hands and feet. Stitched fingers and toes. Extra clean: 16" - $4,800.00; 20" - $6,500.00. Fair, with slight scuffs or soil: 15" - $2,900.00; 23" - $3,400.00. **Columbian type:** 16" - $1,300.00 up; 22" - $2,300.00 up.

Comic Characters: Extra clean: 16" - $625.00 up. Soil and wear: 16" - $200.00 up.

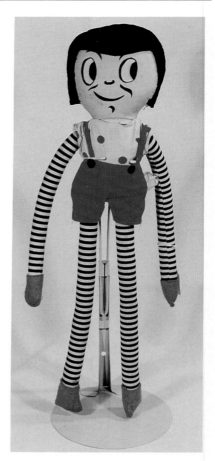

21" flapper-style **"Dutch Boy"** with long limbs. Felt cap, pants, hands, and feet. Printed face. Original cloth clothes. 1929–1930. Tagged "Hollywood Imps. Made by Woodard Co. U.S.A." $275.00.

Deans Rag Book Dolls: Golliwogs (black): (See photo in Series 6, pg. 65.) 12" - $245.00; 14" - $325.00. **Child:** 10" - $300.00; 15" - $625.00; 17" - $825.00. **Printed face:** 10" - $100.00; 15" - $165.00; 17" - $225.00.

Drayton, Grace: Dolly Dingle. 1923 by Averill Mfg. Co. Cloth with printed features, marked on torso. 11" - $375.00; 15" - $525.00. **Chocolate**

Drop: 1923 by Averill. Brown cloth with printed features and three tufts of yarn hair. 11" - $400.00; 16" - $625.00. **Hug Me Tight:** By Colonial Toy Mfg. Co. in 1916. One-piece printed cloth with boy standing behind girl. 12" - $300.00; 16" - $475.00. **Peek-A-Boo:** Made by Horsman in 1913–1915. All cloth with printed features. 10" - $175.00; 12" - $265.00.

Embroidered features, primitive: Home made, all cloth, yarn, lamb's wool or painted hair. **White:** 16" - $265.00 up; 20" - $485.00 up. **Black:** 15" - $365.00 up; 19" - $825.00 up.

Fangel, Maud Toursey: 1938 on. All cloth with printed features. Can have printed cloth body or plain body without "undies." Mitt-style hands with free-formed thumbs. **Child:** Must be near mint condition. 9" - $375.00; 12" - $585.00; 15" - $700.00; 18" - $800.00. **Baby:** 14" - $525.00; 17" - $750.00.

Farnell's Alpha Toys: Marked with label on foot "Farnell's Alpha Toys/ Made in England." (See photo in Series 6, pg. 58.) **Child:** (example: Peggy Ann) 14" - $465.00; 16" - $575.00. **Baby:** 14" - $500.00; 17" - $550.00. **King George VI:** 16" - $1,400.00. **Palace Guard/ Beefeater:** 16" - $800.00.

Georgene Novelties: See Averill, Georgene section.

Kamkins: Made by Louise Kampes. 1928–1934. Marked on head or foot, also has paper heart-shaped label on chest. All cloth with molded face mask and painted features, wigs, boy or girl. Extra clean: 20" - $1,900.00; 25" - $2,600.00. Slight wear/soil: 20" - $925.00; 25" - $1,100.00.

Kewpie Cuddles: See Kewpie section.

Krueger, Richard: New York, 1917 on. All cloth, oil-painted mask face, yarn or mohair wig, oil cloth body. Clean and original. Marked with tag "Krueger, N.Y. Reg. U.S. Pat. Off.

Made in USA. **Child:** 13" - $125.00; 16" - $175.00; 20" - $225.00. **Character:** Such as Pinocchio. 15–16" - $450.00 up.

Kruse, Käthe: See that section.

Lenci: See Lenci section.

Liberty of London Royal Dolls: Marked with cloth or paper tag. Flesh-colored cloth faces with stitched and painted features. All cloth bodies. 1939 Royal Portrait dolls are 10" and include Queen Mary, King George VI, Queen Victoria and Princess Elizabeth. (See photo in Series 7, pg. 53) Extra clean: 10" - $200.00. Slight wear/soil: 10" - $95.00. **Other historical or coronation figures:** Extra clean: 10" - $200.00. Slight wear/soil: 10" - $95.00.

Madame Hendron: See Averill section.

Mammy Style Black Dolls: All cloth with painted or sewn features. **Ca. 1910–1920s:** 14" - $245.00; 17" - $400.00. **Ca. 1930s:** 15" - $185.00 up.

Missionary Babies: See Beecher in this section.

Mollye: See Mollye in Modern section.

Mother's Congress Doll: Patented Nov. 1900. All cloth, printed features and hair. Mitt-style hands without formed thumbs. Designed and made by Madge Mead. Marked with cloth label "Mother's Congress Doll/ Children's Favorite/Philadelphia, Pa./ Pat. Nov. 6, 1900." Extra clean: 17" - $900.00 up; 25" - $1,100.00 up. Slight soil: 17" - $400.00; 22" - $500.00. **Oil-painted faces and hair:** Unidentified, cloth body and limbs. 22" - $700.00; 27" - $950.00.

Old Cottage Doll: England, 1948 on. Cloth and English composition. Later versions have hard plastic heads. Hand painted features. 8" - $125.00 up; 12" - $185.00 up.

Philadelphia Baby: Also called **"Sheppard Doll."** Made by J.B. Sheppard in late 1890s to early 1900s. Stockinette covered body with painted cloth arms and legs. Modeled cloth head is painted. Extra clean: 22" - $4,000.00. Slight soil and wear: 22" - $2,500.00. Very worn: 22" - $1,200.00.

Petzold, Dora: Germany, 1920s. Pressed paper head, painted features, wig, stockinette body filled with sawdust, short torso. Soft stuffed arms, free-formed thumbs, stitched fingers. Legs have formed calves. (See photo in Series 7, pg. 139.) 18" - $600.00; 22" - $800.00; 25" - $900.00.

Poir, Eugenie: 1920s, made in New York and France. All cloth body with felt face and limbs or can be all felt. Painted features, majority of eyes are painted to the side, mohair wig. Stitched four fingers together with free-standing thumb. Unmarked except for paper label. Extra clean: 17" - $725.00; 23" - $950.00. Slight soil and wear: 17" - $400.00; 23" - $500.00. **Photographic faces:** (Also see Babyland in this section) Extra clean: 16" - $750.00. Slight soil and wear: 16" - $350.00.

Printed Cloth Dolls: 1903 on. All cloth with features and/or underwear/clothes printed. These dolls are cut and sew types. **Rastus, Cream of Wheat:** 18" - $145.00. **Aunt Jemima:** Set of four dolls. $100.00 each; **Printed-on underwear (Dolly Dear, Merry Marie, etc.)** Cut: 7" - $95.00; 16" - $175.00; 19" - $200.00. Uncut: 7" - $125.00; 16" - $200.00; 19" - $275.00. **Boys and girls with printed outer clothes:** Cut: 9–10" - $100.00; 14" - $200.00; 19" - $265.00. Uncut: 9" - $125.00; 14" - $200.00; 19" - $300.00. **Black boy or girl:** 17" - $450.00; 21" - $625.00. **Brownies:** By Palmer Cox, 1892. 8" - $100.00; 14" - $200.00. **George/Martha Washington:** 1901 by Art Fabric. Cut: $450.00. Uncut: Set of four - $850.00. **St. Nicholas/Santa Claus:** Marked "Pat. Dec. 28, 1886. Made by E.S. Peck, NY." One arm

11½" mint "Harold Lloyd" is a printed cloth, cut-and-sew doll. "Yours for Happiness" and signature on back. "H.L." on belt buckle. Cut cloth - $175.00. Uncut cloth - $250.00.

stuffed with toys and other arm holds American flag. Cut: 15" - $350.00. Uncut: 15" - $695.00

Raynal: Made in France by Edouard Raynal. 1920s. Cloth body and limbs (sometimes has celluloid hands), felt mask face with painted features. Eyes painted to side. Marked on soles of shoes or will have necklace imprinted "Raynal." Original clothes generally are felt, but can have combination felt/organdy or just organdy. Extra clean: 16" - $600.00; 21" - $875.00. Slight soil and wear: 16" - $250.00; 21" - $400.00.

Rollinson Dolls: Molded cloth with painted features, head and limbs. Molded hair or wig. Designed by Gertrude F. Rollinson, made by Utley Doll Co. Marked with a stamp of doll in a diamond and printed around border "Rollinson Doll Holyoke, Ma." **Molded hair:** Extra clean: 21" - $1,200.00 up. Slight soil and wear: 21" - $500.00. **Wigged by Rollinson:** Extra clean: 18" - $1,600.00 up, 23" - $2,000.00. Slight soil and wear: 20" - $850.00; 26" - $1,000.00. **Toddler with wig:** 18" - $1,800.00.

Smith, Mrs. S.S.: See Alabama in this section.

Soviet Union: 1920–1930s. (See photo in Series 8, pg. 57.) All cloth with stockinette hands and head. Molded face mask with painted features. Dressed in regional costumes. Marked "Made in Soviet Union." Extra clean: 10" - $125.00, 14" - $200.00. Slight soil and wear: 10" - $40.00; 14" - $85.00. **Tea Cozies:** (See photo Series 8, pg. 57.) Doll from waist up and has full skirt that is hollow to be placed over pot to keep contents warm. 17" - $175.00; 22" - $265.00; 28" - $350.00.

Steiff: See Steiff section.

Walker, Izannah: Made in 1870s and 1880s. Modeled head with oil-painted features, applied ears, cloth body and limbs, painted-on boots. Brushstroke or corkscrew curls around face over ears. Hands and feet are stitched. Marked "Patented Nov. 4, 1873." Very good condition: 17" - $21,000.00; 20" - $24,000.00. Fair condition: 17" - $10,000.00; 20" - $14,000.00. Poor condition: 17" - $2,500.00; 20" - $3,400.00.

10" "Chief" and "Squaw" made of all printed material. Tightly stuffed with wool dust. Came ready made but may have also been a cut-and-sew doll. Made by Henderson Glove Co., Akron, Ohio as an advertising doll. 1927–1930. Mint, each - $100.00; Frayed or soiled, each - $50.00.

Two vertical curls in front of ears:
Very good condition: 20" - $23,000.00
up; 26" - $28,000.00 up. Fair condition:
20"- $15,000.00; 26" - $19,000.00.

Wellings, Norah: See Wellings
section.

Wellington: 1883 on. Label on
back: "Pat. Jan. 8, 1883." All stockinette, oil painted features, lower limbs.
Features are needle-sculpted. Hair is
painted. Has distinctive buttocks;
rounded. Excellent condition: 22–23" -
$15,000.00 up. Fair to poor condition:
22–23" - $5,200.00 up.

COMPOSITION DOLLS – GERMANY

Most German manufacturers made
composition-headed dolls as well as
dolls of bisque and other materials.
Composition dolls were made in Germany before World War I, but the
majority were made in the 1920s and
1930s. They can be all composition or
have a composition head with cloth
body and limbs. Prices are for excellent quality and condition.

Child Doll: All composition with
wig, sleep/flirty eyes, open or closed
mouth and jointed composition body.
Unmarked or just have numbers. 14" -
$185.00; 18" - $325.00; 21" - $485.00;
24" - $550.00.

Child: Same as above, but with
name of company (or initials): 14" -
$300.00; 18" - $475.00; 25" - $600.00;
28" - $750.00.

Baby: All composition, open
mouth. 14" - $185.00; 16" - $250.00;
19" - $400.00. **Toddler:** 18" - $485.00;
22" - $625.00.

Baby: Composition head and
limbs with cloth body, open mouth,
sleep eyes. 16" - $165.00; 22" - $285.00;
27" - $450.00.

Painted Eyes: Child: 14" -
$165.00; 18" - $275.00. **Baby:** 14" -
$165.00; 18" - $300.00.

Shoulder Head: Composition
shoulder head, glass eyes, wig, open
or closed mouth, cloth or kidaleen body
with composition arms (full arms or

lower arms only with cloth upper
arms), and lower legs. May have bare
feet or modeled boots. Prices for dolls
in extra clean condition and nicely
dressed. Unmarked. (Also see Wax
Section.) **Excellent Quality:** Extremely
fine modeling. 16" - $475.00; 21" -
$625.00; 24" - $725.00; 29" - $875.00.

24" German composition made by Armand
Marseille. Cloth body with composition
head and limbs. Open mouth, sleep eyes.
Marked "A.M./2549." $350.00–
375.00. *Courtesy Frasher Doll Auctions.*

Average Quality: May resemble a china head doll. 12" - $165.00; 14" - $200.00; 17" - $250.00; 22" - $325.00; 25" - $365.00; 29" - $500.00.

    Painted Hair: 10" - $150.00; 15" - $250.00; 19" - $400.00.

    Swivel Neck: On composition shoulder plate. 14" - $425.00; 17" - $550.00; 23" - $700.00.

Large 24" German composition baby. This black character doll has sleep/flirty eyes, open mouth, and is on five-piece bent limb baby body. $985.00. *Courtesy Frasher Doll Auctions.*

DEP

Many French and German dolls bear the mark "DEP" as part of their mold marks, but the dolls referred to here are marked *only with the DEP and a size number.* They are on French bodies with some bearing a Jumeau sticker. The early 1880s DEP dolls have fine quality bisque and artist workmanship, and the later dolls of the 1890s and-into the 1900s generally have fine bisque, but the color will be higher, and they will have painted lashes below the eyes with most having hair eyelashes over the eyes. The early dolls will have outlined lips but the later ones will not. Prices are for clean, undamaged and nicely dressed dolls.

Marks:

$$\mathrm{DEP}$$
$$10$$

    Open Mouth: 12" - $700.00; 14" - $875.00; 18" - $1,200.00; 21" - $1,500.00; 25" - $1,900.00; 30" - $2,500.00. **Open mouth, very Jumeau looking, red check marks:** 18" - $1,500.00; 23" - $2,000.00; 30" - $3,000.00.

    Closed Mouth: 14" - $2,400.00; 18" - $2,900.00; 25" - $3,800.00; 28" - $3,300.00. Unusually fine example: 18" - $3,900.00; 28" - $5,000.00 up.

    Walking, Kissing, Open Mouth: 16" - $1,300.00; 19" - $1,700.00; 22" - $1,900.00; 26" - $2,500.00.

This 26" doll is on fully jointed French body and has excellent quality bisque. Open mouth, large sleep eyes with lashes, painted lashes below eyes only. Marked "DEP." $1,950.00. *Courtesy Turn of Century Antiques.*

This early 28" doll has unusually fine quality bisque. On fully jointed French body. Open/closed mouth with space between lips. Large glass eyes. Marked "DEP." $5,000.00 up. *Courtesy Turn of Century Antiques.*

DOLL HOUSE DOLLS

Doll House Man or Woman: With molded hair/wig and painted eyes. 6–7" - $160.00–230.00.

Children: All bisque: 3½" - $80.00, 5½" - $125.00. **Bisque/cloth:** 3½" - $95.00; 5½" - $150.00.

Man or Woman with Glass Eyes/Wigs: 6–7" - $350.00–465.00.

Man or Woman with Molded Hair, Glass Eyes: 6–7" - $400.00.

Man with Mustache: 5½–6½" - $165.00–250.00.

Grandparents, Old People, or Molded-on Hats: 6–7" - $265.00.

Military Men: Have mustaches. Original. (See photo in Series 8, pg. 128.) 6–7" - $400.00 up.

Black Man or Woman: Molded hair, all original. 6–7" - $485.00.

Swivel Neck: Wig or molded hair. 6–7" - $800.00 up.

China Glaze with early hairdos: 4–5" - $300.00-385.00; **Low brow/common hairdo:** 1900s and after. $65.00–125.00.

7" bride and groom doll house dolls. She has solid dome and missing wig. He has a modeled-on mustache. Both have painted features and original clothes. Pair - $375.00. *Courtesy Turn of Century Antiques.*

DRESSEL, CUNO & OTTO

Cuno & Otto Dressel operated in Sonneberg, Thuringia, Germany and were sons of the founder. Although the firm was in business in 1700, they are not listed as dollmakers until 1873. They produced dolls with bisque heads or composition over wax heads, which can be on cloth, kid, or jointed composition bodies. Some of their heads were made for them by other German firms, such as Simon & Halbig, Heubach, etc. They registered the trademark for "Jutta" in 1906 and by 1911 were also making celluloid dolls. Prices are for undamaged, clean and nicely dressed dolls.

Babies: 1910 on. Marked "C.O.D." but without the word "Jutta." Allow more for toddler body. 12" - $325.00. 15" - $425.00; 18" - $585.00; 24" - $785.00.

Marks:

C.O.D.

C.O.D 49 D.E.P.
Made in Germany

Child: 1893 on. Jointed composition body, with open mouth. 15" - $325.00; 18" - $495.00; 23" - $585.00; 25" - $625.00; 30" - $950.00; 35" - $1,500.00.

Child: On kid, jointed body, open mouth. 14" - $265.00; 18" - $425.00; 24" - $525.00.

13½" **"The Farmer" is from the portrait series made by Cuno & Otto Dressel with Simon & Halbig doll heads. Character face with glass eyes, closed smiling mouth, grey wig and beard. Has fully jointed body. Original, ca. 1896. Marked "51/ Germany."** $1,750.00. *Courtesy Frasher Doll Auctions.*

Jutta: 1910–1922. **Baby:** Open mouth and five-piece bent limb body. 12" - $500.00; 14" - $565.00; 17" - $650.00; 20" - $950.00; 24" - $1,450.00; 27" - $1,800.00.

Toddler Body: 8" - $585.00; 14" - $665.00; 17" - $800.00; 20" - $1,000.00; 24" - $1,300.00; 26" - $1,500.00.

Child: Marked with **"Jutta"** or with S&H **#1914, #1348, #1349,** etc.: 13" - $525.00; 15" - $625.00; 19" - $700.00; 23" - $900.00; 25" - $1,000.00; 30" - $1,400.00; 38–39" - $2,900.00–3,200.00.

Lady Doll: 1920s with adult face, closed mouth and on five-piece composition body with thin limbs and high heel feet. Original clothes. Marked **#1469.** 14" - $3,800.00; 16" - $4,300.00. **Redressed or Nude:** 14" - $2,900.00; 16" - $3,500.00.

Character Dolls: 1909 and after. Closed mouth, painted eyes, molded hair or wig. May be glazed inside head. 12" - $1,700.00; 14" - $2,200.00; 17" - $2,800.00; 22" - $3,200.00.

Character Dolls: Same as above, but with glass eyes. 14" - $2,400.00; 17" - $3,000.00; 22" - $3,400.00; 24" - $3,500.00.

Character Dolls: Marked with letter and number, such as **B/4, A/2,** or **A/16.** Jointed child or toddler body, painted eyes, closed mouth. No damage, ready to display. 12" - $1,600.00; 15–16" - $2,700.00; 18" - $3,000.00.

Composition: Shoulder head of 1870s, glass or painted eyes, molded hair or wig and on cloth body with composition limbs with molded-on boots. Will be marked with Holz-Masse:

With wig: Glass eyes. 14" - $275.00; 12" - $350.00; 24" - $550.00. **Molded hair:** 17" - $400.00; 24" - $565.00.

Portrait Dolls: 1896. Such as **Uncle Sam, The Farmer, Admiral Dewey, Admiral Byrd, Old Rip, Witch, etc.** Portrait bisque head, glass eyes, composition body. Some will be marked with a **"D"** or **"S."** Heads made for Dressel by Simon & Halbig. Prices for clean, undamaged and origi-nally dressed. **Military dolls:** (See photo in Series 6, pg. 72) 9" - $950.00; 13" - $1,800.00; 16" - $2,500.00. **Old Rip or Witch:** 9" - $750.00; 13" - $1,600.00; 16" - $1,900.00. **Uncle Sam:** 9" - $900.00; 13" - $1,750.00; 16" - $2,500.00.

Fur covered: Glued on body/limbs. 8–9" - $175.00; 12" - $265.00.

E.D.

E. Denamur of Paris made dolls from 1885 to 1898. The E.D. marked dolls seem to be accepted as being made by Denamur, but they could have been made by E. Dumont, Paris. Composition and wood jointed bodies. Prices are for excellent quality bisque, no damage and nicely dressed.

Closed or Open/Closed Mouth: 15" - $2,500.00; 17" - $3,000.00; 22" - $3,700.00; 25" - $4,000.00; 28" - $4,600.00.

Open Mouth: 16" - $1,500.00; 18" - $1,800.00; 22" - $2,200.00; 25" - $2,600.00.

Black: Open mouth. 18" - $2,600.00; 24" - $3,200.00.

Marks:

E 6 D

E 5 D
DEPOSE

18" with open mouth and on jointed French body. Marked "E. 5 D." Shown with two pairs of Gebruder Heubach figurines with one pair back to back and the other kissing. These were used instead of piano babies during the 1910s. 18" - $1,800.00; Pairs, each set – $800.00.
Courtesy Frasher Doll Auctions.

EDEN BÉBÉ

Fleischmann & Bloedel of Fürth, Bavaria; Sonneberg, Thuringia; and Paris, France was founded in 1873 and making dolls in Paris by 1890. The company became a part of S.F.B.J. in 1899. Dolls have composition jointed bodies and can have open or closed mouths. Prices are for dolls with excellent color and quality bisque, no damage and nicely dressed.

Marks:

EDEN BÉBÉ PARIS

Closed or Open/Closed Mouth: Pale bisque. 15" - $2,300.00; 18" - $2,600.00; 22" - $3,000.00; 26" - $3,700.00.
Closed Mouth: High color bisque. 15" - $1,500.00; 18" - $1,800.00; 22" - $2,100.00; 26" - $2,600.00.
Open Mouth: 15" - $1,200.00; 18" - $2,000.00; 22" - $2,400.00; 26" - $3,000.00.
Walking Kissing Doll: Jointed body with walker mechanism, head turns and one arm throws a kiss. Heads by Simon & Halbig using mold **#1039** (and others). Bodies assembled by Fleischmann & Bloedel. Price for perfect, working doll. 21" - $1,250.00 up.

20" with open mouth, heavy feathered eyebrows, and French jointed body. Marked "Eden Bébé Paris 9 Depose." **$2,000.00.** *Courtesy Frasher Doll Auctions.*

ELLIS, JOEL

Joel Ellis made dolls in Springfield, Vermont, in 1873 and 1874 under the name Co-operative Manufacturing Co. All wood jointed body has tenon and mortise joints, arms are jointed in same manner. The hands and feet are made of pewter. Has molded hair and painted features.

Springfield Wooden Doll: It must be noted that dolls similar to the Joel Ellis ones were made in Springfield, Vt. also by Joint Doll Co. and D.M. Smith & Co. They are very much like the Joel Ellis except when standing the knee joint will be flush with the method of jointing not showing. The hips are cut out with the leg tops cut to fit the opening, and the detail of the hands is not as well done. Prices are also for Mason-Taylor dolls. (See example under Bonnet dolls.)

Fair condition: Does not need to be dressed. 11" - $575.00; 13" - $750.00.

Excellent condition: 13" - $950.00 up; 15" - $1,300.00 up.

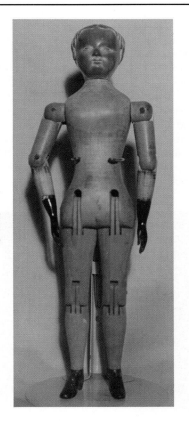

12½" Joel Ellis wooden doll of 1874. Fully jointed with pewter hands and feet. Hair and face have original paint. $950.00 up. *Courtesy Turn of Century Antiques.*

FASHION AND FORTUNE DOLLS, FRENCH

These "adult" style dolls were made by a number of French firms from about 1860 into the 1930s. Many will be marked only with a number or have a stamp on the body, although some of the stamps/labels may be the store from where they were sold and not the maker. The most available fashion doll seems to be marked F.G. dolls. Prices are for dolls in perfect condition with no cracks, chips, or repairs and in beautiful old or newer clothes made of appropriate age materials.

Articulated Wood: Marked or unmarked. Or blown kid bodies and limbs. Some have bisque lower arms. 16" - $6,600.00 up; 20" - $8,500.00 up.

Articulated: Marked or unmarked. With bisque lower legs and arms with excellent modeling detail. 16" - $8,500.00 up; 22" - $9,500.00 up.

Marked "Bru": (Also see Smiling Mona Lisa in this section.) 1860s. Round face, swivel neck, glass eyes: (See photo in Series 6, pg. 79.) 14" - $3,500.00; 17" - $5,500.00; 20" - $6,400.00 up. **Wood body:** 14" - $5,200.00.

Marked "Huret": Bisque or china glazed shoulder head, kid body with bisque lower arms. **Painted eyes:**

15" - $5,600.00; 18" - $6,800.00. **Glass eyes:** 14" - $6,200.00; 17" - $8,000.00. **Wood body:** 15" - $8,700.00 up; 18" - $9,800.00 up. **Gutta Percha body:** 16" - $9,400.00 up; 19" - $11,000.00 up.

Huret Type: China shoulder head, painted eyes, cut pate with cork, wigged, kid fashion body, curved china lower arms. 16" - $4,000.00; 21" - $5,000.00. **Painted Black Hair:** Kid body. 16" - $1,800.00. **Flat Glass Eyes:** Wire controlled to sleep. 25" - $12,000.00.

Huret Child: 16" - $26,000.00 up; 20" - $32,000.00 up.

Marked "Rohmer": (See photo in Series 7, pg. 65 and Series 8, pg. 71.) Bisque or china glazed shoulder head (can be jointed). Kid body with bisque lower arms (or china). **Glass eyes:** 16" - $6,800.00; 19" - $12,500.00. **Painted eyes:** 16" - $6,200.00; 19" - $10,000.00. **Wood body:** 15" - $8,000.00; 18" - $14,000.00.

Unmarked Rohmer or Huret Type: Painted eyes. 16" - $4,000.00; 20" - $4,800.00; 26" - $7,000.00. **Wire controlled sleep eyes:** 27" - $13,000.00.

17" with china glazed head and swivel neck. Leather body with bisque lower arms. Wooden tenon joints at shoulders, gussets at hips, wooden socket joints at knees, and metal eyelet holes in torso. Original clothes. Marked "Rohmer Brevette SGDG Paris" in green stamp on body. $9,600.00 up. *Courtesy Frasher Doll Auctions.*

18" Jumeau Fashion with wooden articulated body with jointed knees and elbows plus rotating joints above knees and elbows. Swivel neck and glass eyes. Original clothes and wig. $9,500.00. *Courtesy Turn of Century Antiques.*

Marked "Jumeau": (See photo in Series 7, pg. 79.) Will have number on head and stamped body. **Portrait-style head:** 15" - $3,400.00; 18" - $5,400.00; 21" - $6,300.00; 24" - $7,200.00. 27" - $8,500.00 **Wood body:** 15" - $6,500.00; 18" - $9,600.00 up; 24" - $12,000.00 up.

Marked "Jumeau": Swivel head. 13–14" - $2,600.00; 17" - $3,200.00; 21" - $3,700.00. **Wood body:** Bisque limbs. 17" - $5,400.00; 21" - $6,500.00. **Very large eyes:** 11–12" - $2,000.00; 15–16" - $2,400.00.

Marked "F.G.": 1860 on. All kid body, one-piece shoulder and head, glass eyes. 11" - $975.00; 13" - $1,100.00; 16" - $1,500.00. **Painted eyes:** 11" - $725.00; 13" - $950.00; 16" - $1,250.00.

Marked "F.G.": 1860 on. All kid body (or bisque lower arms), swivel head on bisque shoulder plate. **Glass eyes:** 12" - $1,400.00; 14" - $2,100.00; 17" - $3,000.00; 21" - $3,500.00; 26" - $4,400.00. **Black:** 14" - $2,500.00; 18" - $3,800.00.

Marked "F.G.": Early face, Gesland cloth-covered body with bisque lower arms and legs. 15" - $5,000.00; 18" - $6,400.00; 23" - $6,800.00; 26" - $7,400.00.

Marked "F.G.": Gesland cloth-covered body with composition or papier maché lower arms and legs. 15" - $3,500.00; 18" - $4,200.00; 23" - $4,600.00; 26" - $5,200.00.

Smiling "Mona Lisa": After 1866. Now being referred to as made by **Bru.** Kid body with leather lower arms, stitched fingers or bisque lower arms. Swivel head on bisque shoulder plate. Marked with letter (example: E, B, D, etc.) 12" - $2,800.00; 15" - $4,300.00; 18" - $6,000.00; 22" - $6,900.00; 26" - $7,700.00; 29" - $12,000.00. (Allow more for wood body or arms.)

Unmarked with Numbers Only: With one-piece head and shoulder. Ex-tremely fine quality bisque, undam-aged. **Glass eyes:** 12" - $1,400.00; 14" - $1,600.00; 22" - $2,200.00. **Painted eyes:** 14" - $950.00; 17" - $1,600.00; 22" - $2,000.00.

Unmarked with Numbers Only: Swivel neck with bisque shoulder plate. Extremely fine quality bisque and un-damaged. 12" - $2,000.00; 14" - $2,600.00; 16" - $3,000.00; 18" - $3,600.00. **Black:** 14" - $3,000.00 up.

Unmarked: Swivel neck, glass eyes, fully jointed wood body. 14" - $3,900.00 up; 17" - $4,500.00 up.

Unmarked: Medium to fair qual-ity. **One-piece head and shoulder:** 11" - $550.00; 15" - $725.00–1,000.00. **Swivel Head:** On bisque shoulder plate. 16" - $1,000.00; 20" - $1,700.00 up.

Marked E.B. (E. Barrois): 1854–1877. (See photo in Series 7, pg. 67.) **Glass eyes:** 16" - $3,600.00; 20" - $5,200.00. **Painted eyes:** 17" -

19" unmarked fashion doll with round early face. One-piece head and shoulder plate. All kid body and original wig. **$3,700.00.** *Courtesy Frasher Doll Auctions.*

$3,000.00; 21" - $3,700.00. (Allow more for bisque or wood arms.) **China Glaze:** (See photo in Series 8, pg. 73.) 16" - $6,000.00.

Marked "Simone": Glass eyes: 20" - $5,700.00; 24" - $6,800.00.

Factory Original Fashion Clothes: Dress: $600.00 up. **Wig:** $250.00 up. **Boots:** $250.00 up. **Cape:** $300.00 up.

Fortune Dolls: French fashion type head with swivel neck, kid body. Open mouth, painted or glass eyes. Underskirt formed by many folded papers written in French. 18" - $3,000.00 up. **Closed mouth:** 18" - $4,800.00 up. **Wooden, German:** Tuck comb of mid-19th century. 17½" - $3,400.00 up.

F.G. BÉBÉ/GESLAND

F. Gaultier (earlier spelled Gauthier) is the accepted maker of the F.G. marked dolls. These dolls are often found on the cloth-covered or all composition bodies that are marked "Gesland." The Gesland firm was operated by two brothers. One of them had the initial "F" (1887–1900).

Marks:

(1887–1900)

F. 8 G.
(1879–1887 Block Letter Mark)

Child with Closed Mouth: Scroll mark. Excellent quality bisque, no damage and nicely dressed. 7–8" - $750.00; 12" - $1,200.00; 15" - $2,600.00; 17" - $3,000.00; 20" - $3,200.00; 23" - $3,600.00; 25" - $4,200.00; 30" - $4,900.00.

Child with Closed Mouth: Same as above, but with high face color, no damage and nicely dressed. 14" - $1,300.00; 16" - $1,900.00; 19" - $2,100.00; 22" - $2,500.00; 25" - $3,000.00.

Beautiful 28" doll with large glass eyes and pale bisque. Pink wash over eyes and closed mouth. On French jointed body. Marked with scroll "F.G." $4,950.00. *Courtesy Ricki Small.*

Child with Open Mouth: Scroll mark. Excellent quality bisque, no damage and nicely dressed. 10–12" - $550.00; 15" - $1,600.00; 17" - $2,000.00; 20" - $2,400.00; 23" - $3,000.00; 27" - $3,400.00.

Child with Open Mouth: Scroll mark. High face color, very dark lips. No damage, nicely dressed. 15" - $800.00; 17" - $1,000.00; 20" - $1,300.00; 23" - $1,800.00; 27" - $2,300.00.

Marked "F.G. Fashion": See Fashion section.

Child on Marked Gesland Body: (See photo is Series 6, pg. 80.) Bisque head on stockinette over wire frame body with composition limbs. **Closed mouth:** 16" - $4,800.00; 19" - $5,300.00; 25" - $6,200.00. **Open mouth:** 17" - $2,800.00; 21" - $3,200.00; 26" - $4,200.00.

Dolls marked with an "F + G" were made by a mother and son in France in the late 1950s to 1961. The dolls were made as fraud items, not just reproductions. The bodies were dirtied and paper labels looked as if they were worn off the chests. If the joint on the kid body is pulled down, they would usually be pure white at the upper end. The ones with composition/wood jointed bodies have old bodies. Some have china glaze heads.

The French government put these people out of business in 1961. The remaining dolls were offered to Kimport Dolls for $10.00 each, but the offer was declined. The New York Doll Hospital did buy them, and in old "Spinning Wheel" magazines and "Doll News" they can be found for sale in New York Doll Hospital ads as "late French Fashions" at $75.00 each.

Information on the F+G dolls can be found in the Sun Flower Antique Doll Club Regional Souvenir, U.F.D.C. (United Federation of Doll Clubs) Doll News, (November, 1967), U.F.D.C. Boston Convention Book (1967), and an article by Virginia Chrostowski in "Yesterday's Children, Region 14" souvenir book (1974). Doll shown valued at $325.00 up. *Courtesy Arthur Michnevitz.*

Block Letter (so called) F.G. Child: 1879–1887. Closed mouth, chunky composition body, excellent quality and condition. 12–13" - $3,900.00; 16–17" - $4,650.00; 19–21" - $5,000.00; 23–24" - $5,400.00; 26–27" - $5,900.00.

Block Letter (so called) F.G. Child: Closed mouth, bisque swivel head on bisque shoulder plate with gusseted kid body and bisque lower arms. 17" - $4,900.00; 21" - $5,200.00; 26" - $6,000.00.

27" marked in block letters "F. 11 G." Has closed mouth with tiny molded tongue. On jointed French body. Shown with 5½" vase of Kewpie holding bear. Marked "9029/WG" and Goebel trademark. Also 3" surprised Kewpie with "O" mouth and 4" Kewpie farmer with hole in fist for rake. 27" - $5,900.00. Vase - $1,200.00. 3" Kewpie - $1,200.00. 4" - $375.00. *Courtesy Frasher Doll Auctions.*

FRENCH BÉBÉ, MAKER UNKNOWN

A variety of French doll makers produced unmarked dolls from the 1880s into the 1920s. These dolls may only have a head size number or be marked "Paris" or "France." Many of the accepted French dolls that have a number are now being attributed to German makers and it will be questionable for some time.

Unmarked French Bébé: Closed or open/closed mouth, paperweight eyes. Excellent quality bisque and artistry on French body. Prices for clean, undamaged and nicely dressed dolls.

Early Desirable, Very French-style Face: Marks such as "J.D.," "J.M. Paris," numbers only. 14" - $15,000.00; 18" - $20,000.00 up; 22" - $25,000.00 up; 26" - $30,000.00 up.

Jumeau or Bru Style Face: May be marked "R.R." 15" - $3,200.00; 18" - $3,600.00; 24" - $4,800.00; 27" - $5,600.00.

Excellent Quality: Unusual face. (See photo in Series 8, pg. 79.) 10" - $1,900.00; 15" - $4,500.00; 18" - $5,000.00; 23" - $6,000.00; 27" - $8,000.00.

Medium Quality: May have poor painting and/or blotches to skin tones: 16" - $1,500.00; 21" - $2,000.00; 26" - $2,450.00.

Open Mouth: 1890s and later. Will be on French body. Excellent quality. 15" - $1,600.00; 18" - $1,900.00; 22" - $2,200.00; 25" - $3,000.00.

Open Mouth: 1920s with high face color and may have five-piece papier maché body. 16" - $650.00; 20" - $825.00; 24" - $1,000.00.

32" very character face French doll with maker unknown. Heavy molded eyelids, open smiling mouth with six upper teeth. On French jointed body. Could have been made by Jumeau during time of S.F.B.J. Marked "F/24 11.10." $8,500.00 up. *Courtesy Frasher Doll Auctions.*

20" doll with long face modeling and closed mouth with white space between lips. French jointed body with straight wrists. $2,900.00. *Courtesy Frasher Doll Auctions.*

Freundlich Novelty Company operated in New York from 1923. Most of their dolls have a cardboard tag and will be unmarked or may have name on the head, but no maker's name.

Baby Sandy: (See photo in Series 6, pg. 85) 1939–1942. All composition with molded hair, sleep or painted eyes. Marked "Baby Sandy" on head. **Excellent condition:** No cracks, craze or chips. Original or appropriate clothes. 8" - $185.00; 12" - $245.00; 16" - $350.00 up; 19" - $600.00. **With light crazing:** Clean, may be redressed. 8" - $85.00; 12" - $100.00; 16" - $125.00; 19" - $200.00.

General Douglas MacArthur: (See photo in Series 6, pg. 85) Ca. 1942. Portrait doll of all composition, painted features and molded hat. Jointed shoulders and hips. **Excellent condition:** Original. 16" - $265.00; 18" - $300.00. **Light craze:** Clothes dirty. 16" - $100.00; 18" - $125.00.

Military Dolls: (See photo in Series 5, pg. 65; Series 6, pg. 85) Ca. 1942 and on. All composition with painted features, molded-on hats and can be a woman or man (W.A.V.E, W.A.A.C., sailor, Marine, etc.) **Excellent condition:** Original and no crazing. 16" - $250.00 up. **Light craze:** Clothes in fair condition: 16" - $95.00.

Ventriloquist Doll: (See photo in Series 7, pg. 73.) **Dummy Dan:** Looks like Charlie McCarthy. 21" - $350.00 up.

FROZEN CHARLOTTE

Frozen Charlotte and Charlie figures can be china, partly china (such as hair and boots), stone bisque or fine porcelain bisque. They can have molded hair, have painted bald heads or take wigs. The majority have no joints, with hands extended and legs separate (some are together). They generally come without clothes and they can have painted-on boots, shoes and socks or be barefooted.

It must be noted that in 1976 a large amount of the 15½–16" "Charlie" figures were reproduced in Germany and their quality is excellent. It is almost impossible to tell that these are reproductions.

Prices are for doll figures without any damage. More must be allowed for any with unusual hairdos, an early face or molded eyelids or molded-on clothes.

All China: Glazed with black or blonde hair, excellent quality of painting and unjointed. 2" - $55.00; 5" - $110.00; 7" - $150.00; 9" - $235.00; 10" - $250.00. **Bald head with wig:** 6" - $165.00; 8" - $195.00; 10" - $275.00. **Charlie:** Molded black hair, flesh tones to neck and head. 12" - $300.00; 14" - $475.00; 17" - $650.00. **All Pink Luster:** 12" - $475.00 up. Luster to head and neck only: $385.00. Blonde: 14–15" - $600.00 up.

Untinted Bisque (Parian): Molded hair, unjointed. 4" - $150.00; 7" - $185.00.

Untinted Bisque: 1860s. Molded hair, jointed at shoulders. 4" - $160.00; 7" - $250.00.

Stone Bisque: Unjointed, molded hair, medium to excellent quality of painting. 4" - $45.00; 8" - $65.00.

Black Charlotte or Charlie: Unjointed, no damage. 3" - $200.00; 5" - $365.00; 7" - $400.00. **Jointed at shoulders:** 4" - $225.00; 7" - $425.00.

Molded Head Band or Bow: Excellent quality: 5" - $225.00; 8" - $350.00. **Medium quality:** 5" - $125.00; 8" - $175.00.

Molded-on Clothes, Shorts, or Bonnet: Unjointed, no damage and medium to excellent quality. 6" - $425.00; 8" - $525.00.

Dressed: In original clothes. Unjointed Charlotte or Charlie. No damage and in overall excellent condition. 5" - $125.00; 7" - $165.00.

Jointed at Shoulder: Original clothes and no damage. 6" - $150.00; 8" - $235.00.

Molded-on, Painted Boots: Unjointed, no damage. 5" - $165.00; 7" - $225.00. **Jointed at shoulders:** 5" - $200.00; 7" - $325.00.

Fulper Pottery Co. of Flemington, N.J. made dolls from 1918–1921. They made children and babies and used composition and kid bodies.

Marks:

Made in
U.S.A.

Child: Fair to medium quality bisque head painting. No damage, nicely dressed. **Composition body, open mouth:** 14" - $400.00; 16" - $600.00; 20" - $750.00. **Kid body, open mouth:** 15" - $400.00; 17" - $575.00; 21" - $600.00.

Child: Poor quality (white chalky look, may have crooked mouth and be poorly painted.) **Composition body:** 16" - $265.00; 21" - $375.00. **Kid body:** 16" - $185.00; 21" - $350.00.

Baby: Bent limb body. Near excellent to medium quality bisque, open mouth, no damage and dressed well. Good artist work on features. 15" - $550.00; 18" - $675.00; 25" - $985.00.

Toddler: Same as baby but has toddler jointed or straight leg body. 18" - $775.00; 26" - $1,100.00.

Baby: Poor quality bisque and painting. 16" - $250.00; 25" - $600.00.

Toddler: Poor quality bisque and painting. 18" - $425.00; 26" - $850.00.

22" doll with open mouth and two upper teeth. Bisque shoulder head on kid body with bisque lower arms. Fairly well painted and good quality bisque. Marked "Fulper." $600.00.

GANS & SEYFARTH

Dolls with the "G.S." or "G & S" were made by Gans & Seyfarth of Germany who made dolls from 1909 into the 1930s. Some dolls will be marked with the full name.

Child: Open mouth, composition body. Good quality bisque, no damage and nicely dressed. 15" - $225.00; 18" - $325.00; 20" - $425.00; 25" - $685.00.

Baby: Bent limb baby body, in perfect condition and nicely dressed. 15" - $400.00; 18" - $585.00; 22" - $700.00; 25" - $800.00. (Add more for toddler body.)

GERMAN DOLLS, MAKER UNKNOWN

Some of these unmarked dolls will have a mold number and/or a head size number and some may have the mark "Germany."

Closed Mouth Child: Excellent bisque. 1880–1890s. Composition jointed body, no damage and nicely dressed. 12" - $1,000.00; 16" - $1,900.00; 21" - $2,800.00; 25" - $3,400.00.

27" very French looking doll but may have been made by Kestner. Closed mouth with space between lips. Large glass eyes. German jointed body. Marked "16" on head. $4,000.00. *Courtesy Frasher Doll Auctions.*

Closed Mouth Child: On kid body (or cloth). May have slightly turned head, bisque lower arms. 12" - $650.00; 15" - $900.00; 20" - $1,400.00; 24" - $1,800.00; 26" - $2,000.00.

Open Mouth Child: Late 1880s to 1900. Excellent pale bisque, jointed composition body. Glass eyes, no damage and nicely dressed. 12" - $365.00; 15" - $450.00; 20" - $600.00; 23" - $700.00; 26" - $800.00; 30" - $1,200.00.

Open Mouth Child: Same as above, but on kid body with excellent quality bisque and bisque lower arms. 12" - $200.00; 15" - $385.00; 20" - $525.00; 23" - $625.00; 26" - $800.00.

Open Mouth Child: 1888–1920s. With very "dolly" type face. Overall excellent condition, composition jointed body. 12" - $200.00; 15" - $365.00; 18" - $485.00; 22" - $575.00; 25" - $625.00; 28" - $850.00; 32" - $1,000.00.

Open Mouth Child: Same as above, but with kid body and bisque lower arms. 12" - $200.00; 15" - $350.00; 18" - $465.00; 22" - $600.00.

Belton Type: May have **mold #132, 136, 137, 138,** etc. Composition jointed body. **Glass eyes:** 12" - $1,400.00; 15" - $1,900.00; 20" - $2,800.00; 24" - $3,200.00.

Glass Eyes, Closed Mouth: May have **mold #132, 136, 137, 138,** etc. Composition jointed body. Excellent overall quality. 16" - $2,600.00; 19" - $3,800.00; 23" - $4,200.00.

All Bisque: See "All Bisque – German" section.

Molded Hair: See that section.

Infants: Bisque head, molded/painted hair, cloth body with composition or celluloid hands, glass eyes. No damage. 10–12" - $325.00; 15" - $475.00; 18" - $625.00.

Babies: Solid dome or wigged, glass eyes, five-piece baby body, open mouth, nicely dressed and no damage. (Allow more for closed or open/closed

mouth or very unusual face and toddler doll.) 8–9" - $265.00; 14" - $475.00; 17" - $600.00; 22" - $765.00. **Toddler:** 14" - $550.00; 17" - $625.00.

Babies: Same as above, but with painted eyes. 8–9" - $185.00; 14" - $300.00; 17" - $400.00; 22" - $650.00.

Bonnet or Hat: See "Bonnet Doll" section.

Tiny Unmarked Doll: Head is bisque of very good quality on five-piece papier maché or composition body, glass eyes, open mouth. No damage. 6" - $225.00; 9" - $300.00; 12" - $400.00. **Poorly painted:** 6" - $125.00; 9" - $185.00; 12" - $285.00.

Tiny Doll: Same as above, but on full jointed composition body. 6" - $350.00; 9" - $450.00; 12" - $525.00.

Tiny Doll: Closed mouth, jointed body. 6" - $350.00; 9" - $500.00; 12" - $650.00. **Five-piece body:** 6" - $250.00; 9" - $350.00; 12" - $425.00.

Character Child: Unidentified, closed mouth, very character face, may have wig or solid dome, glass eyes, closed or open/closed mouth. Excellent quality bisque, no damage and nicely dressed. 16" - $4,200.00 up; 20" - $5,200.00 up.

Character: Closed mouth, glass eyes. **Mold #128, 134,** and others of this quality. 16" - $7,500.00 up; 22" - $10,000.00 up. **Painted eyes:** 16" - $6,000.00 up; 22" - $8,500.00 up. **Mold #111:** (See photo in Series 8, pg. 82.) **Glass eyes:** 22" - $22,000.00 up. **Painted eyes:** 21" - $13,000.00 up. **Mold #163:** 16" - $1,000.00.

10" bisque head doll with five-piece papier maché body. Sleep eyes, open mouth, and has excellent bisque. All original clothes and wig. Marked "1901/DEP/ 9/0." $165.00.

GLADDIE

Gladdie was designed by Helen Jensen in 1929. The German-made doll was distributed by George Borgfeldt. The cloth body has composition limbs, and the head has glass eyes. (See photos in Series 5, pg. 69; Series 6, pg. 92; Series 7, pg. 79.)

Ceramic Style or Biscaloid Head: 16–17" - $1,000.00; 19–20" - $1,300.00 up.

Bisque Head: Mold #1410. 16–17" - $4,400.00; 19–20" - $5,500.00; 25–26" - $6,800.00.

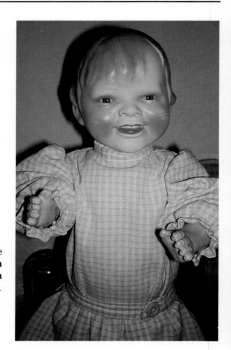

17" "Gladdie" with painted ceramic style head with glass eyes. Smiling mouth with upper teeth. On cloth body with composition limbs. 16–17" - $1,000.00. *Courtesy Ricki Small.*

GOEBEL

The Goebel factory has been operating since 1879 and is located in Oeslau, Germany. The interwoven W.G. mark has been used since 1879. William Goebel inherited the factory from his father, Franz Detlev Goebel. About 1900, the factory only made dolls, dolls heads and porcelain figures. They worked in both bisque and china glazed items.

Child: 1895 and later. Open mouth, composition body, sleep or set eyes with head in perfect condition, dressed and ready to display. 5–6" - $200.00; 14" - $485.00; 18" - $650.00; 22" - $775.00.

Child: Open/closed mouth, wig, molded teeth, shoulder plate, kid body, bisque hands. 17" - $850.00; 20" - $1,000.00.

Marks:

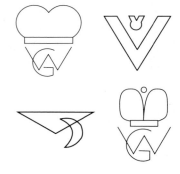

Child: Deeply molded hair; may have molded bows. Intaglio eyes, open/closed mouth, smile, jointed body. (See photo in Series 7, pg. 80.) Rare. 12" - $1,800.00; 15" - $3,200.00; 17" - $4,000.00.

Character: After 1910. Molded hair that can be in various styles, with or without molded flowers or ribbons, painted features and on five-piece papier maché body. No damage and nicely dressed. 7" - $345.00; 9" - $475.00; 12" - $600.00.

Character Baby: After 1909. Open mouth, sleep eyes and on five-piece bent limb baby body. No damage and nicely dressed. 13" - $425.00; 16" - $550.00; 19" - $725.00; 24" - $900.00.

Toddler: 14" - $550.00; 17" - $725.00; 22" - $950.00.

Molded-on Bonnet: Closed mouth, five-piece papier maché body, painted features and may have various molded-on hats or bonnets and painted hair. 7" - $375.00; 9" - $500.00; 12" - $600.00.

24" with sleep eyes and open mouth. On five-piece bent limb baby body. Marked with crown and "W" over "G" B5-11 3/4. $850.00. *Courtesy Frasher Doll Auctions.*

GOOGLY

Bisque head with glass or set eyes to the side, closed smiling mouth, impish or watermelon-style mouth, original composition or papier maché body. Molded hair or wigged. 1911 and after. Not damaged in any way and nicely dressed.

All Bisque: See All Bisque section.

Armand Marseille: #200: (See photo in Series 8, pg. 21.) 8" - $1,650.00; 12" - $2,500.00. **#210:** 8" - $2,100.00; 12" - $3,000.00. **#223:** 7" - $825.00; 10" - $1,000.00. **#240, 241:** 10–11" - $2,300.00; 13" - $2,800.00. **#248:** 9" - $1,000.00. **#252:** 8" - $950.00. **#253, 353:** 7" - $725.00; 9" - $900.00; 12" - $1,200.00. **#254:** 10" - $950.00. **#255–**

#310: (Just Me) Fired-in color. 7–8" - $1,000.00; 10–11" - $1,500.00 up; 13" - $1,700.00 up. **#310: Painted bisque.** 8" - $675.00; 12"- $1,100.00. **#320:** 9" - $1,200.00. **Glass eyes:** $1,200.00. **Painted eyes:** 6" - $700.00; 8" - $850.00. **#323: Fired-in color.** 7" - $1,250.00; 10–11" - $1,650.00; 13" - $1,800.00. **On baby body:** 14" - $1,100.00. **Painted bisque baby:** 9" - $550.00; 14" - $800.00. **#325:** 7" - $650.00; 12" - $950.00.

B.P. (Bahr & Proschild) #686: 10" - $2,100.00; 13" - $2,650.00 **Baby:** 14" - $1,600.00.

Demalcol: (See photo in Series 7, pg. 82) 10" - $525.00; 14" - $725.00.

Elite: See end of this section.

10½" #323 Armand Marseille googly with sleep eyes and excellent bisque. Cute original clothes. $1,250.00. *Courtesy Turn of Century Antiques.*

Hansi: "Gretel." (See photo in Series 8, pg. 87.) Molded hair, shoes and socks. Made of composition/celluloid-type material "prialytine." 12" - $3,500.00.

Hertel Schwab: See that section.

Heubach Einco: 9–10" - $4,800.00; 15" - $7,500.00; 17" - $8,200.00.

Heubach (marked in square): 9" - $950.00; 13" - $1,800.00. **#8676:** 7" - $750.00; 10" - $1,100.00. **#9056:** Full bangs, hair rolled under around head. 8" - $900.00 up; 12" - $1,200.00 up. **#9573:** 7" - $825.00; 9" - $1,500.00; 12" - $2,000.00. **#9578, 11173:** Called "Tiss Me." 8" - $1,500.00; 12" - $1,800.00.

Heubach Koppelsdorf: (See photo in Series 6, pg. 96) **#260, 261, 263, 264:** 7" - $365.00; 10" - $475.00. **#318:** 9" - $1,200.00; 14" - $2,000.00. **#319:** 7" - $675.00; 11" - $1,200.00. **#417:** 7" - $550.00; 13" - $1,250.00.

Kestner: #111. Jointed body. (See photo in Series 8, pg. 8.) 10" - $2,900.00; 14" - $3,400.00.

Kestner: #163, 165: This number now attributed to Hertel Schwab. 13" - $4,600.00; 15" - $5,400.00. **#172–173:** Attributed to Hertel Schwab. 11" - $3,200.00; 14" - $4,300.00. **#217, 221:** 6" - $1,100.00; 10" - $3,200.00; 12–13" - $4,200.00; 14" - $4,900.00; 16" - $5,500.00; 17" - $5,700.00.

Kammer & Reinhardt (K star R): 9" on five-piece body. $2,400.00. **#131:** 10" - $5,200.00; 14" - $7,100.00.

Kley & Hahn (K&H): Mold #180. 15" - $2,700.00; 17" - $3,200.00.

Oscar Hitt: 14" - $6,200.00; 17" - $8,400.00.

Our Fairy: See All Bisque section.

P.M. (Otto Reinecke): #950: 6" - $950.00; 8" - $1,200.00; 12–13" - $1,400.00; 15–16" - $1,800.00 up.

9½" "Just Me" with blue sleep googly eyes. Color fired in and on five-piece body with bent right elbow. $1,650.00. *Courtesy Turn of Century Antiques.*

S.F.B.J.: #245: (See photo in Series 6, pg. 96) **Five-piece body:** 8" - $1,500.00. **Fully jointed body:** 12" - $2,600.00; 15" - $4,800.00 up.

Steiner, Herm: 9" - $900.00; 12" - $1,100.00.

Composition Face: Very round composition face mask or all composition head with wig, glass eyes to side and closed impish watermelon-style mouth. Body is stuffed felt. In original clothes. **Excellent condition:** 8" - $450.00; 12" - $650.00; 14" - $950.00; 16" - $1,300.00; 20" - $1,800.00. **Fair condition:** Cracks or crazing, nicely redressed. 7" - $165.00; 11" - $300.00; 13" - $450.00; 15" - $525.00; 19" - $750.00.

Painted Eyes: Composition or papier maché body with painted-on shoes and socks. Bisque head with eyes painted to side, closed smile mouth and molded hair. Not damaged and nicely dressed. **A.M. 320, Goebel, R.A., etc.:** 6" - $350.00; 8" - $500.00; 10" - $600.00; 12" - $700.00. **Heubach, Gebruder:** 7–8" - $500.00 up.

Disc Eyes: Bisque socket head or shoulder head with molded hair (can have molded hat/cap), closed mouth and inset celluloid discs in large googly eyes. (See photo in Series 8, pg. 85.) 10" - $1,000.00; 14" - $1,200.00; 17" - $1,500.00; 21" - $1,900.00.

Molded-on Military Hat: (See photo in Series 5, pg. 71; Series 7, pg. 82; Series 8, pg. 86.) Marked "Elite." 12" - $2,700.00; 16" - $4,200.00. **Japanese Soldier:** 12" - $3,000.00. **Two faced:** 12" - $4,000.00.

14" "Sweetie" with sticker and name on bottom of foot. All composition with spring jointed arms. Molded, painted hair under wig. One leg and foot have been broken and glued on; one large toe is chipped off. This condition - $150.00; mint and original - $650.00.

14" mask face googly that is all original and in excellent condition. Glass eyes, composition head, cloth body with stitches to indicate fingers. $950.00. *Courtesy Turn of Century Antiques.*

GREINER

Ludwig Greiner of Philadelphia, PA, made dolls from 1858 into the late 1800's. The heads are made of papier maché, and they can be found on various bodies. Some can be all cloth; many are homemade. Many have leather arms or can be found on Lacmann bodies that have stitched joints at the hips and the knees and are very wide at the hip line. The Lacmann bodies will be marked "J. Lacmann's Patent March 24th, 1874" in an oval. The Greiner heads will be marked "Greiner's Patent Doll Heads/ Pat. Mar. 30, '58." Also "Greiner's/ Improved/Patent Heads/Pat. Mar. 30, '58." The later heads are marked "Greiner's Patent Doll Heads/Pat. Mar. 30, '58. Ext. '72."

Greiner Doll: Can have black or blonde molded hair, blue or brown painted eyes and be on a nice home-made cloth body with cloth arms or a commerical cloth body with leather arms. Dressed for the period and clean, with head in near perfect condition with no paint chips and not repainted.

With '58 Label: 18" - $825.00; 24" - $1,100.00; 27" - $1,250.00; 30" - $1,500.00; 35" - $1,700.00; 38" - $2,100.00. **With chips/flakes or repainted:** 17" - $500.00; 23" - $700.00; 26" - $825.00; 29" - $925.00; 34" - $1,000.00; 37" - $1,400.00.

With '72 Label: 19" - $500.00; 22" - $600.00; 27" - $800.00; 32" - $1,200.00. **With chips/flakes or repainted:** 19" - $250.00; 22" - $350.00; 27" - $450.00; 32" - $525.00.

Glass Eyes: 22" - $2,000.00; 27" - $2,500.00. **With chips/flakes or repainted:** 22" - $975.00; 27" - $1,200.00.

Unmarked: Ca. 1850. So called "Pre-Greiner." Papier maché shoulder head, cloth body can be home made. Leather, wood or cloth limbs. Painted hair, black eyes with no pupils. Glass eyes, old or original clothes. **Good condition:** 19" - $1,400.00; 27" - $1,500.00; 32" - $1,900.00. **Fair condition:** 19" - $500.00; 27" - $700.00; 32" - $900.00.

Unusual 26" Greiner has fully modeled eyelids around eyes and painted curly hair. Bears the 1872 label. $850.00 up. *Courtesy Turn of Century Antiques.*

This 19" doll is attributed to Halopeau (France), ca. 1882. Has outline eyes, blushed eyelids, open/closed mouth with white space between lips, and original human hair wig. Original wood and composition jointed French body with straight wrists. (See photo in Series 7, pg. 84.) Marked "H." 19–20" - $78,000.00; 24–25" - $88,000.00; 20" unmarked - $20,000.00; 26" unmarked - $30,000.00.
Courtesy Frasher Doll Auctions.

HALF DOLLS

Half dolls can be made of any material including bisque, papier maché and composition. Not all half dolls were used as pincushions. They were also used for powder box tops, brushes, tea cozies, etc. Most date from 1900 into the 1930s. The majority were made in Germany, but many were made in Japan. Generally, they will be marked with "Germany" or "Japan." Some have numbers; others may have the marks of companies such as William Goebel or Dressel, Kister & Co.

The most desirable are the large figures, or any size for that matter, that have both arms molded away from the body or are jointed at the shoulder. (Allow more if marked by maker.)

Arms and hands extended: Prices can be higher depending on detail and rarity of figure. Marked; china or bisque. 3" - $145.00 up; 5" - $285.00 up; 8" - $650.00 up; 12" - $950.00 up.

Arms extended: Hands attached to figure. **China or bisque:** 3" - $75.00; 5" - $115.00; 8" - $160.00. **Papier maché or composition:** 5" - $35.00; 7" - $85.00.

Bald head, arms away: 4" - $145.00 up. **Arms attached:** 4" - $75.00 up.

Common Figures: Arms and hands attached. **China:** 3" - $22.00; 5" - $35.00; 8" - $45.00. **Papier maché or composition:** 3" - $20.00; 5" - $30.00; 8" - $40.00.

Jointed Shoulders: China or bisque: 5" - $125.00; 8" - $165.00; 10" - $185.00. **Papier maché:** 4" - $40.00; 7" - $85.00. **Wax over papier maché:** 4" - $45.00; 7" - $100.00.

Children or Men: 3" - $45.00; 5" - $90.00; 7" - $110.00. **Jointed shoulders:** 3" - $75.00; 5" - $110.00; 7" - $185.00.

Japan marked: 3" - $20.00; 5" - $35.00; 7" - $55.00.

7½" German half doll with legs. Made together as "doll" at factory. Most likely meant to be skirted because doll has white strapless dress molded on. Legs have painted-on gold slippers. $160.00.

Half doll atop box of drawers. Cloth skirt opens to reveal three drawers. 20" tall overall and 15" across at base. Original, 1890s. Marked "Meissen." (See photo in *Patricia Smith's Album of All Bisque Dolls.*) $2,000.00 up. *Courtesy Ivy A. Koehn.*

The figures on these lamps are 5" tall. They are made of a composition style material with painted features, mohair wigs, and wire attached arms. Wire lamp base frames. The face on the blonde doll has a very self-satisfied expression with flirty side glance eyes. There a secret smile with cheek dimple. Her wig is original. In contrast, the brunette doll has very haughty expression with turned up nose and head with partly closed eyes. The base of blonde doll lamp is marked "Leviton 9062." Base of brunette doll lamp is marked "175 P." Each - $95.00. *Courtesy Glorya Woods.*

All of these porcelain half dolls were made in Germany and range in size from 2½" to 4½". Some of the figures have their arms modeled away from their bodies. The large center figure has an unusual hat and holds two long stem flowers. *Courtesy Glorya Woods.*

HANDWERCK, HEINRICH

Heinrich Handwerck began making dolls and doll bodies in 1876 at Gotha, Germany. The majority of their heads were made by Simon & Halbig. In 1897 they patented, in Germany, a ball jointed body #100297 and some of their bodies will be marked with this number.

Mold numbers include: **12x, 19, 23, 69, 79, 89, 99, 100, 109, 118, 119, 124, 125, 139, 152, 189, 199, 1001, 1200, 1290.**

Child: No mold number. After 1885. Open mouth, sleep or set eyes, on ball jointed body. Bisque head with no cracks, chips or hairlines, good wig and nicely dressed. 14" - $325.00; 16" - $485.00; 19" - $550.00; 23" - $675.00; 25" - $750.00; 32" - $1,250.00; 36" - $1,450.00; 41–42" - $2,400.00.

Sample mold marks:

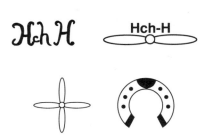

Child: Same as above but with mold marks. 12" - $450.00; 14" - $475.00; 17" - $525.00; 21" - $650.00; 24" - $725.00; 28" - $985.00; 32" - $1,400.00; 35–36" - $1,650.00; 42" - $3,200.00; 45" - $4,200.00.

Kid Body: Bisque shoulder head, open mouth. All in good condition and

HANDWERCK, HEINRICH

nicely dressed. 16" - $295.00; 19" - $385.00; 25" - $500.00; 27" - $700.00.

Mold #79, 89: With closed mouth. 14" - $1,600.00; 17" - $1,950.00 up; 21" - $2,300.00 up.

Mold #189: With open mouth. 14" - $465.00; 17" - $825.00; 21" - $975.00.

42" large doll is on fully jointed body and has excellent bisque and open mouth. Marked "421 21/Handwerck/Germany." $3,200.00. *Courtesy Frasher Doll Auctions.*

HANDWERCK, MAX

Max Handwerck started making dolls in 1900 and his factory was located at Waltershausen, Germany. In 1901, he registered "Bébé Elite" with the heads made by William Goebel. The dolls from this firm are marked with the full name, but a few are marked with "M.H."

Child: Bisque head, open mouth, sleep or set eyes, on fully jointed composition body, no damage and nicely dressed. **Mold #283, 287, 291, etc.:** 16" - $365.00; 20" - $450.00; 24" - $550.00; 28" - $800.00; 32" - $1,000.00; 40" - $2,000.00.

Bébé Elite: (See photo in Series 7, pg. 88.) Bisque heads with no cracks or chips, sleep or set eyes, open mouth. Can have a flange neck on cloth body with composition limbs or be on a bent leg composition baby body. Upper teeth and smile: 15" - $450.00; 21" - $750.00. **Toddler:** 17" - $700.00; 22" - $900.00; 26" - $1,300.00. **Socket head on fully jointed body:** 17" - $625.00; 21" - $850.00.

HERTEL, SCHWAB & CO.

Hertel, Schwab & Co. has been recognized by the German authors Jurgen and Marianne Cieslik as the maker of many dolls that were attributed to other companies all these years. There does not seem to be a "common denominator" to the Hertel, Schwab doll lines and any style can be included.

Babies: Bisque head, molded hair or wig, open or open/closed mouth, sleep or painted eyes, bent limb baby body. Good condition with no damage.

Mold #125, 127 ("Patsy"): 14" - $1,000.00; 17" - $1,400.00.

Mold #126 ("Skippy"): 12" - $1,000.00; 15" - $1,300.00.

Mold numbers: 130, 136, 142, 150, 151, 152, 153, 154: 10" - $325.00; 15" - $475.00; 17" - $600.00; 23" - $845.00; 26" - $950.00.

Child: Bisque head, painted or sleep eyes, closed mouth, jointed composition body, no damage and nicely dressed.

#119, 134, 140, 141, 149: 16" - $4,900.00; 18" - $6,000.00.

#154, closed mouth: 16" - $2,400.00; 22" - $2,800.00. **Open mouth:** 18" - $1,200.00; 22" - $1,600.00.

#169, closed mouth: 18" - $3,200.00; 22" - $3,600.00. **Toddler:** 22" - $4,000.00; 26" - $5,200.00. **Baby:** Open mouth. 21", $1,300.00; 24" - $1,500.00.

All Bisque: One-piece body and head, glass eyes, closed or open mouth. All in perfect condition.

Prize Baby, #208: 6" - $300.00; 8" - $525.00.

Swivel Neck: 6" - $450.00; 8" - $700.00; 10" - $800.00. (See #222 below.)

Googly: Large, side glance sleep or set eyes. Wig or molded hair. Closed mouth, no damage and nicely dressed.

#163: 12" - $3,000.00; 15" - $5,600.00.

#165: 12" - $3,000.00; 16" - $5,600.00.

#168: Looks like Campbell Kid. **Open/closed mouth:** 16" - $6,300.00. **Two-faced:** 15" - $7,000.00.

#172: 14–15" - $6,300.00.

#173: 12" - $3,200.00; 14" - $4,000.00.

#189: 8" - $600.00.

#217: 7½" - $725.00.

#222 (Our Fairy): Painted eyes, molded hair. 9–10" - $1,700.00; 12" - $2,250.00 up. **Wig, glass eyes:** 9–10" - $2,100.00; 12" - $2,600.00 up.

15" attributed to Hertel, Schwab but most likely made by one of the better German firms. Open/closed mouth, painted features, and on fully jointed body. Marked "140." $4,700.00. *Courtesy Ellen Dodge.*

The Heubach Brothers (Gebruder) made dolls from 1863 into the 1930's at Lichte, Thuringia, Germany. They started producing character dolls in 1910. Heubach dolls can reflect almost every mood and are often found on rather crude, poor quality bodies, and many are small dolls.

Marks:

Character Dolls: Bisque head, open/closed or closed mouth, painted eyes (allow more for glass eyes), on kid, papier maché or jointed composition bodies. Molded hair or wig. No damage and nicely dressed.

Marked "Heubach": No mold number. Open/closed mouth, deep dimples. (See photo in Series 9, pg. 98.) 20" - $4,850.00; 30" - $7,900.00.

#1017: Baby faced toddler with open mouth. 18" - $1,500.00; 22" - $1,800.00; 28" - $2,300.00.

#2850, 8058: Open/closed mouth, two rows teeth. Molded braided hair, blue ribbon bow. 16" - $9,400.00 up; 20" - $11,000.00 up.

#5636: Laughing child. Two lower teeth, intaglio painted eyes. 9" - $850.00; 12" - $1,100.00. **Glass eyes:** 12" - $1,400.00; 16" - $2,100.00.

#5689: Open mouth, smiling. Glass eyes. 16" - $1,700.00; 18" - $2,100.00; 23" - $2,300.00.

#5730 (Santa): 14" - $1,500.00; 17" - $2,300.00; 24" - $2,700.00.

#5777, 7307, 9355 (Dolly Dimples): Ball jointed body. 12–13" - $2,200.00; 16" - $2,600.00; 22" - $3,300.00; 24" - $3,500.00.

#6692: Shoulder head, smiling, intaglio eyes. 15" - $900.00 up.

#6736, 6894: Laughing, wide open/closed mouth, molded lower teeth. 10" - $900.00; 16" - $1,800.00.

#6894, 6898: Baby, closed mouth, pouty. 5" - $235.00; 6½" - $265.00; 9½" - $400.00; 12–13" - $525.00.

#6896: Pouty, jointed body. 16" - $900.00; 20" - $1,200.00.

#6969, 6970, 7246, 7248, 7347, 7407, 7602, 7802, 8017, 8420: Pouty boy or girl, jointed body, painted eyes. 6½" - $350.00; 10" - $950.00; 12" - $1,300.00; 15" - $1,900.00;

Right: 22" rare character with mischievous expression. Molded hair, intaglio eyes, and on jointed toddler body. Marked "10" with Heubach in square and "9145." Shown with 20" Kestner with open mouth. Marked "H Germany 12/J.D.K. 249." 22" - $7,000.00; 20" - $1,800.00. *Courtesy Frasher Doll Auctions.*

21" - $3,000.00. **Glass eyes:** 14" - $2,600.00; 17" - $3,200.00; 20" - $3,700.00. **Toddler, painted eyes:** 21" - $2,600.00; 25" - $3,200.00. **Toddler, glass eyes:** 20" - $3,700.00; 24" - $4,300.00.

#7172, 7550: 15" - $1,600.00.

#7448: Open/closed mouth, eyes half shut. 15" - $2,850.00.

#7134: See #7634.

#7602: Painted eyes and hair. Long face pouty. Closed mouth. 16" - $2,200.00; 20" - $2,800.00 up. **Glass eyes:** 16" - $2,700.00; 20" - $3,300.00.

#7604: Laughing expression. Jointed body, intaglio eyes. 10" - $525.00; 12" - $675.00. **Baby:** 14" - $800.00. **Walker:** Key wound. 14" - $1,600.00.

#7606: Open/closed mouth. 14" - $950.00; 20" - $1,350.00.

#7616: Open/closed mouth with molded tongue. Socket or shoulder head. Glass eyes. 12" - $1,500.00; 16" - $2,000.00.

#7620: Open/closed mouth, dimples, protruding ears. 20" - $1,460.00.

#7622, 8793, 76262: Molded hair, intaglio eyes. Closed mouth, light cheek dimples. 14" - $1,800.00; 16" - $2,200.00. **Pouty:** 14" - $985.00; 17" - $1,300.00.

#7623: Molded hair, intaglio eyes, open/closed mouth, molded tongue, on bent limb baby body. 12" - $850.00; 16" - $1,200.00. **Jointed body:** 15" - $1,500.00; 21" - $2,000.00.

#7634, 7134: Crying, squinting eyes. Wide open/closed mouth. 14" - $1,000.00; 16" - $1,500.00.

#7636: 10" - $825.00; 13" - $1,000.00.

#7644: Laughing expression. Socket or shoulder head, intaglio eyes. 14" - $850.00; 17" - $1,150.00.

#7665, 8724: Smile expression. 16" - $1,600.00.

#7666: Squinting eyes, crooked smile. 16" - $3,500.00 up.

11" Gebruder Heubach laughing character with mold number 7669. Jointed body and glass eyes. Open/closed mouth with molded tongue. $1,300.00. *Courtesy Turn of Century Antiques.*

#7661, 7686: Wide open/closed mouth, deeply molded hair. 14" - $2,300.00; 17" - $3,700.00.

#7669, 7679: Laughing expression with open/closed mouth. Glass eyes. Walker doll. 11–12" - $1,300.00; 15" - $1,750.00; 18" - $2,300.00.

7668, 7671: See Black or Brown Doll section.

#7679: Whistler with socket head. 15" - $1,200.00; 17" - $1,600.00.

#7684: Screamer with molded tongue and painted eyes. 12" - $900.00; 16" - $1,500.00

#7701: Pouty with intaglio eyes. 16" - $1,500.00; 19" - $1,900.00.

#7711: Open mouth, jointed body. 12" - $465.00; 15" - $875.00; 22" - $900.00.

#7745, 7746: Wide open/closed mouth, two painted lower teeth, molded hair. Baby or toddler: 16" - $2,000.00.

#7748: Protruding ears, open/closed mouth, two lower teeth, dimples, painted laughing eyes partly closed. Row of baby fat on back of neck. Chunky toddler body. 16" - $5,000.00 up.

#7751: Squinting eyes, open/closed mouth modeled as yawn. Molded hair, jointed body. 15" - $3,300.00; 18" - $4,000.00.

#7759: Closed mouth pouty baby. 6" - $235.00; 8" - $265.00; 10" - $400.00; 12" - $525.00.

#7763: Same description as #7768, 7788.

#7764: Wide open/closed mouth, intaglio eyes to side, deeply sculptured hair, large molded bow. Five-piece body or toddler body. 14" - $1,300.00 up; 17" - $2,000.00 up.

#7768, #7788 ("Coquette"): Tilted head, molded hair and can have ribbon modeled into hairdo. 8½" - $485.00; 10" - $750.00; 15" - $1,100.00. **Swivel neck:** 8" - $565.00; 10" - $885.00. **All Bisque:** 9" - $1,450.00 up.

#7781 Baby: Squinted eyes, wide yawn mouth. 15" - $1,800.00.

#7849: Closed mouth, intaglio eyes. 14" - $800.00.

#7851: Same description as #7764. Cloth body, composition limbs. 12" - $1,200.00.

#7852, 7862, 119: (See photo in Series 8, pg. 96.) Braids coiled around ear (molded), intaglio eyes. 16" - $2,800.00 up; 18" - $3,300.00 up.

#7911: Grin. 15" - $1,300.00.

#7925, 7926 (Adult): Painted eyes: 15" - $3,500.00 up. **Glass eyes:** 17" - $4,400.00.

#7958: Deeply modeled hair and bangs. Dimples, open/closed mouth, intaglio eyes. 15" - $3,600.00; 18" - $4,200.00.

#7959: Intaglio eyes, molded-on bonnet, deeply molded hair, open/closed mouth. 17" - $3,500.00; 21" - $4,600.00 up.

#7975 (Stuart Baby): Glass eyes, removable porcelain bonnet. 11–12" - $1,900.00.

#7977, #7877 (Stuart Baby): Molded baby bonnet. Painted eyes. 10" - $1,100.00; 12" - $1,600.00; 14" - $2,200.00; 16" - $2,800.00. **Glass eyes:** 12" - $2,000.00, 14" - $2,500.00; 16" - $3,000.00.

#8035: Boy with molded hair, painted eyes, and jointed body. Long cheeks, short chin, full lips (closed mouth). 16–17" - $9,000.00.

#8050: Lightly modeled hair, intaglio eyes, open/closed laugh mouth with two rows of teeth. 16" - $2,500.00.

#8053: Round cheeks, closed mouth, painted eyes to side, large ears. 19" - $3,500.00.

#8058: Laughing expression. Open/closed mouth, two rows teeth, painted eyes, molded hair with ribbon around head. 16–17" - $9,000.00.

22½" Gebruder Heubach child with sleep eyes and original lashes. Open mouth and fully jointed body. Marked "8191." $765.00. *Courtesy Turn of Century Antiques.*

#8145: Toddler with closed smile mouth. Eyes painted to side. Painted hair. 16" - $1,500.00 up; 20" - $1,900.00 up.

#8191: Smiling openly. Jointed body. 12" - $1,000.00; 14" - $1,200.00; 17" - $1,500.00.

#8191: "Dolly" style face, glass eyes, open mouth. Composition jointed body. 14" - $525.00; 17" - $625.00; 22" - $765.00

#8192: Open/closed smiling mouth with tongue molded between teeth. 9" - $525.00; 12" - $800.00; 16" - $1,300.00; 23" - $2,000.00. **Open mouth:** 15" - $750.00; 18" - $1,000.00.

#8197: Deeply molded curls. Molded loop for bow. Pretty face with closed mouth and full lips. Shoulder head, kid body, bisque lower arms, composition legs. 16–17" - $8,700.00 up.

#8316: Smiling expression. Open/closed mouth, molded teeth. Glass eyes, wig. 16" - $3,500.00 up; 19" - $4,700.00 up. **Painted eyes:** 14" - $1,000.00 up.

#8381: Closed mouth, pensive expression, painted eyes, molded hair, ribbon around head with bow, exposed ears. 17–18" - $3,400.00 up.

#8420: Pouty, painted eyes. 14" - $750.00; 17" - $825.00. **Glass eyes:** 9" - $825.00; 14" - $1,400.00; 16" - $1,600.00; 19" - $2,600.00.

#8459, 8469: Wide open/closed laughing mouth, two lower teeth, glass eyes. 12" - $2,500.00; 15" - $3,000.00.

#8555: Shoulder head, painted bulging eyes. (See photo in Series 8, pg. 97.) 14" - $4,900.00.

#8556: Bulging painted eyes to side and looking down. Very puckered small mouth. Deeply molded hair with top knot. Hair wave near front and onto forehead. 12" - $1,400.00; 16" - $2,200.00.

#8556: Open/closed mouth, two rows teeth, molded hair, ribbon. 18" - $8,400.00; 21" - $9,200.00.

#8590: Closed mouth, puckered lips. 14" - $1,300.00; 17" - $1,800.00. **Baby:** 14" - $1,200.00; 16" - $1,500.00.

#8596: Smile, intaglio eyes. 14" - $825.00; 16" - $1,000.00.

#8648: Extremely pouty closed mouth, intaglio eyes to side. 20" - $2,800.00; 24" - $3,600.00.

#8724: See #7665.

#8774 ("Whistling Jim"): Eyes to side and mouth modeled as if whistling. 12" - $750.00; 14" - $985.00; 17" - $1,450.00.

#8868: Molded hair, glass eyes, closed mouth, very short chin. 16" - $2,300.00; 20" - $2,900.00.

#8991: Molded hair, painted eyes to side, open/closed mouth with molded tongue, protruding ears. **Toddler body:** 15" - $2,600.00. **Kid body:** 12–13" - $1,100.00.

#9141: Winking. **Glass eyes:** 9" - $1,500.00. **Painted eyes:** 7-8" - $950.00.

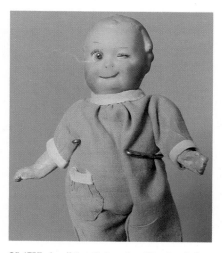

8" "Winker" by Gebruder Heubach has one eye painted closed and the other is an intaglio googly eye. Has closed "watermelon" crooked mouth. On five-piece toddler body. $985.00. *Courtesy Turn of Century Antiques.*

#9189: Same description as #7764 but no bun in molded hair. Cloth body, composition limbs. 11–12" - $1,250.00.

#9355: Shoulder head. 17" - $1,000.00; 23" - $1,800.00.

#9457 (Indian): 16–17" - $4,800.00 up.

#9891: Molded-on cap, intaglio eyes. **Aviator:** 12–13" - $1,600.00. **Sailor:** 12–13" - $1,300.00. **Farmer:** 12–13" - $1,100.00.

#10532: Open mouth, jointed body. 10" - $450.00; 14" - $700.00; 17" - $950.00; 20" - $1,300.00.

#10586, #10633: Child with open mouth, jointed body. 16" - $650.00; 19" - $800.00; 23" - $1,000.00.

#11173: Glass eyes, five-piece body, pursed closed mouth with large indented cheeks. Called **"Tiss-Me."** 8" - $1,500.00 up; 12" - $1,800.00.

Child with dolly-type face (non-character): Open mouth, glass sleep or set eyes. Jointed body, bisque head with no damage. Nicely dressed. 14" - $425.00; 16" - $525.00; 19" - $650.00; 24" - $875.00; 27" - $985.00.

Googly: See that section.

Indian Portrait, #8467: Man or woman. 14" - $4,200.00 up.

Babies or Infants: Bisque head, wig or molded hair, sleep or intaglio eyes, open/closed pouty-type mouths.

#6894, #6898, #7602: 6" - $265.00; 8" - $350.00; 12" - $450.00; 15" - $550.00; 17" - $725.00; 22" - $1,000.00; 25" - $1,300.00; 27" - $1,700.00.

#7604: Laughing expression. 12–13" - $700.00.

#7745, 7746: Laughing expression. 15–16" - $4,400.00 up.

#7959, Molded bonnet: Deep modeling to pink or blue bonnet. Molded hair to front and sides of face. 11–12" - $2,000.00 up.

#7975: See #7977 "Stuart Baby."

Animals: Bisque head on five-piece body or fully jointed body. Usually smiling with painted teeth. 8" - $900.00 up.

10" Gebruder Heubach figurine that holds dress over head and arms are modeled away from head. Excellent quality. $900.00. *Courtesy Ellen Dodge.*

Ernst Heubach began making dolls in 1887 in Koppelsdorf, Germany. Marks of this firm can be the initials "E.H." or the dolls can be found marked with the full name, Heubach Koppelsdorf, or:

Some mold numbers from this company: **27X, 87, 99, 230, 235, 236, 237, 238, 242, 250, 251, 262, 267, 271, 273, 275, 277, 283, 300, 302, 312, 317, 320, 321, 330, 335, 338, 339, 340, 342, 349, 350, 367, 399, 407, 410, 417, 438, 444, 450, 452, 458, 616, 1310, 1342, 1900, 1901, 1906, 1909, 2504, 2671, 2757, 3027, 3412, 3423, 3427, 7118, 32144.**

Child: #250, 275, 302 etc.: After 1888. Jointed body, open mouth, sleep or set eyes. No damage and nicely dressed. 8" - $165.00; 10" - $200.00; 14" - $250.00; 18" - $450.00; 22" - $500.00; 26" - $625.00; 30" - $900.00; 38" - $1,300.00.

Child: On kid body with bisque lower arms, bisque shoulder head, some turned head, open mouth. No damage and nicely dressed. 14" - $200.00; 20" - $350.00; 24" - $400.00; 30" - $750.00.

Child: Painted bisque. 8" - $100.00; 12" - $135.00.

Babies: #300, 320, 342, etc. 1910 and after. On five-piece bent limb baby body, open mouth with some having wobbly tongue and pierced nostrils. Sleep eyes. No damage and nicely dressed. (Allow more for toddler body.) 6" - $185.00; 10" - $285.00; 14" - $400.00; 16" - $500.00; 19" - $600.00; 25" - $975.00.

#300, 320: Fully jointed body. 18" - $525.00; 23" - $675.00.

Baby, #267: Typical baby with open mouth but has flirty eyes and metal eyelids that drop down over eyes. 14" - $485.00; 17" - $600.00; 20" - $785.00; 24" - $900.00.

Baby, painted bisque: 10" - $125.00; 16" - $245.00. **Toddler:** 16" - $400.00.

Infant: 1925 and after. Molded or painted hair, sleep eyes, closed mouth, flange neck bisque head on cloth body with composition or celluloid hands. No damage and nicely dressed.

#338, #340: 13" - $675.00; 15" - $925.00.

#339, #349, #350: 12" - $600.00; 14" - $800.00.

#399: White only. (See Black doll in Black or Brown Dolls section.) 14" - $465.00.

Left: 16" girl with sleep eyes and open mouth. On five-piece bent limb baby body. Marked "Heubach Koppelsdorf 300 Germany." Right: 17" boy baby by Kestner, mold #257. Flirty eyes, open mouth. 16" - $500.00; 17" - $850.00.
Courtesy Frasher Doll Auctions.

HEUBACH, (ERNST) KOPPELSDORF

Infant: 1925. Cloth body, celluloid or composition hands. Painted hair, sleep eyes, closed mouth. No damage, nicely dressed.

#339, 349, 350: 9½" - $425.00; 12" - $565.00.

#338, 340: 14" - $700.00; 16" - $800.00.

#320, 335, 339, 340, 349, 350, 399: See Black or Brown Doll section.

Character Child: 1910 on. Molded hair, painted eyes and open/closed mouth. No damage. **#262, #330 and others:** 12" - $550.00; 16" - $1,000.00.

JULLIEN

Jullien marked dolls were made in Paris, France from 1875 to 1904. The heads will be marked Jullien and a size number. In 1892, Jullien advertised "L'Universal" and the label can be found on some of his doll bodies. (See photo in Series 7, pg. 96.)

Child: Closed mouth, paperweight eyes. French jointed body of composition and papier maché with some having wooden parts. Undamaged bisque head and in excellent condition. 12" - $2,500.00; 14" - $2,900.00; 16" - $3,800.00; 18" - $4,200.00; 22" - $4,600.00; 25" - $5,200.00; 28" - $5,900.00.

Child: Same as above but with open mouth. 15" - $1,300.00; 17" - $1,700.00; 20" - $2,000.00; 22" - $2,300.00; 25" - $2,800.00. **Poor quality, high color:** 15" - $1,100.00; 20" - $1,750.00; 22" - $1,950.00; 25" - $2,300.00.

30" doll with open mouth and six teeth. French jointed body is marked "Jullien 11." $3,500.00.
Courtesy Frasher Doll Auctions.

Known Jumeau Sizes: 0 - 8–9"; 1 - 10"; 2 - 11"; 3 - 12"; 4 - 13"; 5 - 14–15"; 6 - 16"; 7 - 17"; 8 - 19"; 9 - 20"; 10 - 21–22"; 11 - 24–25"; 12 - 26–27"; 13 - 29–30".

Tete Jumeau: 1879–1899 and later. Marked with red stamp on head and oval sticker on body. Closed mouth, paperweight eyes, jointed body with full joints or jointed with straight wrists. Pierced ears with larger sizes having applied ears. No damage at all to bisque head, undamaged French body, dressed and ready to place into collection. (Allow more for original clothes and marked shoes.) 9–10" - $3,000.00 up; 12" - $3,500.00; 14" - $3,800.00; 16" - $4,100.00; 18" - $4,400.00; 20" - $4,600.00; 22" - $5,000.00; 24" - $5,400.00; 28" - $6,200.00; 30" - $6,800.00.

1907 Jumeau: Incised "1907," sometimes has the Tete Jumeau stamp. Sleep or set eyes, open mouth, jointed French body. No damage, nicely dressed. 14" - $1,800.00; 16" - $2,400.00; 19" - $2,800.00; 22" - $3,000.00; 25" - $3,500.00; 29" - $4,000.00; 34" - $5,000.00.

Tete Jumeau: Open mouth. Not incised "1907." May or may not have number. Will have marked Jumeau body. (See photo in Series 8, pg. 103, Series 9, pg. 105–107.) 16" - $2,500.00; 21" - $3,100.00; 24" - $3,600.00; 27" - $4,000.00; 30" - $4,600.00.

Tete Jumeau on adult body: Closed mouth. (See photo in Series 5, pg. 87.) Allow more for original clothes. 19–20" - $6,900.00; 25" - $7,700.00.

Tete Jumeau on adult body: Open mouth. Allow more for original clothes. (See photo in Series 9, pg. 104.) 14" - $2,200.00; 16" - $2,500.00; 19" - $2,600.00; 20" - $2,800.00; 22" - $3,200.00; 24" - $3,500.00; 28" - $4,000.00; 30" - $4,400.00; 34" - $5,000.00.

E.J. Child: Ca. early 1880s. Head incised "Depose/E. 6 J." Paperweight eyes, closed mouth, jointed body with straight wrist (unjointed at wrist). Larger dolls will have applied ears. No damage to head or body and nicely dressed in excellent quality clothes. 10" - $5,600.00 up; 14" - $5,800.00; 16" - $6,200.00; 18" - $6,600.00; 22" - $7,500.00; 26" - $8,500.00 up.

E.J. Child: Mark with number over the E.J. (Example: E.^{6}J.) 17–18" - $11,000.00; 22–23" - $18,000.00.

E.J./A Child: 19" - $15,000.00; 22" - $20,000.00; 26" - $25,000.00 up.

Depose Jumeau: (Incised) 1880. Head will be incised "Depose Jumeau" and body should have Jumeau sticker. Closed mouth, paperweight eyes and on jointed body with straight wrists,

14" doll on marked Jumeau body with straight wrists. Open/closed mouth with space between lips. Marked "Depose E. 5 J." Shown with antique doll hat and original box plus two other hats. Doll - $5,800.00; hat/box - $350.00; other hats, each - $175.00 up.

although a few may have jointed wrists. No damage at all and nicely dressed. 15" - $5,200.00; 18" - $6,000.00; 22" - $6,700.00; 25" - $7,400.00.

Long Face (Triste Jumeau): 1870s. Closed mouth, applied ears, paperweight eyes and straight wrists on Jumeau marked body. Head is generally marked with a size number. No damage to head or body, nicely dressed. 20–21" - $24,000.00 up; 25–26"- $26,000.00 up; 29–30" - $30,000.00 up; 33–34" - $36,000.00.

Portrait Jumeau: 1870s. Closed mouth, usually large almond-shaped eyes and jointed Jumeau body. Head marked with size number only and body has the Jumeau sticker or stamp. Allow more for original clothes. 10" - $5,800.00; 12" - $6,100.00; 15" - $6,800.00; 21" - $8,000.00; 25" - $12,000.00; 28" -

$16,000.00. **Very almond-shaped eyes:** 12" - $6,000.00; 15–16" - $7,200.00; 19" - $9,000.00; 24" - $14,000.00.

Phonograph Jumeau: Bisque head with open mouth. Phonograph in body. No damage, working and nicely dressed. 20" - $8,200.00; 25" - $12,000.00 up.

Wire Eye (Flirty) Jumeau: Lever in back of head operates eyes. Open mouth, jointed body, straight wrists. 18" - $6,800.00; 21" - $8,200.00; 26" - $9,600.00.

Walker: Open mouth: 20" - $2,600.00; 24" - $3,000.00. **Throws kisses:** 20" - $2,800.00; 24" - $3,200.00.

Celluloid Head: Incised Jumeau. 14" - $625.00 up.

Mold #200 Series: Examples: **201, 203, 205, 208, 211, 214, 223.** (See photo in Series 7, pg. 100.)

30" doll on Jumeau marked jointed body. Applied ears, closed mouth with space between lips. Old factory costume. Marked with incised "Depose Tete Jumeau Bte S.G.D.G. 13." $7,900.00. *Courtesy Frasher Doll Auctions.*

Beautiful 29" "Long Face Triste" Jumeau with closed mouth. On marked Jumeau body with straight wrists. Clothes are possibly original. $30,000.00 up. *Courtesy Frasher Doll Auctions.*

Very character faces and marked Jumeau. Closed mouth. No damage to bisque or body. 16" - $40,000.00 up; 20" - $68,000.00 up. (**At auction:** Original dressed African with scowl lines - $115,000.00 Smiling woman - $120,000.00.)

Mold #230 Series: Ca. 1906. Open mouth. 14" - $1,200.00; 16–17" - $1,500.00; 20" - $1,800.00 up.

S.F.B.J. or UNIS: Marked along with Jumeau. Open mouth, no damage to head and on French body. 16" - $1,400.00; 20" - $1,800.00. **Closed mouth:** 16" - $2,400.00; 20" - $3,000.00.

Two-Faced Jumeau: Has two different faces on same head, one crying and one smiling. Open/closed mouths, jointed body. No damage and nicely dressed. 15" - $11,000.00 up.

Fashion: See Fashion section.

Mold #221: Ca. 1930s. Small 10" dolls will have a paper label "Jumeau." Adult style bisque head on five-piece body with painted-on shoes. Closed mouth and set glass eyes. Dressed in original ornate gown. No damage and clean. 10–11" - $850.00 up.

Mold #306: Jumeau made after formation of Unis and mark will be "Unis/France" in oval and "71" on one side and "149" on other, followed by "306/Jumeau/1939/Paris." Called "Princess Elizabeth." Closed mouth, flirty or paperweight eyes. Jointed French body. No damage and nicely dressed. 20" - $2,700.00; 30" - $4,500.00.

Marked Shoes: #5 and up - $400.00 up.

24" all original "Bébé Phonograph" with box. Tin door in torso covers mechanism. Box has instructions in French, English, and Spanish. Doll marked "Tete Jumeau 11" on head and "Bébé Jumeau Diplome d'Honneur Brevette SGDG" on torso. Phonograph disc marked "Jumeau." $12,000.00. *Courtesy Frasher Doll Auctions.*

Beautiful 15" Jumeau doll with almond-shaped eyes and closed mouth. On marked Jumeau jointed body. Marked "Depose Tete Jumeau Bte. S.G.D.G." $3,900.00. *Courtesy Turn of Century Antiques.*

KAMMER & REINHARDT

Kammer and Reinhardt dolls generally have the Simon and Halbig name or initials incised along with their own name or mark, as Simon & Halbig made most of their heads. They were located in Thuringia, Germany, at Waltershausen and began in 1895, although their first models were not on the market until 1896. The trademark for this company was registered in 1895. In 1909, a character line of fourteen molds (#100 – #114) was exhibited at the Leipzig Toy Fair.

Marks:

Character Boy or Girl: Closed or open/closed mouth. Jointed body or five-piece body. No damage and nicely dressed.

#101: Boy "Peter"; girl "Marie." **Five-piece body:** 9" - $1,400.00; 11" - $2,100.00. **Fully jointed body:** 9"- $1,600.00; 11" - $2,000.00. 14" - $2,600.00; 16" - $3,300.00; 18" - $4,200.00; 22" - $5,300.00. **Glass eyes:** 14" - $6,400.00; 17" - $7,600.00; 21" - $10,000.00.

#102: Boy "Karl," extremely rare. 12" - $28,000.00 up; 15" - $34,000.00. **Glass eyes:** 17" - $38,000.00 up.

#103: Closed mouth, sweet expression, painted eyes **or #104:** Open/closed mouth, dimples, mischievous expression, painted eyes. Extremely rare. 19" - $56,000.00 up.

#105: Extremely rare. Open/closed mouth. Much modeling around intaglio eyes. 19" - $85,000.00 up.

#106: Extremely rare. Full round face, pursed closed full lips, intaglio eyes to side, and much chin modeling. 21" - $58,000.00 up.

#107: Pursed, pouty mouth. Intaglio eyes. 15" - $17,000.00 up; 22" - $38,000.00 up. **Glass eyes:** 17" - $36,000.00.

#109: "Elise." Very rare. (See photo in Series 8, pg. 105.) 15" - $16,000.00; 20" - $23,000.00. **Glass eyes:** 20" - $28,000.00.

#112, #112X, #112A: (See photo in Series 5, pg. 91.) Very rare. 15" - $9,800.00; 18" - $19,000.00; 23" - $26,000.00. **Glass eyes:** 15" - $16,000.00; 18" - $22,000.00; 24" - $30,000.00.

#114: Girl "Gretchen"; boy "Hans." 8" - $1,600.00; 10" - $2,800.00; 15" - $4,100.00; 19" - $5,400.00; 23" - $8,200.00. **Glass eyes:** 18" - $7,800.00; 24" - $12,000.00.

#117: Closed mouth. 14" - $4,000.00; 17" - $4,800.00; 22" - $6,200.00; 25" - $7,200.00; 28" - $8,200.00.

16" "Elise" with mold #109. Painted eyes with droopy, molded eyelids. Closed mouth, fully jointed body. Original mohair wig in coiled braids at ears. Possible original costume. **$16,000.00.** *Courtesy Frasher Doll Auctions.*

#117A: Closed mouth. 15" - $4,200.00; 18" - $5,000.00; 22" - $6,400.00; 25" - $7,400.00; 28" - $8,400.00.

#117n: Open mouth, flirty eyes. (Subtract $200.00 for sleep eyes only.) 16" - $1,200.00; 20" - $1,600.00; 23" - $1,800.00; 28" - $2,400.00; 32" - $2,700.00.

#123, #124 (Max & Moritz): (See photo in Series 8, pg. 107.) 17" - $27,000.00 up each.

#127: Molded hair, open/closed mouth. Toddler or jointed body. 16" - $1,900.00; 20" - $2,500.00; 24" - $3,100.00.

Character Babies: Open/closed mouth or closed mouth on five-piece bent limb baby body, solid dome or wigged. No damage and nicely dressed.

#100: Called "Kaiser Baby." Intaglio eyes, open/closed mouth. 12" - $550.00; 15" - $650.00; 18" - $950.00; 21" - $1,250.00. **Glass eyes:** 14" - $1,900.00; 19" - $2,500.00. **Black:** 15" - $1,100.00; 17" - $1,800.00.

#115, #115a "Phillip": 15" - $4,000.00; 18" - $4,500.00; 24" - $5,000.00; 26" - $5,500.00. **Toddler:** 16" - $4,600.00; 18" - $5,000.00; 24" - $5,500.00.

#116, #116a: 15" - $3,800.00; 18" - $4,300.00; 25" - $5,000.00. **Toddler:** 16" - $4,500.00; 21" - $5,000.00; 25" - $5,400.00. **Open Mouth:** 16" - $1,400.00; 18" - $2,300.00. **Toddler:** 20" - $3,500.00.

#127: 12" - $800.00; 16" - $1,200.00; 21" - $1,800.00; 24" - $2,200.00. **Toddler:** 15" - $1,400.00; 20" - $1,900.00; 26" - $2,500.00. **Child:** 14" - $1,450.00; 17" - $2,000.00; 22" - $2,500.00; 25" - $3,300.00.

Babies with Open Mouth: Sleep eyes on five-piece bent limb baby body. Wigs, may have tremble tongues or "mama" cryer in body. No damage and nicely dressed. Allow more for flirty eyes.

#118a: 15" - $1,600.00; 18" - $2,000.00. 20" - $2,300.00.

#119: 16" - $4,000.00; 20" - $4,900.00.

#121: 12" - $550.00; 15" - $750.00; 18" - $1,200.00; 23–24" - $1,400.00. **Toddler:** 14"- $1,000.00; 21" - $1,700.00; 25" - $2,000.00; 28" - $2,500.00.

#122, #128: 12" - $550.00; 15" - $750.00; 18" - $1,100.00; 22" - $1,300.00. **Toddler:** 14" - $1,300.00; 18" - $1,600.00; 24" - $2,000.00.

#126: 8" - $425.00; 12" - $550.00; 16" - $750.00; 20"- $900.00; 24" - $1,200.00; 28" - $1,700.00. **Toddler:**

11" all original doll with sleep eyes, pouty expression, and closed mouth. On toddler body. Marked "K * R Simon & Halbig 115A." Shown with Ginny doll and Steiff Ginny's pup. Doll is a walker and original. K * R - $4,750.00, Ginny - $385.00, pup - $165.00.
Courtesy Frasher Doll Auctions.

6½–7" - $650.00; 9" - $700.00; 16" - $975.00; 21" - $1,300.00; 24" - $1,700.00; 29" - $2,000.00. **Child Body:** 22" - $950.00; 34" - $1,800.00.

#135: 14" - $1,400.00; 20" - $2,300.00.

#172: Ca. 1925. Five-piece baby body. (Allow more for flirty eyes.) 16" - $3,000.00; 20" - $3,500.00.

19" doll with sleep eyes and original wig. On fully jointed body. Marked "K * R/Simon & Halbig." $750.00.
Courtesy Turn of Century Antiques.

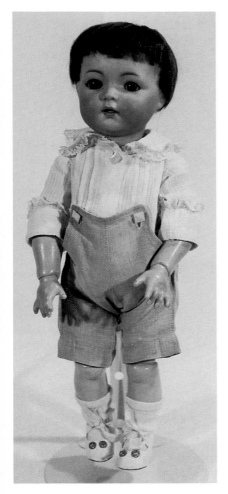

12" cute little toddler with sleep eyes and open mouth. Marked "K * R 121." $550.00 up. *Courtesy Claudia Meeker.*

Child Dolls: 1895–1930s. Open mouth, sleep or set eyes. Fully jointed body. No damage, nicely dressed. Most often found mold numbers are: **#109, 191, 290, 400, 403:** (Add more for flirty eyes. Add more for all original clothes.) 8" - $485.00; 12" - $500.00; 15" - $650.00; 18" - $700.00; 21" - $775.00; 24" - $1,150.00; 29" - $1,250.00; 34" - $1,650.00; 39" - $2,800.00; 42" - $3,400.00.

#192: Closed mouth, sleep eyes, fully jointed body. No damage. 6–7" - $625.00; 16" - $2,100.00; 22"- $2,800.00; 25" - $3,400.00. **Open mouth:** 7–8" - $475.00; 14" - $825.00; 20" - $1,250.00; 25" - $1,500.00.

Small Child Dolls: Open mouth, sleep eyes (some set). On five-piece bodies. No damage. 6" - $365.00; 8" - $500.00. **Jointed body:** 8" - $565.00; 10" - $675.00.

KAMMER & REINHARDT

Small Child Doll: Open mouth, flapper style, painted bisque. 8" - $450.00.
Small Child Doll: Closed mouth. 6" - $525.00; 8" - $650.00.
Googly: See Googly section.

Celluloid: See Celluloid section.
Infant: 1924 on. Molded hair, glass eyes, open mouth. Cloth body with composition hands. 14" - $1,850.00; 17" - $2,800.00.

KESTNER, J.D.

Johannes Daniel Kestner's firm was founded in 1802, and his name was carried through the 1920s. The Kestner Company was one of the few that made entire dolls, both bodies and heads. In 1895, Kestner started using the trademark of the crown and streamers. (Also see German - All Bisque.)

Sample marks:

B MADE IN 6	J.D.K.
GERMANY	208
J.D.K.	GERMANY
126	

F GERMANY 11

9" cute pouty doll from Kestner mold #169. Sleep glass eyes, closed mouth. Original wig and shoes. On jointed body. $1,400.00. *Courtesy Ricki Small.*

Child Doll, Closed mouth: Ca. 1880. Some appear to be pouties, some may have very sweet expression. Sleep or set eyes, jointed body with straight wrist. No damage and nicely dressed.
#X, XII, XV, 1003: 15" - $3,200.00; 18" - $3,600.00; 22" - $4,000.00; 25" - $4,400.00.
#XI, 103: Very pouty. (See photo in Series 7, pg. 106.) Price will be less for kid body. 11–12" - $2,200.00; 16" - $3,100.00; 18" - $3,800.00; 22" - $4,000.00; 25" - $4,300.00.
#128 Pouty, #169, or unmarked Pouty: #128 can have sweet expression. On five-piece body. 6½–7" - $1,000.00; 10" - $1,400.00; 12" - $1,700.00; 14" - $2,100.00; 17" - $2,400.00; 19" - $2,600.00; 23" - $3,000.00; 26" - $3,500.00.
Turned Shoulder Head: Ca. 1880s. **Closed mouth:** Set or sleep eyes, on kid body with bisque lower arms. No damage and nicely dressed. (Allow more for swivel neck.) 16" - $1,500.00; 18" - $1,700.00; 23" - $2,200.00; 26" - $2,600.00. **Open mouth:** 16" - $650.00; 18" - $725.00; 23" - $975.00.

Early Child: Square cut porcelain teeth. Jointed body. Marked with number and letter. 15" - $1,200.00; 18" - $1,800.00; 22" - $2,100.00 up; 25" - $2,300.00 up.

A.T. Type: (See photo in Series 8, pg. 111.) Composition jointed body with straight wrists. **Closed mouth:** 11" - $12,000.00; 13" - $15,000.00; 15" - $18,000.00; 17" - $21,000.00. **Open Mouth:** 13" - $2,100.00; 15" - $2,900.00; 17" - $3,300.00.

Bru Type: (See photo in Series 7, pg. 107; Series 8, pg. 112.) Open/closed mouth, modeled teeth. **Composition lower arms, kid body:** 16" - $2,500.00; 22" - $3,200.00. **Bisque lower arms:** 17" - $5,200.00; 24" - $6,400.00. **On jointed composition body, straight wrists:** 18" - $4,800.00; 23" - $5,800.00; 26" - $6,400.00.

11" Kestner character with painted brown eyes, closed mouth, mohair wig, and original leather boots. Fully jointed body. Marked "178." $2,000.00. *Courtesy Turn of Century Antiques.*

Character Child: 1910 and after. Closed mouth or open/closed unless noted. Glass or painted eyes, jointed body and no damage and nicely dressed. **#175, 176, 177, 178, 179, 180, 181, 182, 183, 184, 185, 187, 188, 189, 190:** These mold numbers can be found on the boxed set doll that has one body and interchangable four heads. (See photos in Series 5, pg. 96; Series 6, pg. 124.) **Boxed set with four heads:** 12–13" - $9,000.00 up. **Larger size with painted eyes, closed or open/closed mouth:** 12" - $2,000.00; 15" - $2,800.00;

14" with sleep eyes, full cheeks with open mouth and square cut teeth. Original wig. Jointed body with straight wrists. Marked "7 Kestner." $1,200.00. *Courtesy Frasher Doll Auctions.*

18" - $3,500.00. **Same as previous listing but with glass eyes:** 12" - $2,800.00; 15" - $3,600.00; 18" - $4,600.00. **Glass eyes, molded-on bonnet:** 16" - $4,800.00 up.

#151: 16" - $2,700.00; 20" - $3,600.00.

#155: Five-piece body: 8–9" - $565.00. **Jointed body:** 8–9" - $800.00.

#206: Fat cheeks, closed mouth. (See photo in Series 8, pg. 112.) **Child or toddler:** 15" - $10,000.00; 21" - $18,000.00; 25" - $23,000.00.

#208: Painted eyes: 16" - $5,000.00; 19" - $9,400.00; 26" - $14,000.00. **Glass eyes:** 18" - $11,000.00; 24" - $14,500.00.

#212: 10" - $2,100.00; 15" - $3,800.00.

#239: Child or toddler. (Also see "Babies."): 17" - $3,800.00; 21" - $4,800.00; 26" - $6,400.00.

#241: Open mouth, glass eyes. (See photo in Series 7, pg. 108.) 16" - $4,400.00; 22"- $5,800.00.

#249: 17" - $1,400.00; 20" - $1,800.00.

#260: Jointed or toddler body. 8" - $675.00; 12" - $975.00; 16" - $1,700.00; 22" - $2,400.00.

Child Doll: Late 1880s to 1930s. Open mouth on fully jointed body, sleep eyes, some set, with no damage and nicely dressed.

#128, 129, 134, 136, 141, 142, 144, 146, 152, 156, 159, 160, 161, 162, 164, 168, 174, 196, 211, 214, 215: 10" - $485.00; 14" - $700.00; 17" - $800.00; 20" - $900.00; 22" - $975.00; 25" - $1,200.00; 30" - $1,500.00; 33" - $1,850.00; 37" - $2,800.00.

#143, 189: (See photo in Series 6, pg. 126.) Character face, open mouth. 8" - $685.00; 12" - $825.00; 16" - $975.00; 18" - $1,200.00; 20" - $1,500.00; 24" - $1,900.00 up.

#192: 15" - $675.00; 18" - $800.00; 21" - $975.00.

Child: Open mouth, square cut teeth part of head (not separate). 10–11" - $650.00; 14" - $800.00; 16–17" - $950.00; 20–21" - $1,600.00; 24" - $2,000.00.

Child Doll, Kid Body: "Dolly" face, open mouth, sleep or set eyes, bisque shoulder head, bisque lower arms. No damage and nicely dressed.

#145, 147, 148, 149, 155, 166, 167, 170, 195, etc. (Add more for fur eyebrows): 8" - $200.00; 12" - $300.00; 16" - $400.00; 19" - $485.00; 22" - $525.00; 25" - $700.00; 29" - $985.00.

#142, 144, 146, 154, 164, 167, 168, 171, 196, 214: Jointed body: Open mouth. 10" - $650.00; 14" - $600.00; 17" - $700.00; 22" - $825.00; 25" - $925.00; 30" - $1,100.00; 35" - $1,350.00; 42" - $1,800.00 up. **Swivel bisque head:** Bisque shoulder head. Open mouth. 17" - $565.00; 21" - $800.00; 26" - $1,100.00. **Kid body:** 17" - $450.00; 21" - $525.00; 26" - $700.000.

#171 (Daisy), some #154: Blonde, side part mohair wig. White dress, red hooded cape. 18" only. Original - $965.00; Redressed - $600.00.

Character Babies: 1910 and later. Bent limb baby bodies, sleep or set eyes, open mouth. Can be wigged or have solid dome with painted hair. No damage and nicely dressed.

#121, 142, 150, 151, 152, 153, 154: Now attributed to Hertel, Schwab & Co. 10" - $325.00; 14" - $465.00; 17" - $600.00; 20" - $750.00; 24" - $900.00.

#211, 226, 236, 260, 262, 263: 9" - $600.00; 15"- $625.00; 18" - $750.00; 20" - $975.00; 24" - $1,300.00.

#220: 15" - $5,200.00; 18" - $6,200.00. **Toddler:** 17" - $6,350.00; 25" - $7,600.00.

#234, 235, 238: 13" - $625.00; 16" - $725.00; 20" - $900.00; 24" - $1,100.00.

#237, 245, 1070 (Hilda): Wigged or solid dome. 12" - $2,800.00; 16" - $3,600.00; 19" - $4,600.00; 22" - $5,300.00; 24" - $6,500.00. **Toddler:** 16" - $5,300.00; 21" - $5,600.00; 24" - $6,700.00.

#239: 15" - $2,500.00; 17" - $3,000.00; 23" - $3,500.00.

#247: 12" - $1,200.00; 16" - $1,700.00; 19" - $2,000.00; 22" - $4,000.00.

#249: 16" - $1,800.00; 20" - $2,200.00.

#257: 9" - $500.00; 14" - $675.00; 18" - $900.00; 21" - $1,000.00; 25" - $1,600.00. **Toddler:** 22" - $1,450.00; 27" - $2,100.00.

#279, 200 (Century Doll): Molded hair with part, bangs, cloth body, composition hands. 15" - $1,100.00; 18" - $2,200.00; 23" - $4,800.00.

#281 (Century Doll): Open mouth: 20" - $1,000.00.

J.D.K. Marked Baby: Called "Sally," "Jean," or "Sammy." Solid dome, painted eyes and open mouth. 13" - $825.00; 15" - $1,100.00; 20" - $2,000.00; 25" - $2,500.00.

Adult Doll, #162: Sleep eyes, open mouth, adult jointed body (thin waist and molded breasts) with slender limbs. No damage and very nicely dressed. 14" - $1,400.00; 17" - $1,600.00; 22" - $2,300.00.

Adult #172: 1910, "Gibson Girl." Bisque shoulder head with closed mouth, kid body with bisque lower arms, glass eyes. No damage and beautifully dressed. 10–11" - $1,150.00; 14" - $2,000.00; 16" - $3,600.00; 20" - $4,200.00.

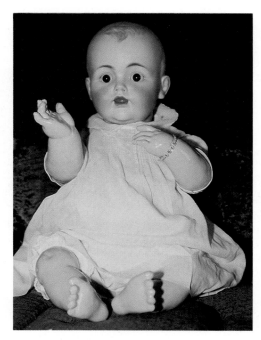

26" solid dome head baby with sleep eyes, open mouth, and molded tongue. On five-piece bent limb baby body. Marked "Made in Germany 49." **$2,500.00.** *Courtesy Jeannie Mauldin.*

Oriental #243: Olive fired-in color to bisque. Matching color five-piece bent limb baby body (or jointed toddler-style body), wig, sleep or set eyes. No damage and dressed in oriental style. 14" - $4,600.00; 17" - $6,000.00. **Child:** Same as above, but on jointed Kestner olive-toned body. 15" - $5,200.00; 18" - $7,200.00. **Molded hair baby:** 14" - $4,800.00.

Small Dolls, open mouth: Five-piece bodies or jointed bodies, wigs, sleep or set eyes. No damage and nicely dressed. 7" - $500.00; 9" - $650.00. **Closed mouth:** 8–9" - $1,200.00.

#133: 9" - $850.00.

#155: Five-piece body: 8–9" - $500.00. **Jointed body:** 8–9" - $785.00.

KEWPIES

Designed by Rose O'Neill and marketed from 1913. All prices are for dolls that have no chips, hairlines or breaks. (See Modern section for composition and vinyl Kewpies.)

Labels:

All Bisque: One-piece body and head, jointed shoulders only. Blue wings, painted features with eyes to one side. 2½" - $125.00; 4½" - $185.00; 6" - $225.00; 7" - $250.00; 8" - $400.00; 10" - $625.00. **With any article of clothing:** 3" - $250.00; 5" - $300.00; 7" - $350.00; 9" - $650.00 up.

All Bisque: Jointed at hips and shoulders. 4" - $300.00; 9" - $695.00; 12" - $1,100.00. **Painted shoes and socks:** 4–5" - $425.00.

Shoulder Head: Cloth or stockinette body. 6–7" - $650.00. **Head Only:** 3" -$175.00.

Action Kewpie: Arms folded: 4½" - $525.00.

Confederate Soldier: 4½" - $500.00.

Cowboy: Big hat, gun. Made as lamp. (See photo in Series 7, pg. 11.) 10½" - $700.00.

Farmer: 4" - $425.00.

Very large 7" "Thinker" Kewpie that is extremely well detailed and painted. Shown with 5" standing Kewpie that is jointed at shoulders only. 7" - $600.00; 5" - $185.00. *Courtesy Shirley Bertrand.*

Gardener: 4" - $425.00.
Governor: 4" - $425.00.
Groom with Bride: 4" - $365.00.
Guitar Player: 3½" - $325.00.
Holding pen: 3" - $325.00.
Holding cat: 4" - $475.00.
Holding butterfly: 4" - $550.00.
Hugging: 3½" - $300.00.
On stomach: Called "Blunderboo."
4" - $475.00.
Soldier: 4½" - $500.00.
Thinker: 4" - $265.00; 6" - $400.00.
Traveler: Tan or black suitcase.
3½" - $325.00.
With broom: 4" - $425.00.
With dog, Doodle: 3½" - $1,200.00.
With helmet: 6" - $550.00.
With outhouse: 2½" - $1,200.00.
With pumpkin: 4" - $350.00.
With rabbit: 2½" - $365.00.
With rose: 2" - $400.00.
With teddy bear: 4" - $500.00.
With turkey: 2" - $325.00.
With umbrella and dog: 3½" -
$1,8300.00.
Kewpie soldier and nurse: 6" -
$2,300.00 up.
Kewpie tree: Or mountain. 17
figures. $20,000.00 up.
Kewpie driving chariot:
$2,800.00 up.

**3½" log vase with 1" Kewpie and 1½"
Doodle dog attached to it. $725.00.**
Courtesy Shirley Bertrand.

Kewpie on inkwell: Bisque: 3½" -
$550.00. Cast metal: 3½" - $425.00; 6" -
$750.00.
Kewpie in basket with flowers:
3½" - $550.00.
Kewpie with drawstring bag:
4½" - $525.00.
Buttonhole Kewpie: $165.00.
Sitting in chair: Arms crossed.
(See photo in Series 8, pg. 96.) 3½" -
$475.00.
Kewpie and dog on bench: 4" -
$2,600.00 up.

Three 4" Kewpies. The one laying on stomach is called "Blunderboo." Its eyes and
facial look are painted slightly different from the others. All have tiny blue wings.
Each - $485.00 up. *Courtesy Shirley Bertrand.*

Kewpie Doodle Dog: (See photo in Series 8, pg. 117.) 1½" - $500.00; 3" - $1,200.00.

Hottentot (Black Kewpie): 3½" - $400.00; 5" - $500.00; 9" - $900.00.

Kewpie perfume bottle: 3½" - $375.00 up.

Pincushion Kewpie: 2½" - $300.00.

Celluloid Kewpies: 2" - $40.00; 5" - $85.00; 9" - $165.00. Black: 5" - $145.00. **Jointed shoulders:** 3" - $70.00; 5" - $110.00; 9" - $175.00; 12" - $250.00; 16" - $600.00 up; 22" - $900.00 up. **Soldier or Action:** 4" - $100.00 up.

Cloth Body Kewpie: Bisque head, painted eyes. 10" - $1,700.00; 14" - $2,200.00. **Glass eyes:** 12" - $2,600.00 up; 16" - $4,500.00 up. **Composition head and half arms:** 13" - $350.00.

Glass Eye Kewpie: Chubby jointed toddler body. Bisque head. Marked "Ges. Gesch./O'Neill J.D.K." 10" - $4,000.00; 12" - $4,400.00; 16" - $6,200.00; 20" - $7,900.00.

All Cloth: (Made by Kreuger) All one-piece with body forming clothes, mask face. **Mint condition:** 7–8" - $175.00; 12" - $200.00; 15" - $350.00; 21" - $550.00; 26" - $1,100.00. **Fair condition:** 12" - $90.00; 15" - $150.00; 21" - $250.00; 26" - $450.00.

All Cloth: Same as above but with original dress and bonnet. Mint condition. 12" - $265.00; 15" - $450.00; 21"- $700.00; 26" - $1,300.00.

Kewpie Tin or Celluloid Talcum Container: Excellent condition: 7–8" - $185.00.

Kewpie Soaps: 4" - $95.00 each. Boxed set of five: $525.00.

Japan: Bisque. 2" - $40.00; 3" - $60.00; 4" - $80.00; 5" - $100.00; 6" - $125.00.

4½" tall paperweight with Kewpie in center. Has painted-on blue wings. Marked on base "Gibson 1935." $325.00 up. *Courtesy Kathy Tvrdik.*

4" Kewpies - one with painted-on boots; the other with shoes and socks. Note how painted eyes are different. Boots - $265.00; shoes - $200.00. *Courtesy Shirley Bertrand.*

Kley & Hahn operated in Ohrdruf, Germany from 1895 to 1929. They made general dolls as well as babies and fine character dolls.

Marks:

K & H   > K&H <

Character Child: Boy or girl. Painted eyes (some with glass eyes), closed or open/closed mouth; on jointed body. No damage and nicely dressed.

#320, 520, 523, 525, 526, 531, 536, 546, 547, 548, 549, 552: 12" - $3,600.00; 15" - $3,500.00; 18" - $4,400.00; 22" - $5,300.00; 25" - $6,000.00.

Same mold numbers on toddler bodies: 16" - $2,800.00; 20" - $3,900.00; 24" - $4,900.00.

Same mold numbers on bent limb baby body: 14" - $1,000.00; 16" - $1,800.00; 20" - $2,600.00; 23" - $3,000.00.

Same mold numbers with glass eyes: Child. 14" - $4,000.00; 18" - $6,500.00; 21" - $7,200.00; 25" - $8,000.00.

Character Baby: Molded hair or wig, glass sleep eyes or painted eyes. Can have open or open/closed mouth. On bent limb baby body, no damage and nicely dressed. **#130, 132, 138, 142, 150, 151, 158, 160, 161, 162, 167, 176, 199, 458, 522, 525, 531, 538, 585, 680:** 10" - $500.00; 16" - $625.00; 20" - $900.00; 24" - $1,100.00; 26" - $1,350.00.

Same mold numbers on toddler bodies: 14" - $625.00; 16" - $825.00; 20" - $1,100.00; 24" - $1,450.00; 28" - $1,700.00.

18½" with round pouty face, full closed mouth, and glass eyes. Marked "K&H 547 8½ Germany." $6,500.00. *Courtesy Frasher Doll Auctions.*

#547: Closed mouth, glass eyes. 16" - $6,200.00.

#538, 568: 15" - $700.00; 17" - $800.00; 20" - $950.00. **Toddler:** 22" - $1,500.00; 26" - $1,900.00.

#162, talker mechanism in head: 17" - $1,500.00; 23" - $2,300.00; 25" - $2,800.00.

#162, flirty eyes and clockworks in head: 18" - $1,800.00; 26" - $3,200.00.

#680: 16" - $850.00. **Toddler:** 20" - $1,500.00.

#153, 154, 157, 166, 169: Child, closed mouth. (See photo in Series 7, pg. 114.) 16" - $3,200.00; 22" - $4,000.00. **Open mouth:** 16" - $1,300.00; 22" - $1,700.00.

#159 Two-faced Doll: 12" - $1,900.00; 15" - $2,400.00.

#166: Molded hair and open mouth. 17–18" - $1,500.00. **Closed mouth:** 18" - $3,000.00.

#169: Closed mouth. **Toddler:** 14" - $2,300.00; 18" - $3,600.00. **Open mouth:** 20" - $1,400.00.

#119: Child, glass eyes, closed mouth. 20" - $5,000.00. **Painted eyes:** 20" - $3,500.00. **Toddler:** Glass eyes. 20" - $4,800.00.

Child Dolls, Walküre, and/or #250: Sleep or set eyes, open mouth, jointed body. No damage and nicely dressed. 8" - $345.00; 14" - $450.00; 17" - $550.00; 20" - $685.00; 24" - $800.00; 28" - $1,000.00; 32" - $1,600.00.

KNOCH, GEBRUDER

Gebruder Knoch porcelain factory operated in Neustadt, Germany from 1887 into the 1920's. Most of their dolls have bisque shoulder heads and kid or cloth bodies, but some will be on jointed bodies and/or have kid bodies with composition jointed limbs.

Marks:

Left: Cute 9¾" child with closed mouth and jointed body. Incised "3920 G.K." Right: 7¾" unmarked doll with open mouth and on five-piece body. 9¾" - $850.00; 7¾" - $295.00. *Courtesy Turn of Century Antiques.*

Character Doll: No damage and ready to display in collection.

#206: 10" - $950.00; 15" - $1,450.00.

#216, 218: 14" - $2,300.00; 18" - $3,000.00.

#246: Winking, has molded cap. 13–14" - $3,250.00.

#237: Molded decorated bonnet. 9–10" - $825.00; 14" - $1,300.00.

Child Doll: Perfect, no damage, nicely dressed. Sleep eyes, wig, open mouth, ball-jointed body. 14" - $275.00; 17" - $425.00; 20" - $525.00.

Käthe Kruse began making dolls in 1910. In 1916, she obtained a patent for a wire coil doll, and in 1923 she registered a trademark of a double "K" with the first one reversed, along with the name Käthe Kruse. The first heads were designed after her own children and copies of babies from the Renaissance period. The dolls have molded muslin heads that are handpainted in oils, and jointed cloth bodies. These early dolls will be marked "Käthe Kruse" on the foot and sometimes with a "Germany" and number.

Early Marked Dolls, Model I: 1910. Wide hips, painted hair. In excellent condition and with original clothes. (See photo in Series 7, pg. 116; Series 8, pg. 120.) 16" - $3,200.00; 19" - $3,700.00. **Fair condition:** Not original. 16" - $1,600.00; 19" - $1,900.00. **Ball-jointed knees:** (See photo in Series 8, pg. 120.) 16" - $3,600.00; 19" - $4,100.00.

Model II: 1922 on. Smile, baby. 14" - $2,450.00.

Model III, IV: 1923 on. Serious child. 16" - $2,000.00 up.

Model V, VI: 1925 on. Typical Kruse. 16" - $1,500.00; 19" - $1,800.00. **Baby:** Painted open or closed eyes. 20" - $3,400.00 up.

Model VII: 1927 on. (See photo in Series 7, pg. 116; Series 8, pg. 120.) 15–16" - $1,400.00; 19" - $1,850.00.

18" Käthe Kruse Model #1 that is in near mint condition. Never played with and all original clothes. Brown oil-painted eyes, cupped cloth hands and rather pouty expression. **$2,200.00.** *Courtesy Turn of Century Antiques.*

Model VIII, IX: 1929 on. (See series 9, pg. 123.) 16" - $1,600.00; 21" - $2,400.00. **Good condition:** 21" - $1,300.00.

Model X: 1935 on. 14–15" - $1,200.00.

1920s Dolls: Model IH and others. (See photo in Series 7, pg. 116; Series 8, pg. 121.) Molded hair or wigged, hips are wide. **Excellent condition:** Original. 16" - $1,800.00; 21" - $2,600.00. **Fair condition:** Not original. 16" - $1,000.00; 21" - $1,600.00.

U.S. Zone: Germany 1945–1951 (Turtle mark.) 14" - $975.00; 17" - $1,100.00.

Plastic Dolls: 1950s–1975. Glued-on wigs, sleep or painted eyes. Marked with turtle mark and number on head and back "Modell/Käthe Kruse/" and number. 15" - $450.00; 18" - $600.00.

Celluloid: 12" - $265.00; 16" - $450.00.

1975 to date: 9" - $185.00; 13" - $365.00; 17" - $465.00.

KUHNLENZ, GEBRUDER

Kuhnlenz made dolls from 1884 to 1930 and was located in Kronach, Bavaria. Marks from this company include the "G.K." plus numbers such as 56-38, 44-15, 44-26, 41-28, 56-18, 44-15, 38-27.

Other marks now attributed to this firm are:

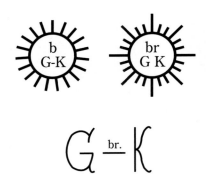

Left: Gebruder Kuhnlenz doll on early jointed body with straight wrists. Has vivid blue glass eyes. Open mouth with six teeth. Marked "44.27." Right: 16" Kestner with open mouth and two upper teeth. Fully jointed body. Marked "D Germany 143." Kuhnlenz - $525.00; Kestner - $900.00. *Courtesy Frasher Doll Auctions.*

Mold #31, 32, Child with closed mouth: Bisque head in perfect condition, jointed body and nicely dressed. 10" - $600.00; 15" - $1,000.00; 19" - $1,500.00; 23" - $1,800.00.

Mold #34: Bru type. 13" - $1,300.00; 17" - $2,600.00.

Mold #38: Kid body, bisque shoulder head. 15" - $600.00; 22" - $900.00.

Mold #41, 44, 56, Child with open mouth: Bisque head in perfect condition, jointed body and nicely dressed. 15" - $550.00; 19" - $825.00; 23" - $1,000.00.

Mold #61: Shoulder head, kid body. 20" - $800.00.

Mold #165: Bisque head in perfect condition, jointed body and nicely dressed. 18" - $500.00; 24" - $700.00.

Mold #44, 46 and others, Tiny dolls: Bisque head in perfect condition, five-piece body with painted-on shoes and socks, open mouth. 8" - $250.00. **Closed mouth:** 8" - $500.00. **Fully jointed body:** 8" - $325.00 up.

LANTERNIER (LIMOGES)

A. Lanternier & Cie of Limoges, France made dolls from about the 1890's on into the 1930s. Before making dolls, they produced porcelain pieces as early as 1855. Their doll heads will be fully marked and some carry a name such as "LaGeorgienne Favorite," "Lorraine," "Cherie," etc. They generally are found on papier maché bodies but can be on fully jointed composition bodies. Dolls from this firm may have nearly excellent quality bisque to very poor quality. (See photo on cover of this book. Photo description and price under Photo Credits on pg. 3.)

Marks:

FABRICATION FRANCAISE

AL & CIE
LIMOGES

Child: 1915. Open mouth, set eyes on jointed body. No damage and nicely dressed. Good quality bisque with pretty face. 15" - $565.00; 20" - $775.00; 24" - $975.00; 27" - $1,100.00. **Poor quality bisque:** Very high coloring or blotchy color bisque. 16" - $365.00; 20" - $425.00; 24" - $550.00; 27" - $700.00.

Jumeau style face: Has a striking Jumeau look. Good quality bisque. 18" - $1,300.00; 21" - $1,600.00. **Poor quality bisque:** 19" - $750.00; 23" - $950.00.

Character: 1915. Open/closed mouth with teeth, smiling fat face, glass eyes, on jointed body. No damage and nicely dressed. Marked "Toto." 17" - $950.00; 21" - $1,400.00.

Lady: 1915. Adult-looking face, set eyes, open/closed or closed mouth. Jointed adult body. No damage and nicely dressed. 14" - $1,000.00; 17" - $1,500.00.

Lenci dolls are all felt with a few having cloth torsos. They are jointed at neck, shoulders and hips. The original clothes will be felt, organdy, or a combination of both. Features are oil painted and generally eyes are painted to the side. Other characteristics are sewn together middle and fourth fingers and the steam-molded head is seamless with sewn-on felt ears. Size can range from 5" to 45". (Mint or rare dolls will bring higher prices.)

Marks: On cloth or paper label "Lenci Torino Made in Italy." "Lenci" may be written on bottom of foot or underneath one arm.

Children: No moth holes, very little dirt, doll as near mint as possible and all in excellent condition. 14" - $800.00 up; 16" - $1,200.00 up; 18" - $1,200.00 up; 20" - $1,600.00 up. **Dirty, original clothes in poor condition or redressed:** 14" - $300.00; 16" - $450.00; 18" - $625.00; 20" - $750.00.

Baby: (See photos in Series 5, pg. 108.) 16" - $1,800.00; 20" - $2,300.00. **Fair condition:** $800.00-1,200.00.

Tiny Dolls (Called Mascottes): (See photos in Series 7, pg. 120; Series 8, pg. 126.) **Excellent condition:** 5" - $250.00; 8–9" - $365.00. **Dirty, redressed, or original clothes in poor condition:** 5" - $95.00; 8–9" - $165.00.

Ladies with adult faces: "Flapper" or "Boudoir" style with long limbs. (See photos in Series 5, pg. 107, Series 6, pg. 136.) **Excellent condition:** 14–15" - $1,000.00; 24" - $2,200.00 up; 27" - $2,600.00 up. **Dirty or in poor condition:** 24" - $750.00; 28" - $875.00.

14" Lenci that is very mint and original. Apparently never played with. Ca. 1920s. $800.00 up. *Courtesy Shirley Bertrand.*

14" "Lucia" face on mint and all original Lenci. Has extremely pale blue eyes. Original tag from Kimport Exports of 1929–1930. Dress tagged "Bruxelles." (*Bruxelles* is French for *Brussels.*) $1,100.00 up. *Courtesy Ricki Small.*

Clowns: Excellent condition: 18" - $1,600.00; 27" - $2,000.00. **Poor condition:** 18" - $600.00; 27" - $950.00.

Indians or Orientals: Excellent condition: 17" - $3,800.00. **Dirty and poor condition:** 17" - $1,000.00.

Golfer: Excellent, perfect condition. 16" - $2,400.00. **Poor condition:** 16" - $950.00.

Pan: Has hooved feet. 9½–10" - $2,100.00. **Dirty and fair condition:** 9½–10" - $500.00.

Shirley Temple type: Excellent condition: 24" - $2,100.00. **Dirty and poor condition:** 24" - $800.00.

Bali Dancer: Excellent condition: 18" - $1,800.00. **Poor condition:** 18" - $550.00.

Smoking Doll: Painted eyes. **Excellent condition:** 25" - $2,100.00 up. **Poor condition:** 25" - $1,000.00.

Glass eyes: Excellent condition: 17" - $2,800.00; 22" - $3,500.00. **Poor condition:** 17" - $9500.00; 22" - $1,100.00.

"Surprise Eyes" Doll: Very round painted eyes and O-shaped mouth. (See photo in Series 9, pg. 128.) 15" - $1,900.00; 19" - $2,500.00. **Flirty glass eyes:** 15" - $2,600.00; 19" - $3,200.00.

Teenager: Long-legged child. 16–17" - $1,000.00 up; 25" - $1,550.00; 36" - $2,200.00.

Boys: Side part hairdo. **Excellent condition:** 18" - $2,200.00 up; 23" - $2,600.00. **Poor condition:** 18" - $850.00; 23" - $975.00. **In Fascist uniform:** 17" - $1,800.00 up. **Winking:** 1920s. Open/closed mouth, painted teeth. (See photo in Series 9, pg. 127.) 11" - $2,800.00; 14" - $3,100.00.

Petite 15" "Salon Boudoir" lady by Lenci that is very mint and all original. Has adult face and long slim limbs. Gown is combination of organdy and felt. $1,000.00. *Courtesy Ricki Small.*

LENCI

Lenci type: Can be made in Italy, Germany, France, Spain, or England. 1920s through 1940s. Felt and cloth. **Child:** Felt or cloth, mohair wig, cloth body. Original clothes. 16" - $600.00; 18" - $725.00.

Small Dolls: Dressed as child. 7 – 8" - $60.00; 12" - $100.00. **In foreign costume:** 7–8" - $45.00.

LIMBACH

These dolls were made mostly from 1893 into the 1920's by Limbach Porzellanfabrik, Limbach, Germany. Allow more for excellent bisque and artist workmanship.

Mark:

MADE IN GERMANY

Child: 1893–1899, 1919 and after. Incised with clover mark. Bisque head, open mouth, glass eyes. Jointed body. No damage and nicely dressed. 14" - $500.00; 17" - $765.00; 21" - $950.00; 24" - $1,100.00.

Same as above, with closed mouth: 15" - $1,600.00; 17" - $1,900.00; 20" - $2,200.00; 23" - $2,800.00.

Same as above, with incised name: Ca. 1919. Incised names such as "Norma," "Rita," "Wally," etc. 16" - $600.00; 21" - $825.00; 24" - $965.00.

LORI

The "Lori Baby" was made by Swaine & Co. and can be marked "232," "DIP," "DV," "DI," "Geschuz S & Co." with green stamp, or incised "D Lori 4." It has lightly painted hair, sleep eyes, open/closed mouth, and is on five-piece bent limb baby body.

Glass Eyes: 12" - $1,000.00; 16" - $1,500.00; 20" - $2,300.00; 23" - $2,900.00; 26" - $3,400.00.

Intaglio Eyes: (See photo in Series 6, pg. 138.) 20" - $2,000.00; 24" - $2,500.00.

Flocked Hair: 16" - $1,850.00; 20" - $2,700.00; 25" - $3,400.00.

23½" marked "D Lori 232 11." Has solid dome, sleep eyes, open mouth, two upper teeth, and five-piece bent limb baby body. $2,900.00. *Courtesy Frasher Doll Auctions.*

Mascotte Dolls were made by May Freres Cie. They operated from 1890 to 1897, then became part of Jules Steiner in 1898. This means the dolls were made from 1890 to about 1902, so the quality of the bisque as well as the artist painting can vary greatly. Dolls will be marked "BÉBÉ MASCOTTE PARIS" and some will be incised with "M" and a number.

Child: Closed mouth and marked "Mascotte." Excellent condition and no damage. (See photo in Series 8, pg. 128.) 14" - $3,500.00; 18" - $4,500.00; 21" - $4,800.00; 24" - $5,600.00; 28" - $6,100.00.

Child: Same as above, but marked with "M" and a number. 14" - $2,800.00; 17" - $3,400.00; 19" - $3,900.00; 23" - $4,500.00; 27" - $5,000.00.

20" "Mascotte" with closed mouth and on French jointed body. Incised "M 8." **$4,700.00.** *Courtesy Marcia Jarmush.*

MAXINE

12½" all composition doll with painted features and molded painted hair. Right arm molded bent at elbow like the "Patsy" doll family. All original. Marked "MITZI/ by Maxine/Pat. Pend." $400.00.

A. Theroude mechanical walker: Patented 1840. Papier maché head, bamboo teeth in open mouth. Stands on three wheels (two large and one small.) Tin cart with mechanism attached to legs. 16" - $3,200.00.

Autoperipatetikos: Base is like clockworks and has tin feet. When key wound, the doll walks. Heads can be china, untinted bisque or papier maché. **Early China Head:** 11" - $1,800.00. **Untinted Bisque:** 11" - $1,300.00. **Papier maché:** 11" - $900.00.

Hawkins, George: Walker with pewter hands and feet and wood torso. Hands modeled to push a carriage, which should be a Goodwin, patented in 1867–1868. Carriage has two large wheels and a small one in front. Molded hair and dolls head will be marked "X.L.C.R./Doll head/Pat. Sept. 8, 1868." (China heads may not be marked.) 11" - $2,400.00.

French Portrette faces: Such as "Vichy," "Fournier," etc. 24" - $16,000.00.

Jumeau: Raises and lowers both arms; head moves. Holds items, such as a hankie and bottle; book and fan, one in each hand. Key wound music box in base. Closed mouth, marked "Jumeau." 15" - $4,200.00 up; 20" - $5,000.00 up. **Same with open mouth:** 15" - $2,400.00 up; 20" - $3,500.00 up.

15" waltzing Steiner. When key is wound, doll glides across floor in circles and raises and lowers bisque arms. Glass eyes with pink wash. Open mouth with two rows of teeth. Baby has painted features. Adult head marked "J. Steiner Paris." $8,900.00. *Courtesy Turn of Century Antiques.*

Jumeau: Marked "Jumeau." Standing or sitting on key wound music box and doll plays an instrument. 14" - $4,200.00 up; 18" - $5,800.00 up.

Jumeau: Marked "Jumeau" walker with one-piece legs, arms jointed at elbows. She raises her arm to an open mouth to throw kisses as head turns. 15" - $2,200.00 up; 22" - $3,200.00 up.

Jumeau: Marked "Jumeau" and stands on three-wheel cart and when cart is pulled, doll's head turns from side to side and arms go up and down. 15" - $3,800.00 up; 18" - $4,800.00 up.

Paris Bébé, R.D., E.D., Eden Bébé: Marked doll standing on key wound music box. Has closed mouth. Holds items in hands and arms move and head nods or moves from side to side. 21" - $5,400.00 up.

Jumeau: 18–20" doll stands at piano built to scale and hands attached to keyboard with rods. Key wound piano. $20,000.00 up.

Steiner, Jules: Bisque head, open mouth with two rows of teeth. Key wound, waltzes in circles, original clothes. Glass eyes, arms move as it dances. 17" - $10,000.00 up.

Steiner, Jules: Bisque head on composition torso chest. Composition lower legs and full arms. Twill-covered sections between parts of body. Key wound, cries, moves head and kicks legs. Open mouth, two rows of teeth. 17" - $2,400.00; 24" - $3,000.00. **Same as above, but bisque torso sections:** 18" - $7,700.00 up.

German Makers: One or two figures on music box, key wound, or pulling cart. Dolls have open mouths. **Marked with name of maker:** $1,800.00 up. **1960s, 1970s:** German-made reproductions of this style dolls. $300.00.

METAL HEADS

Metal heads made in Germany, 1888-on; United States, 1917 on.

Marks:

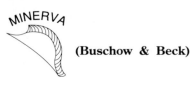

(Buschow & Beck)

(Alfred Heller)

JUNO (Karl Standfuss)

Metal Shoulder Head: Cloth or kid body. Molded hair, painted eyes. 14" - $150.00; 17" - $200.00. **Molded hair, glass eyes:** 14" - $200.00; 17" - $265.00. **Wig, glass eyes:** 14" - $265.00; 17" - $325.00; 21" - $425.00.

All Metal Child: Wig or molded hair, fully jointed. Some are also jointed at wrist, elbow, knee, and ankle. Open/closed mouth with painted teeth. Some have metal hands and feet with composition body. 15–16" - $465.00; 19–20" - $600.00.

All Metal Jointed Dolls: Made in Switzerland. Metal ball joints, patented 1921–1940. **Man:** 6" - $185.00; 10" - $250.00. **Comic character:** 6" - $165.00; 10" - $225.00. **Hitler:** 6" - $225.00; 10" - $285.00. **Chauffeur:** 6" - $145.00; 10" - $185.00. **Animal Head:** 6" - $165.00; 10" - $200.00.

METAL HEADS

Same as previous listing, but with composition heads, hands, and feet: 6" - $100.00 up; 10" - $150.00 up.

Metal Baby: All metal bent baby body. Some are spring jointed. Painted features, wig or molded hair. 13–14" - $150.00. **Glass eyes:** 13–14" - $200.00.

Very large 30" tin head doll. Has cloth body, leather hands, glass eyes, and open mouth. Marked "D.R.G.M." plus six unreadable numbers. **$850.00.** *Courtesy Ellen Dodge.*

MOLDED HAIR BISQUE

The molded hair bisque dolls are just like any other flesh-toned dolls, but instead of having wigs, they have molded hair, glass set eyes or finely painted and detailed eyes, and generally they will have closed mouths. They almost always are one-piece shoulder heads on kid or cloth bodies with bisque lower arms. Some will have compostion lower legs. These dolls are generally very pretty. Many molded hair dolls are being attributed to A.B.G. (Alt, Beck & Gottschalck) but are recognizably Kling dolls. (See photo in Series 9, pg. 135.) Such dolls are from mold **#890, 1000, 1008, 1028, 1064, 1142, 1256, 1288,** etc.

Child: Closed mouth. 6½" - $145.00; 10" - $225.00; 16" - $525.00; 21" - $850.00; 24" - $1,300.00; 26" - $1,700.00.

Boy: 17" - $650.00; 20" - $975.00; 23" - $1,500.00.

Decorated Shoulder Plate: With elaborate hairdo. 20" - $2,400.00 up.

Japan: Marked ℱ𝒴 or ⊛. Bows on sides of head. Cloth body, long legs, black silk feet, oilcloth arms. 17" - $325.00; 20" - $425.00.

Left: 12½" all celluloid with glass eyes and molded hair. Marked "Minerva, Germany 4." Right: 14" molded hair bisque with glass eyes, kid body and bisque lower arms. Center: 8" black painted bisque child with open mouth. Marked "Heubach Koppelsdorf 414-15 DRGM." 12½" - $125.00; 14" - $465.00; 8" - $265.00.

Alexandre Mothereau made dolls in Paris, France from 1880 to 1895. Dolls are marked "B.M." with size number and trademarked "Bébé Mothereau." 18" - $17,000.00; 25" - $24,000.00; 30" - $29,000.00.

"Bébé Mothereau" with pale bisque, blush over eyelids, and closed mouth. Jointed French body with straight wrists. Factory costume in faded pink silk. Marked "B.M. 9." $24,000.00. *Courtesy Frasher Doll Auctions.*

MOTSCHMANN (SONNEBERG TÄUFLING)

Charles Motschmann has always been credited as the manufacturer of a certain style doll, but now his work is only being attributed to the making of the voice boxes in the dolls. Various German makers such as Heinrich Stier and others are being given the credit for making the dolls. They date from 1851 into the 1880s.

The early dolls were babies, children and Orientals. They have glass eyes, closed mouths, heads of papier maché, wax over papier maché or wax over composition. They can have lightly brush stroked painted hair or come with a wig. If the mouth is open, the doll will have bamboo teeth. The larger dolls will have arms and legs jointed at wrists and ankles. The lower torso and lower arms and legs are composition or wood; the upper torso and upper arms and legs are twill cloth. The mid-section will also be cloth. If the doll is marked, it can be found on the upper cloth of the leg and will be stamped:

PATENT 29 APRIL
1857
CH. MOTSCHMANN
SONNEBERG

Baby: Motschmann marked or type. **Extremely fine condition:** 13" - $600.00; 16" - $800.00; 20" - $1,200.00; 25" - $1,500.00. **Fair condition:** 13" - $400.00; 16" - $525.00; 20" - $675.00; 25" - $800.00.

MOTSCHMANN (SONNEBERG TÄUFLING)

Child: Extremely fine condition: 15" - $900.00; 18" - $1,200.00; 23" - $1,600.00. **Fair condition:** 15" - $425.00; 18" - $685.00; 23" - $825.00.

Child: Bisque with cloth at waist and mid-limbs. (See photo in Series 9, pg. 136.) 18" - $6,500.00 up.

Petite 10" Motschmann china glazed boy with swivel neck, brown eyes, china shoulders/upper body, hips, and lower arms and legs. Cloth between these sections. Brush stroke around face and painted-on shoes. **$1,200.00 up.** *Courtesy Ellen Dodge.*

MUNICH ART DOLL

Munich Art character dolls are very rare and were designed by Marion Kaulitz, 1908–1912, who had them modeled by Paul Vogelsanger. Dolls have composition or fabric heads, painted features, and are on fully jointed bodies.

Excellent condition: 13–14" - $2,600.00; 18–19" - $3,600.00. **Fair condition:** 13–14" - $1,000.00; 18–19" - $1,500.00.

14" "Munich Art Dolls" with composition heads that have oil-painted features. On fully jointed bodies. Each - $2,100.00. *Courtesy Jane Walker.*

ORIENTAL DOLLS

Bisque dolls with fired-in Oriental color and on jointed yellowish tinted bodies were made in Germany by various firms. They could be children or babies and most were made after 1900. Must be in excellent condition and in Oriental clothes with no damage to head.

Amusco, Mold #1006: Bisque head. (See photo in Series 9, pg. 138.) 16" - $1,100.00.

Armand Marseille: Girl or boy marked only "A.M." 6" - $575.00; 8–9" - $750.00. **Painted bisque:** Excellent condition. 8" - $265.00; 12" - $475.00.

#353 Baby: 12" - $1,000.00; 15" - $1,200.00; 17" - $1,400.00. **Painted bisque:** 15" - $600.00.

Belton type: #193, 206, etc. Closed mouth. Small doll may have painted-on slippers. 10" - $2,600.00 up; 14" - $3,400.00 up; 17" - $4,200.00 up.

Bruno Schmidt (BSW) #220: Closed mouth. 14" - $2,700.00; 17" - $3,900.00.

#500 (BSW): 14" - $2,100.00; 16" - $2,400.00. **All bisque:** 6" - $685.00.

Jumeau: Very rare. Closed mouth, very almond-shaped angled eyes, and upward painted eyebrows. Early body with straight wrists. 26" - $58,000.00 up.

Kestner (J.D.K.) #243: Baby: 14" - $4,600.00; 17" - $6,000.00. **Molded hair baby:** 14" - $4,800.00. **Child:** 15" - $5,200.00; 18" - $7,200.00. **All bisque:** 7" - $1,250.00.

Schoenau & Hoffmeister, #4900: Marked "S" PB in star "H." (See photo in Series 5, pg. 116.) 16" - $1,800.00; 20" - $2,100.00.

Simon & Halbig (S & H) #164: 16" - $2,400.00; 19" - $2,800.00 up.

#220: (See photo in Series 6, pg. 145.) Solid dome or "Belton" type. Closed mouth. 16" - $3,700.00.

#1099, 1129, 1159, 1199: (See photo in Series 7, pg. 129; Series 8, pg. 132; Series 9, pg. 138.) 15" - $3,000.00; 19" - $3,600.00.

#1329: (See photo in Series 7, pg. 129.) 15" - $2,200.00; 20" - $3,400.00.

All Bisque: Unmarked. 7–8" - $800.00 up.

Unmarked: Open mouth. 14" - $1,300.00; 18" - $2,000.00. **Closed mouth:** 14" - $1,800.00; 18" - $2,600.00. **All bisque:** Glass eyes. 6" - $485.00; 10–11" - $885.00 up.

Nippon – Caucasian Dolls made in Japan: 1918–1922. Most made during World War I. These dolls can be near excellent quality to very poor quality. Morimura Brothers mark is ⊛. Dolls marked 𝔉𝓎 were made by Yamato. Others will just be marked with NIPPON along with other marks such as "J.W."

15" with slanted glass eyes and eyebrows. Open mouth with four teeth. On fully jointed body. Made by Simon & Halbig and marked "S & H 1199 DEP." **$3,000.00.** *Courtesy Frasher Doll Auctions.*

Large 19" Nippon baby with sleep eyes and high face color. Taken from the "Hilda" mold. Five-piece bent limb baby body. **$800.00.** *Courtesy Turn of Century Antiques.*

Nippon Marked Baby: Good to excellent bisque, well painted, nice body and no damage. 10" - $185.00; 12" - $245.00; 15" - $325.00; 21" - $500.00; 24" - $850.00. **Poor quality:** 12" - $125.00; 16" - $175.00; 20" - $265.00; 25" - $365.00. **"Hilda" look-alike, excellent quality:** 15" - $800.00; 18" - $1,000.00. **Medium quality:** 15" - $500.00; 18" - $745.00.

Nippon Child: Good to excellent quality bisque, no damage and nicely dressed. 14" - $300.00; 17" - $375.00; 22" - $700.00. **Poor quality:** 15" - $135.00; 19" - $225.00; 23" - $325.00.

Molded Hair: Molded bows on side, cloth body, oilcloth lower arms, silk feet. Marked 𝔉𝓎 or ⊛. 1920–1930s. 14" - $300.00; 17" - $500.00.

Traditional Doll: Made in Japan. Papier maché swivel head on shoulder plate, cloth mid-section and upper arms and legs. Limbs and torso are papier maché, glass eyes, pierced nostrils. The early dolls will have jointed wrists and ankles and will be slightly sexed.

Early fine quality: Original dress, 1890s. 14" - $365.00; 19" - $600.00; 26" - $1,100.00.

Early Boy: With painted hair. 17" - $500.00; 22" - $900.00; 26" - $1,200.00 up. **1930s or later:** 14" - $145.00; 17" - $265.00. **1940s:** 13" - $85.00.

Lady: All original and excellent quality. 1920s: 12" - $200.00; 16" - $285.00. **Later Lady:** 1940s–1950s. 12" - $85.00; 14" - $100.00.

9" Samurai Warrior that is all original. Wooden limbs and stand. He may have been part of an old Boy's Day set. **$400.00 up.** *Courtesy Turn of Century Antiques.*

Emperor or Empress in sitting position: 1920s–1930s. 4–5" - $150.00; 8" - $200.00 up; 12" - $375.00 up.

Warrior: 1880s–1890s. 16–18" - $650.00 up. **On horse:** 16" - $1,200.00 up. **Early 1920s:** 12" - $300.00 up. **On horse:** 12" - $800.00 up.

Japanese Baby: Bisque head, sleep eyes, closed mouth, and all white bisque. **Papier maché body:** Original and in excellent condition. Late 1920s. 8" - $65.00; 12" - $95.00. **Glass eyes:** 8" - $125.00; 12" - $225.00.

Japanese Baby: Head made of crushed oyster shells painted flesh color, papier maché body, glass eyes and original. 8" - $65.00; 12" - $95.00; 16" - $145.00; 19" - $200.00.

6" traditional Japanese baby with stone bisque head, crushed oyster shell limbs and pupilless sleep eyes. Original. **$60.00.** *Courtesy Kathy Tvrdik.*

Two 15" bent limb babies with glass sleep eyes, open mouth, and two upper teeth. Each marked "Morimura Brothers." Doll on left has dimples and papier maché body. One on right has good composition German body. Each - $325.00 up. *Courtesy Frasher Doll Auctions.*

7" "Katsuraningyo" with six wigs. Crushed oyster shell paste head with glass eyes. Cloth and oyster shell limbs. Original. Wigs can vary and usually denote different times in the life of a Japanese woman. Ca. pre-World War II. Set in box - $90.00. *Courtesy Kathy Tvrdik.*

Oriental Dolls: All composition, jointed at shoulder and hips. Painted features and hair. Can have bald head with yarn braid down back with rest covered by cap, such as "Ling Ling" or "Ming Ming" made by Quan Quan Co. in 1930s. Painted-on shoes. 10" - $165.00.

Chinese Traditional Dolls: Man or woman. Composition-type material with cloth-wound bodies or can have wooden carved arms and feet. In traditional costume and in excellent condition. 9" - $350.00; 12" - $575.00.

Door of Hope Dolls: Created at the Door of Hope Mission in China from 1901 to 1910s. Cloth bodies with head and limbs carved of wood by carvers who came from Ning-Po providence. Chinese costume. (See photo in Series 8, pgs. 63–65.)

Adult: 9" - $600.00; 11" - $675.00 up. **Child:** 6" - $425.00; 8" - $500.00. **Mother and baby:** 11" - $625.00. **Man:** 9" - $625.00. **Carved flowers in hair:** 12" - $725.00. **Bride or bridesmaid:** 12" - $650.00. **Groom:** $600.00. **Widow:** $700.00. **Mourner:** $650.00. **Grandfather:** $700.00. **Amah (Governess):** $625.00.

12" Emperor and Empress from the Girl's or Boy's Day sets. Crushed oyster shell paste heads with glass eyes and painted emblems and brows. Both are all original. They sit on wicker and wooden bases. Set - $550.00. *Courtesy Turn of Century Antiques.*

P.D.

P.D. marked dolls were made in Paris, France by Petit & DuMontier, 1878–1890. (See Series 8, pg. 77.)

Child: Closed mouth, jointed body, metal hands. No damage, nicely dressed. 15" - $8,000.00; 18" - $9,500.00; 21" - $13,000.00; 23" - $16,000.00; 27" - $20,000.00.

24" Petit & Dumontier of 1878–1890. Full closed mouth, very full cheeks, large glass eyes and on French jointed body with metal hands. Marked "P. 5 D." $16,000.00.
Courtesy Frasher Doll Auctions.

P.G.

Pintel & Godchaux of Montreuil, France made dolls from 1890 to 1899. They held one trademark – "Bébé Charmant." Heads will be marked "P.G."

Child, closed mouth: 16" - $2,600.00; 21" - $3,000.00; 25" - $3,900.00. **Child, open mouth:** 15" - $1,300.00; 20" - $2,000.00; 23" - $2,500.00.

PAPIER MACHÉ

Papier maché dolls were made in U.S., Germany, England, France and other countries. Paper pulp, wood and rag fibers containing paste, oil or glue are formed into a composition-like moldable material. Flour, clay and/or sand is added for stiffness. The hardness of papier maché depends on the amount of glue added.

Many so called papier maché parts were actually laminated paper with several thicknesses of molded paper bonded (glued) together or pressed after being glued.

"Papier maché" means "chewed paper" in French, and as early as 1810, dolls of papier maché were being mass produced by using molds.

Marked "M&S Superior": (Muller & Strassburger) Papier maché shoulder head with blonde or black molded hair, painted blue or brown eyes, old cloth body with kid or leather arms and boots. Nicely dressed and head not repainted, chipped or cracked. 16" - $400.00; 18"- $600.00; 24" - $750.00. **Glass eyes:** 20" - $850.00. **With wig:** 18" - $775.00. **Repainted**

nicely: 16" - $275.00; 21" - $450.00. **Chips, scuffs or not repainted well:** 16" - $95.00; 21" - $110.00.

French or French Type: (See photos in Series 5, pg. 151; Series 7, pg. 133; Series 9, pg. 142.) Painted black hair, some with brush marks, on solid dome. Some have nailed-on wigs. Open mouths have bamboo teeth. Inset glass eyes. All leather/kid body. Very good condition, nice old clothes. 16" - $1,400.00; 19" - $1,800.00; 23" - $2,200.00; 26" - $2,600.00; 30" - $3,400.00. **Wooden jointed body:** 7–8" - $865.00. **Painted eyes:** 7" - $450.00; 15" - $950.00.

Early Papier Maché: (See photo in Series 6, pg. 153.) Cloth body and wooden limbs. Early hairdo with top knots, buns, puff curls or braiding. Not restored and dressed in original

or very well made clothes. Very good condition; may show a little wear. 12" - $600.00; 14" - $700.00; 18" - $1,000.00; 21" - $1,400.00; 25" - $1,500.00. **Glass eyes:** 20" - $2,200.00. **Flirty eyes:** 20" - $2,800.00 up.

Long Curls: 9" - $525.00; 13" - $650.00.

Covered Wagon or Flat Top Hairdo: 7" - $275.00; 11" - $400.00; 14–15" - $600.00.

Milliner's Models: 1820s –1860s. **Braided bun, side curls:** 9–10" - $785.00; 13–14" - $1,250.00. **Side**

Papier maché "Red Riding Hood" with sleep eyes and open mouth. All original. Marked "S.F.B.J. Paris." Came with wolf that was made by Effanbee. Wolf is on "Patsy" body with right arm bent at elbow. Original - $385.00; redressed - $275.00; Wolf - $450.00 up. *Courtesy Marcia Jarmush.*

17" early papier maché called "Milliner's Model" with cloth and wooden limbs. All original clothes. Exposed ears, center part with hair in long curls. Brown painted eyes. $1,200.00. *Courtesy Ricki Small.*

curls, high top knot: 12" - $1,000.00; 17" - $1,900.00. **Coiled braids over ears, braided bun:** 19–20" - $2,200.00 up. **Braided bun, coiled braids at ears:** 18" - $1,800.00. **Center part:** Sausage curls. 15" - $700.00; 18" - $900.00. **Molded bonnet:** Very rare. Kid body, wood limbs, bonnet painted to tie under chin. 15" - $2,000.00 up.

Marked "Greiner": Dolls from 1858 on. Blonde or black molded hair, brown or blue painted eyes, cloth body with leather arms, nicely dressed and with very little minor scuffs. See Greiner section.

Motschmann Types: With wood and twill bodies. Separate hip section, glass eyes, closed mouth and brush stroke hair on solid domes. Nicely dressed and ready to display. 15" - $725.00; 21" - $975.00; 25" - $1,500.00.

German Papier Maché: 1870–1900s. Various molded hairdos, painted eyes and closed mouth. May be blonde or black hair. Nicely dressed and not repainted. 14" - $200.00; 17" - $325.00; 19" - $425.00; 23" - $475.00; 25" - $525.00; 30" - $700.00. **Glass eyes:** 14" - $525.00; 17" - $775.00. **Showing wear and scuffs, but not touched up:** 17" - $225.00; 21" - $300.00; 25" - $350.00; 30" - $450.00; 35" - $700.00.

Wax over papier maché: See Wax section.

Turned Shoulder Head: Solid dome, glass eyes, closed mouth. Twill cloth body with composition lower arms. Very good condition and nicely dressed. 17" - $750.00; 22" - $950.00.

24" German wax over papier maché head doll with large glass eyes and the remains of original wig. Cloth body with composition lower limbs. Modeled-on boots. $465.00. *Courtesy Turn of Century Antiques.*

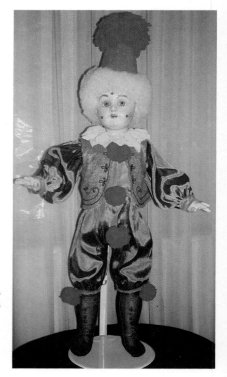

28" French papier maché clown with glass eyes, open mouth, and detailed face. Has S.F.B.J. style five-piece papier maché body. All original and very mint condition. $1,000.00 up. *Courtesy Ricki Small.*

German Character Heads: (See photo in Series 6, pg. 152.) These heads are molded just like the bisque ones. Glass eyes, closed mouth and on fully jointed body. Excellent condition and nicely dressed. 15" - $1,100.00 up; 21" - $1,700.00 up.

Papier maché, 1920s on: Head usually has bright coloring and wigged. Usually dressed as a child or in provincial costumes. Stuffed cloth body and limbs or have papier maché arms.

Excellent overall condition. 8" - $80.00; 12" - $135.00; 14" - $185.00. **Marked by maker: German:** 8" - $95.00; 12" - $165.00. **French:** 8" - $115.00; 12" - $195.00; 14" - $275.00.

Clowns: Papier maché head with painted clown features. Open or closed mouth. Molded hair or wigged. Cloth body with some having composition or papier maché lower arms or five-piece body. Excellent condition. 10" - $265.00; 14" - $500.00; 20" - $825.00; 26" - $965.00.

PARIAN-TYPE (UNTINTED BISQUE)

"Parian-type" dolls were made from the 1850s to the 1880s, with the majority being made during the 1870s and 1880s. There are hundreds of different heads, and all seem to have been made in Germany. If there is a mark, it will be found on the inside of the shoulder plate. It must be noted that the very rare and unique unglazed porcelain dolls are difficult to find and their prices will be high.

"Parian-type" dolls can be found with every imaginable thing applied to the head and shirt tops – flowers, snoods, ruffles, feathers, plumes, etc. Many have inset glass eyes, pierced ears and most are blonde, although some will have from light to medium brown hair, and a few will have glazed black hair.

Various Fancy Hairstyles: (See photo in Series 5, pg. 121.) With molded combs, ribbons, flowers, head bands, or snoods. Cloth body with cloth/Parian-type limbs. Glass eyes. Perfect condition and very nicely dressed. 16" - $1,700.00 up; 21" - $2,300.00 up. **Painted eyes, unpierced ears:** 18" - $1,200.00; 22" - $1,600.00.

Swivel Neck: Glass eyes. 17" - $3,100.00; 21" - $3,700.00.

Molded Necklaces: Jewels or standing ruffles, undamaged. **Glass eyes, pierced ears:** 16" - $1,900.00 up; 21" - $2,500.00 up. **Painted eyes, unpierced ears:** 18" - $1,200.00; 22" - $1,600.00.

14" "Blue Scarf" Parian with deeply modeled hair and scarf. Painted features. Cloth body with parian lower limbs. Has modeled-on boots. $1,000.00. *Courtesy Turn of Century Antiques.*

PARIAN-TYPE (UNTINTED BISQUE)

Bald Head: Solid dome, takes wigs, full ear detail. 1850s. Perfect condition and nicely dressed. 14" - $775.00; 18" - $995.00; 22" - $1,600.00.

Molded Head Band: (See photo in Series 5, pg. 121; Series 7, pg. 137; Series 9, pg. 146.) Called **"Alice."** 14" - $400.00; 17" - $625.00; 20" - $925.00.

Very Plain Style: With no decoration in hair or on shoulders. No damage and nicely dressed. 10" - $175.00; 15" - $350.00; 20" - $485.00; 24" - $575.00.

Men or Boys: Hairdos with center or side part, cloth body with cloth/Parian-type limbs. Decorated shirt and tie. 16" - $900.00; 19" - $1,400.00.

Undecorated Shirt Top: 16" - $300.00; 19" - $500.00; 25" - $825.00.

Molded Hat: (See photos in Series 8, pg. 140.) Blonde or black hair. **Painted eyes:** 15" - $2,200.00; 18" - $2,800.00 up. **Glass eyes:** 14" - $2,600.00; 16" - $3,100.00; 20" - $3,900.00.

20" bald head (solid dome) Parian lady with unusual facial modeling. Cobalt blue eyes. Open/closed mouth with white space between lips. Pierced ears. Cloth body with parian lower limbs. Shown with wig. **$1,600.00 up.** *Courtesy Turn of Century Antiques.*

PARIS BÉBÉ

These dolls were made by Danel & Cie in France from 1889 to 1895. The heads will be marked "Paris Bébé" and the body's paper label will be marked with a drawing of the Eiffel Tower and "Paris Bébé/Brevete."

Paris Bébé Child: Closed mouth, no damage and nicely dressed. 16" - $4,600.00; 20" - $5,100.00; 24" - $5,800.00; 27" - $6,000.00. **High color to bisque, closed mouth:** 17" - $3,200.00; 21" - $3,600.00; 25" - $4,000.00; 27" - $4,300.00.

20" with large glass eyes, closed mouth, and full cheeks. On French jointed body. Old mohair wig. Marked "Paris Bébé." **$5,100.00.** *Courtesy Ricki Small.*

Bébé Phénix dolls were made by Henri Alexandre of Paris who made dolls from 1885 to 1901. The company was sold to Tourel in 1892 and Jules Steiner in 1895.

Mark:

(1885–1891)

Child, closed mouth: #81: 10" - $1,800.00. **#85:** 14" - $3,200.00. **#88:** 17" - $4,400.00. **#90:** 18" - $4,600.00. **#91:** 19–21" - $4,900.00. **#93:** 22" - $5,400.00. **#94:** 23-24" - $5,500.00. **#95:** 23–25" - $5,600.00.

Child, open mouth: 17" - $2,000.00; 19" - $2,300.00; 23" - $2,700.00; 25" - $3,000.00.

1885–1891: Perfect, early jointed body, beautiful clothes, closed mouth, glass eyes. 15" - $3,600.00; 17½" - $4,800.00. Marked:

25" "Bébé Phenix" with open mouth and on jointed French body with straight wrists. Original with red label across front with name. Marked "91" with star symbol. **$5,500.00.** *Courtesy Frasher Doll Auctions.*

PIANO BABIES

Piano babies were made in Germany from the 1880s into the 1930s. One of the finest quality makers of piano babies was Gebruder Heubach. They were also made by Kestner, Dressel, Limbach, etc. A number of these figures were reproduced in the late 1960s to late 1970s. Painting and skin tones will not be as "soft" as old ones.

Piano Babies: All bisque, unjointed. Molded hair, painted features, molded-on clothes. Figures come in variety of poses.

Excellent Quality or marked "Heubach": Extremely good artist workmanship and excellent detail to modeling. 4" - $200.00; 6" - $600.00; 8" - $750.00 up; 12" - $825.00 up; 16" - $1,100.00 up.

Medium Quality: May not have painting finished on back side of figure. 4" - $125.00; 8" - $265.00; 12" - $400.00; 16" - $550.00.

With animal, pot, flowers, on chair, or with other items: (See photos in Series 6, pg. 158; Series 7, pg. 141.) Excellent quality. 4" - $250.00; 8" - $450.00; 12" - $825.00 up; 16" - $1,200.00 up.

Black: Excellent quality: 4" - $365.00; 8" - $475.00; 12" - $825.00; 16" - $1,200.00 up. **Medium quality:** 4" - $165.00; 8" - $250.00; 12" - $400.00; 16" - $800.00.

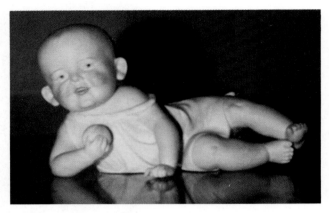

Piano baby that is 9½" long and 6" high. Protruding ears and open/closed mouth. Marked "Germany ⊡ DEP/1292." **$700.00.** *Courtesy Mike Head.*

Right: 15" piano baby with molded eyelids. Has very detailed features and clothes. Made in Germany by either Revalo or Goebel. Left: 27" S.F.B.J. Jumeau with open mouth. On Jumeau jointed body. Original. **15" - $950.00; 27" - $1,300.00.** *Courtesy Frasher Doll Auctions.*

Rabery & Delphieu began making dolls in 1856. The very first dolls have kid bodies and are extremely rare. Most of their dolls are on French jointed bodies and are marked "R.D." A few may be marked "Bébé de Paris."

Child, closed mouth: Excellent condition with no chips, breaks or hairlines in bisque. Body in overall good condition and nicely dressed. Pretty face. 12" - $2,600.00; 16" - $3,200.00; 19" - $3,600.00; 22" - $4,000.00; 24" - $4,400.00; 27" - $5,300.00.

Child, open mouth: Same condition as above. 15" - $1,300.00; 19" - $2,000.00; 22" - $2,500.00; 24" - $3,000.00; 28" - $3,500.00. **With two rows of teeth:** Excellent condition. 22" - $2,900.00. **Bisque:** 28" - $4,000.00; 36" - $5,000.00.

Child, high color: Lesser quality, poor artist workmanship. **Closed mouth:** 16" - $1,800.00; 19" - $2,200.00; 22" - $2,400.00. **Open mouth:** 15" - $675.00; 19" - $900.00; 22" - $1,050.00.

24" walker in original box. Head turns as legs move. Has closed mouth and early straight wrists. On jointed French body. Doll marked "R. 2 D." Box marked "L'Intrepide - Marchant." $4,600.00; original in box - $5,000.00. *Courtesy Turn of Century Antiques.*

37" with open mouth and two rows of teeth. French jointed body and excellent quality bisque. Marked "R. 6 D." $5,000.00. *Courtesy Frasher Doll Auctions.*

Bernard Ravca made dolls in Paris from 1924 to the mid-1930's when he moved to New York. The dolls were stitched stockinette characters and personalities. If made in France, doll will bear a label marked "Original Ravca/ Fabrication Francaise" or a wrist tag "Original Ravca" plus handwritten name of doll. Some of the dolls will be cloth and stockinette, some with cloth body and limbs, and others will be a gesso/ papier maché combination. His dolls can range in size from 7" to 35."

Peasants/Old People: 7" - $85.00; 9" - $95.00; 12" - $125.00; 15" - $200.00 up.

Character from books/poems: 7" - $100.00 up; 9" - $125.00 up; 12" - $165.00 up; 15" - $200.00 up; 17" - $285.00 up.

Gesso/papier maché/cloth dolls: Personality figures. 12" - $400.00; 15" - $565.00; 17" - $985.00; 20" - $1,425.00.

Military Figures: Such as Hitler, Mussolini. 17" - $1,000.00; 20" - $1,800.00; 27" - $4,000.00 up.

Left: "Marshall Chiang Kai Shek." Head is gessoed and hand painted in oils. Body is cloth with mitt-type hands. Original. **Right: "Madame Chiang Kai Shek."** Head modeled in papier maché and hands in gesso. Painted features, cloth body. Both are true Ravca "personality" dolls. Marshall - **$985.00;** Madame - **$565.00.** *Courtesy Christine Pericho.*

Left: 15" "Mary Martin" is made of combination papier maché and gesso with painted features and molded hair. Tray includes tiny packages of cigarettes and flowers. She carries doll over arm. Right: 17" "Joan Crawford" has gesso head with oil-painted features. Papier maché fingers with inset nails look rather claw like. Mohair wig. Ca. 1942. Both personalities are all original figures by Bernard Ravca. "Mary Martin" - $565.00; "Joan Crawford" - $985.00.

RECKNAGEL OF ALEXANDRINENTHAL

Dolls marked with "R.A." were made by Recknagel of Alexandrinenthal, Thuringia, Germany. The R.A. dolls date from 1886 to after World War I. Bisque quality and artist workmanship can range from very poor to excellent. Prices are for dolls with good artist workmanship, such as nice lips and eyebrows painted straight, feathered, and not off center. Original or nicely dressed and no damage.

Child: 1890s–1914. Set or sleep eyes, open mouth. Small dolls have painted-on shoes and socks. 8" - $175.00; 12" - $225.00; 16" - $375.00; 20" - $525.00; 23" - $700.00.

#1907, 1909, 1914, etc.: 8" - $185.00; 12" - $275.00; 16" - $385.00; 20" - $545.00; 23" - $775.00.

Baby: Ca. 1909–1910 on. Five-piece bent limb baby body or straight leg, curved arm toddler body and with sleep or set eyes. No damage and nicely dressed. 7" - $185.00; 9" - $225.00; 12" - $300.00; 16" - $450.00; 20" - $550.00.

Character: Painted eyes, modeled bonnet, and open/closed mouth. Some dolls are smiling; some have painted-in

teeth. No damage and nicely dressed. 8" - $700.00; 12" - $1,100.00.

Character: Glass eyes, closed mouth, and composition bent limb baby body. 7" - $685.00; 10" - $865.00; 14" - $1,000.00.

Character dolls by Recknagel. Both have painted features and open/ closed mouths with molded teeth and tongue. Five-piece papier maché bodies. Left: Rare 9" figure with molded-on bonnet and marked "26-12/0." Right: 7" child with molded hair and attached porcelain hair ribbon. Has painted-on shoes and socks. 9" - $950.00 up; 7" - $785.00 up. *Courtesy Jane Walker.*

REINECKE, OTTO

Dolls marked "P.M." were made by Otto Reinecke of Hof-Moschendorf, Bavaria, Germany from 1909 into the 1930s. The mold number found most often is the **#914** baby or toddler. (See photo in Series 7, pg. 144.)

Child: Bisque head with open mouth. On five-piece papier maché body or fully jointed body. Can have sleep or set eyes. No damage and nicely dressed. 10" - $145.00; 14" - $265.00; 17" - $475.00; 21" - $600.00.

Baby: Open mouth, sleep eyes or set eyes. Bisque head on five-piece bent limb baby body. No damage and nicely dressed. Can be incised "DEP - P.M. - Grete." 10" - $275.00; 12" - $325.00; 15" - $450.00; 21" - $600.00; 26" - $800.00.

Left: 16" baby with sleep eyes/ lashes and open mouth with two teeth. Marked "P.M. 23 Germany 7½." Right: 14" "Dream Baby" mold #341 by Armand Marseille. 16" - $525.00; 14" - $500.00.
Courtesy Frasher Doll Auctions.

REVALO

Revalo marked dolls were made in Germany by Gebruder Ohlhaver from 1921 to the 1930s. Prices are for nicely dressed and no damage.

Child: Open mouth. 15" - $425.00; 18" - $575.00; 21" - $675.00.

Molded hair child: With and without molded ribbon and/or flower. Painted eyes and open/closed mouth. (See photo in Series 7, pg. 146.) 12" - $685.00; 15" - $875.00.

Baby: Open mouth. On five-piece baby body. 14" - $475.00; 17" - $675.00.

Toddler: 16" - $750.00; 18" - $900.00.

14" Revalo "Coquette" type doll with painted features and open/closed mouth. Deeply molded hair with molded headband. On jointed German body. $850.00
Courtesy Ricki Small.

Bruno Schmidt's doll factory was located in Waltershausen, Germany and many of the heads used by this firm were made by Bahr & Proschild, Ohrdruf, Germany. They made dolls from 1898 on into the 1930s.

Mark:

2033-6

Child: Bisque head on jointed body, sleep eyes, open mouth, no damage and nicely dressed. 16" - $500.00; 20" - $700.00; 25" - $950.00. **Flirty eyes:** 21" - $900.00; 29" - $1,500.00.

Character Baby, Toddler or Child: Bisque head, glass eyes or painted eyes, jointed body, no damage and nicely dressed.

#2025, 2026: Closed mouth, glass eyes. 20" - $4,500.00. **Painted eyes:** 16" - $1,800.00.

#2052: Intaglio eyes with molded eyelids, glass eyes. Closed smile mouth. Molded hair or wig. 17" - $5,600.00 up.

#2069: Closed mouth, glass eyes, sweet face, jointed body. 13" - $4,200.00; 17" - $6,700.00.

#2048, 2094, 2096: Called **"Tommy Tucker."** (See photo in Series 6, pg. 163; Series 8, pg. 146.) Molded, painted hair, open mouth. 14" - $1,300.00; 18" - $1,600.00; 23" - $1,800.00; 26" - $2,100.00.

#2048, 2094, 2096: "Tommy Tucker" with closed mouth. Otherwise, same as above. (See photo in Series 8, pg. 146.) 14" - $2,000.00; 18" - $2,600.00; 23" - $3,000.00.

#2072: Closed mouth, glass eyes, wig. 18" - $3,800.00. **Toddler:** 22" - $4,350.00.

#2097: Toddler: 15" - $775.00; 21" - $1,100.00. **Baby:** 14" - $575.00; 18" - $875.00.

Character Child: Closed mouth, painted eyes or glass eyes, jointed child body, no damage and nicely dressed.

Marked "BSW" in heart: No mold number. (See photo in Series 6, pg. 164.) 17" - $2,800.00; 21" - $3,400.00.

#529: Marked with "BSW" in heart. Closed mouth, painted eyes, molded eyelids. (See photo in Series 9, pg. 154.) 17" - $6,000.00.

#2033, 531, 537 "Wendy": (See photo in Series 6, pg. 163; Series 9, pg. 154.) 13" - $16,000.00; 16" - $19,000.00 up; 20" - $22,000.00 up.

19" doll with painted features, closed mouth, and molded tongue. On fully jointed body. Marked "2025/B.S.W." in heart "529". $7,500.00. *Courtesy Frasher Doll Auctions.*

Franz Schmidt & Co. began in 1890 at Georgenthal, near Waltershausen, Germany. In 1902, they registered the cross hammers with a doll between and also the F.S.&Co. mark.

Mark:

1310

F.S. & Co.

Made in
Germany

10

Baby: Bisque head on bent limb baby body, sleep or set eyes, open mouth and some may have pierced nostrils. No damage and nicely dressed. (Add more for toddler body.)

#1255, 1271, 1272, 1295, 1296, 1297, 1310: 12" - $365.00; 14" - $500.00; 20" - $725.00; 25" - $1,200.00. **Toddler:** 8-9" - $625.00; 15" - $725.00; 21" - $1,100.00; 25" - $1,300.00.

#1267: Painted eyes, Open/closed mouth. (See photo in Series 5, pg. 126.) 14" - $2,800.00; 19" - $3,800.00. **Glass eyes:** 16" - $3,600.00; 21" - $4,600.00.

#1285: 16" - $850.00; 22" - $1,000.00.

Child: Papier maché and composition body with walker mechanism with metal rollers on feet. Open mouth, sleep eyes. Working and no damage to head, nicely dressed.

#1250: 14" - $750.00; 20" - $975.00.

#1262: Child with closed mouth, almost smiling. Painted eyes, wig, jointed body. 16" - $6,800.00; 21" - $15,000.00 up.

19" very character baby by Franz Schmidt, mold #1267. Has painted hair and features and open/closed mouth with two molded upper teeth. Bent limb baby body. May be original. $4,000.00.
Courtesy Frasher Doll Auctions.

16" with sleep eyes, open mouth, and on five-piece bent limb baby body. Marked "1295 F.S. & Co." $585.00. *Courtesy Frasher Doll Auctions.*

SCHMIDT, FRANZ

#1263: Closed mouth, painted eyes, rather downcast expression. 20" - $9,700.00 up; 24" - $15,000.00 up.

#1266, 1267: Child with open mouth and sleep eyes. 22" - $2,400.00.

#1286: Molded hair, ribbon, open mouth smile, glass eyes. 15–16" - $3,650.00.

SCHMITT & FILS

Schmitt & Fils produced dolls from the 1870s to 1891 in Paris, France. The dolls have French jointed bodies and came with closed or open/closed mouths.

Mark:

Child: 1880 – on. Bisque head with long, thin face. Jointed body with closed mouth or open/closed mouth. No damage and nicely dressed. Marked on head and body. (See photo in Series 8, pg. 149; Series 9, pg. 156.) 11–12" - $9,700.00; 16" - $16,000.00 up; 18" - $18,000.00 up; 22" - $23,000.00 up; 25" - $26,000.00 up; 28" - $29,000.00.

Child: Round face, full cheeks. (See photo in Series 6, pg. 166.) 11–12" - $9,600.00; 18" - $18,000.00 up; 23" - $20,000.00 up.

Adorable 11" closed mouth Schmitt & Fils with both head and body marked with the shield mark and "4/0." Straight wrists. Dress, wig, and bonnet are possibly original. **$9,700.00.** *Courtesy Ellen Dodge.*

Schoenau & Hoffmeister began making dolls in 1901 and were located in Bavaria. The factory was called "Porzellanfabrik Burggrub" and this mark will be found on many of their doll heads. Some of their mold numbers are **21, 169, 170, 769, 900, 914, 1271, 1800, 1906, 1909, 1923, 4000, 4900, 5000, 5300, 5500, 5700, 5800, 5900** and also **Hanna.**

Mark:

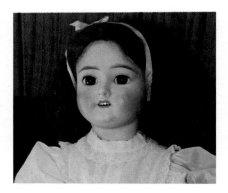

24" doll with sleep eyes, open mouth, and jointed body. Marked "1909 Germany" and Schoenau & Hoffmeister mark. **$700.00.** *Courtesy Jeannie Mauldin.*

Princess Elizabeth: Smiling open mouth, set eyes, bisque head on jointed five-piece body and marked with name on head or body. 16" - $1,800.00; 22" - $2,600.00; 25" - $2,900.00.

Hanna: Child with black or brown fired-in color to bisque head. Sleep or set eyes, five-piece body or jointed body. Marked with name on head. 8" - $385.00; 14" - $750.00.

Hanna Baby: Bisque head, open mouth, sleep eyes. On five-piece bent limb baby body. 9" - $300.00; 11" - $400.00; 14" - $525.00; 15" - $700.00; 22" - $1,200.00; 24" - $1,500.00. **Toddler:** 7–8" - $375.00–425.00; 15" - $850.00; 19" - $1,000.00.

Character Baby: #169, 769, 1271, etc. 1910–on. Bisque head on five-piece bent limb baby body. Can also be marked with "Burggrub." 13" - $365.00; 16" - $550.00; 18" - $675.00; 24" - $800.00. **Toddler:** 20" - $950.00; 23" - $1,100.00.

Child: #1800, 1906, 1909, 5500, 5700, 5900, 5800, etc. Bisque head with open mouth, sleep or set eyes, jointed body. No damage and nicely dressed. 10" - $200.00; 14" - $325.00; 17" - $475.00; 21" - $550.00; 28" - $900.00; 30" - $1,000.00; 34" -

28" doll with sleep eyes, open mouth, and on fully jointed body. Marked "S," "pb" in star, "H. 1906 12 Germany." **$900.00.** *Courtesy Frasher Doll Auctions.*

$1,500.00; 38" - $2,500.00; 42" - $3,700.00 up. **Kid body:** Open mouth. 14" - $225.00; 17" - $325.00; 21" - $400.00.

Painted Bisque: Painted head on five-piece body or jointed body. 9" - $150.00; 12" - $250.00.

Das Lachende Baby (The Laughing Baby): 23" - $2,500.00; 26" - $3,000.00.

SCHOENHUT

Albert Schoenhut & Co. was located in Philadephia, PA, from 1872 until the 1930's. The dolls are all wood with spring joints, have holes in the bottoms of their feet to fit in a metal stand.

Marks:

(1911–1913)   **(1913–1930)**

SCHOENHUT DOLL
PAT. JAN. 17, '11, USA
& FOREIGN COUNTRIES
(Incised 1911–on)

Child With Carved Hair: May have comb marks, molded ribbon, comb or bow. Closed mouth. Original or nice clothes. **Excellent condition:** 14" - $2,500.00; 21" - $2,800.00. **Very**

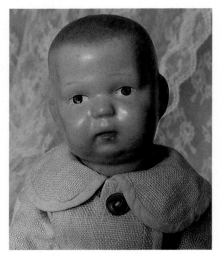

13½" mint Schoenhut boy with early "pouty" baby-style head. Really cute in this tiny size. **$885.00.** *Courtesy Turn of Century Antiques.*

good condition: Some wear. 14" - $1,450.00; 17" - $1,750.00; 21" - $2,200.00. **Poor condition:** With chips and dents. 14" - $600.00; 21" - $700.00.

Child: Rare, 1911. Looks exactly like Kammer & Reinhardt's #101 pouty. (See photo in Series 8, pg. 152.) 21" - $5,200.00 up.

Man With Carved Hair: Mint: 19" - $3,000.00 up. **Some wear:** 19" - $1,800.00. **Chips, dirty:** 19" - $800.00.

Baby Head: Can be on regular body or bent limb baby body. Bald spray painted hair or wig, painted decal eyes. Nicely dressed or original. **Excellent condition:** 12" - $525.00; 16" - $685.00; 18" - $725.00. **Good condition:** 16" - $425.00; 18" - $525.00. **Poor condition:** 16" - $175.00; 18" - $225.00.

Toddler: Excellent condition. 12" - $850.00; 16" - $1,000.00.

Child, character face: 1911–1930. Wig, intaglio eyes. Open/closed mouth with painted teeth. Suitably redressed or original. **Excellent condition:** 14" - $1,600.00; 17" - $1,750.00; 21" - $2,000.00. **Good condition:** 14" - $900.00; 17" - $1,100.00; 21" - $1,200.00. **Poor condition:** 14" - $325.00; 17" - $485.00; 21" - $600.00.

Cap Molded To Head: (See photo in Series 8, pg. 152.) 16" - $3,800.00 up.

Tootsie Wootsie: (See photo in Series 6, pg. 170.) Molded, painted hair, open/closed mouth with molded tongue and two upper teeth. Toddler or regular body. 14" - $2,100.00; 17" - $2,500.00; 20" - $2,800.00 up.

"Dolly" Face: 1915–1930. Common doll, wigged, open/closed mouth with painted teeth, decal painted eyes. Original or nicely dressed. **Excellent condition:** 14" - $675.00; 17" - $750.00; 20" - $875.00. **Good condition:** 14" - $450.00; 17" - $625.00; 21" - $750.00. **Poor condition:** 14" - $175.00; 16" - $285.00.

Sleep Eyes: Has lids that lower down over the eyes. Open mouth with teeth or just slightly cut open mouth with carved teeth. Original or nicely dressed. **Excellent condition:** 13–14" - $1,200.00; 17" - $1,350.00; 22" - $1,500.00. **Good condition:** 14" - $650.00; 18" - $800.00. **Poor condition:** 17" - $225.00; 22" - $300.00.

Walker: 1919–1930. One-piece legs with "walker" joints in center of legs and torso. Painted eyes, open/closed or closed mouth. Original or nicely dressed. **Excellent condition:** 15" - $900.00; 18" - $1,100.00; 21" - $1,400.00. **Good condition:** 15" -

$550.00; 18" - $650.00; 21" - $850.00. **Poor condition:** 15" - $125.00; 18" - $185.00; 21" - $250.00.

All Composition: Molded curly hair, "Patsy" style body, paper label on back, 1924. 13" - $600.00.

Circus Animals: $95.00–500.00.

Circus Parade Set, #18: 1950s. Tent and all figures/animals - $1,900.00.

Circus Humpty Dumpty: Tent, figures, and animals. $2,800.00 up.

Clowns: $150.00–300.00.

Ringmaster: $200.00–350.00.

Roly-Poly figures: 1914, marked. (See photo in Series 8, pg. 155.) $300.00 up.

14" and 17" walkers. Both have the "baby" face heads with painted features. Doll on left has original walking shoes with wooden soles and no holes. 14" - $800.00; 17" - $1,000.00. *Courtesy Shirley Bertrand.*

19" girl and boy with closed mouths and painted features. Both have very detailed mouths with character lips. Girl is all original. $1,800.00. *Courtesy Shirley Bertrand.*

SCHUETZMEISTER & QUENDT

Schuetzmeister & Quendt made dolls from 1893 to 1898. This short term factory was located in Boilstadt, Germany.

Marks:

Child: Mold #251, 252, etc. Can have cut pate or be a bald head with two string holes. No damage and nicely dressed, open mouth. 14" - $425.00; 20" - $545.00; 23" - $650.00.

Baby: Includes mold #201 & 301. Five-piece bent limb baby body. Not damaged and nicely dressed. Open mouth. 12" - $325.00; 14" - $450.00; 17" - $525.00; 22" - $725.00. **Toddler:** 16" - $950.00; 20" - $1,100.00; 24" - $1,500.00.

SIMON & HALBIG

Simon & Halbig began making dolls in the late 1860s or early 1870s and continued until the 1930s. Simon & Halbig made many heads for other companies and they also supplied some doll heads from the French makers. They made entire dolls, all bisque, flange neck dolls, turned shoulder heads and socket heads.

All prices are for dolls with no damage to the bisque and only minor scuffs to the bodies, well dressed, wigged and with shoes. Dolls should be ready to place in a collection.

Marks:

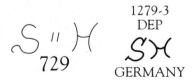

1279-3
DEP
SH
GERMANY

20" Simon & Halbig child with mold #550. Sleep eyes, open mouth. On fully jointed body. Clothes and wig may be original. **$765.00.** *Courtesy Frasher Doll Auctions.*

#130, 530, 540, 550, 570, 600, 1039, 1040, etc: Child, 1890 to 1930's, open mouth. (More for flirty eyes.) 12" - $475.00; 16" - $565.00; 19" - $725.00; 23" - $800.00; 27" - $1,150.00; 32" - $1,800.00; 35" - $2,000.00; 40" - 800.00.

#1049, 1059, 1069, 1078, 1079, 1099: Open mouth, jointed body. 12" - $525.00; 15" - $650.00; 19" - $700.00; 21" - $785.00; 24" - $825.00; 26" - $1,000.00; 30" - $1,300.00; 32" - $1,500.00; 35" - $1,900.00; 42" - $3,800.00. **Pull string sleep eyes:** 19" - $950.00 up.

#1009: Kid body. 19" - $975.00; 24" - $1,100.00; 26" - $1,400.00. **Jointed body:** 16" - $950.00; 19" - $1,300.00; 21" - $1,500.00; 24" - $1,900.00.

#1019, open mouth: Smiling. Jointed body. 16" - $6,300.00. Composition shoulder plate, ball-jointed arms, cloth body and upper legs. Ball-jointed lower legs. 18" - $7,500.00.

#1010, 1029, 1040, 1080, 1170, etc: Open mouth and kid body. 10" - $325.00; 14" - $425.00; 21" - $650.00; 25" - $725.00; 28" - $975.00.

#1109: 16" - $725.00; 23" - $975.00.

#1250, 1260: Open mouth, kid body. 16" - $575.00; 19" - $700.00; 25" - $975.00.

Characters: 1910 and after. Wig or molded hair, glass or painted eyes, with open/closed, closed, or open mouth. On jointed child bodies.

#IV: 20" - $22,000.00 up.

#IV: Open mouth. 23" - $5,500.00.

#120: 15" - $1,850.00; 23" - $2,850.00; 28" - $3,700.00.

#150: Full, closed mouth. Intaglio eyes. (See photo in Series 7, pg. 155; Series 9, pg. 163.) 16" - $12,000.00 up; 19" - $16,000.00 up; 23" - $21,000.00 up.

#151, 1388: Open/closed mouth, painted teeth. (See photo in Series 7, pg. 155; Series 9, pg. 163.) 15" - $5,300.00; 20" - $7,400.00.

#153 "Little Duke": (See photo in Series 8, pg. 157.) 15" - $32,000.00; 17" - $41,000.00; 21" - $48,000.00 up.

20" with sleep eyes/lashes, open mouth, and on fully jointed body. Marked "1059 Simon & Halbig." $775.00. *Courtesy Turn of Century Antiques.*

Large 36" doll with excellent bisque. Sleep eyes, open mouth. On fully jointed body. Marked "S&H 1079." $2,400.00. *Courtesy Frasher Doll Auctions.*

#540, 550, 570, Baby Blanche: 17" - $625.00; 23" - $725.00.

#600: 14" - $950.00; 18" - $1,400.00; 22" - $1,900.00. **Open mouth:** 17" - $650.00; 21" - $800.00.

#603: 10–12" - $5,600.00.

#718, 719, 720: 16" - $2,400.00; 22" - $3,500.00. **Open mouth:** 13" - $1,200.00; 18" - $1,800.00; 25" - $2,600.00.

#729: Slight open mouth, smiling. 16" - $3,200.00 up; 19" - $4,600.00.

#729: Closed mouth. 16" - $3,000.00; 20" - $3,700.00. **Kid body:** 16" - $1,400.00; 20" - $1,850.00; 25" - $2,200.00.

#739: 13" - $1,200.00; 18" - $2,100.00; 26" - $3,000.00. **Open mouth:** 17" - $1,450.00; 21" - $1,750.00; 26" - $2,200.00.

#740: Kid body, closed mouth. 10" - $600.00; 16" - $1,500.00; 18" - $1,700.00.

#720, 740: Jointed body. 10" - $675.00; 17" - $1,600.00; 21" - $2,200.00.

#749: Closed mouth, jointed body. 18" - $2,800.00; 22" - $3,400.00. **Open mouth:** 12" - $1,200.00; 18" - $1,800.00; 25" - $2,500.00. **Kid body:** 17" - $1,400.00; 21" - $2,000.00.

#759: Open mouth, deep cheek dimples, rare. (See photo in Series 9, pg. 164.) 24" - $18,000.00 up.

#905, 908: (See photo in Series 6, pg. 173.) Closed mouth. 16" - $2,800.00; 19" - $3,300.00. **Open mouth:** 14" - $1,600.00; 20" - $1,800.00; 25" - $2,450.00.

28" with closed mouth, jointed body, and large paperweight eyes. Marked "S. 15 H. 949." $3,700.00. *Courtesy Frasher Doll Auctions.*

#919: Open/closed mouth. 17" - $5,200.00; 21" - $7,200.00.

#929: Closed mouth. 17" - $3,600.00; 22" - $4,800.00. **Open mouth:** 18" - $2,400.00; 21" - $3,500.00.

#939: Closed mouth. **Composition body:** 15" - $2,600.00; 18" - $2,900.00; 21" - $3,500.00; 26" - $4,600.00; 40" - $4,500.00. **Kid body:** 18" - $1,600.00; 21" - $2,300.00; 26" - $2,900.00. **Open mouth:** 13" - $1,200.00; 18" - $1,900.00; 26" - $2,800.00; 40" - $3,700.00.

#939, Black: Closed mouth. 18"- $3,000.00; 21" - $3,900.00. **Open mouth:** (See photo in Series 5, pg. 132.) 18" - $1,700.00; 21" - $2,000.00; 26" - $2,600.00.

#940, 950: Kid body. (See photo in Series 7, pg. 156.) 10" - $565.00; 15" - $1,300.00; 21" - $1,700.00. **Jointed body:** 10" - $850.00; 15" - $1,700.00; 21" - $2,200.00.

#949: Closed mouth. (See photo in Series 9, pg. 165.) 16" - $2,300.00; 21" - $2,900.00; 25" - $3,400.00; 32" - $4,200.00. **Open mouth:** 18" - $1,800.00; 21" - $2,400.00; 26" - $2,800.00. **Kid body:** 15" - $1,400.00; 18" - $1,700.00; 21" - $2,100.00.

#949, Black: Closed mouth. 18" - $3,200.00; 21" - $4,000.00. **Open mouth:** 18" - $1,700.00; 21" - $2,100.00. **Kid body:** 18" - $1,400.00; 21" - $1,900.00; 26" - $2,000.00.

#969, 970: Slighty open mouth grin, square cut teeth, puffed cheeks. 17" - $9,800.00.

#979: Closed mouth. 13" - $2,600.00; 16" - $3,400.00; 19" - $3,700.00. **Open mouth:** 17" - $1,800.00; 21" - $2,400.00.

#979: Open mouth, square teeth, slight smile. 16" - $3,750.00. **Kid body:** 17" - $2,800.00; 21" - $3,200.00.

#1248, 1249, 1250, 1260, Santa: 14" - $1,000.00; 17" - $1,200.00; 22" - $1,500.00; 26" - $1,800.00; 30" - $2,100.00; 34" - $2,500.00.

30" with sleep eyes and open mouth with accent in center of lower lip. Fully jointed body. 12" "Bobby Ann, " a Kiddipal Dolly. Composition with sleep eyes and closed mouth. Mint in box, ca. 1929–1932. 8" poodle cut "Ginny" by Vogue. Original. 30" - $2,100.00; 12" - $365.00; 8" - $425.00. *Courtesy Frasher Doll Auctions.*

#1269, 1279: (See photo in Series 5, pg. 134; Series 9, pg. 166.) 12" - $1,700.00; 15" - $2,300.00; 18" - $3,000.00; 22" - $3,600.00; 25" - $4,000.00; 30" - $5,500.00; 34" - $5,900.00.

#1299: 17" - $1,200.00; 21" - $1,400.00.

#1302: See Black Dolls section.

#1303: Also see Black Dolls section. Closed mouth, thin lips. 18" - $7,600.00 up.

#1304: 14" - $6,500.00; 17" - $8,200.00.

#1305: Open/closed mouth, long nose. 18" - $14,000.00.

#1308: 20" - $6,600.00 up.

#1309: Character with open mouth. 10" - $1,500.00; 16" - $2,000.00; 20" - $3,100.00.

Very character faced doll with molded short eyebrows and eyes that slant upward. Molded upper and lower eyelids. Open mouth with accent in center of lower lip. Has dimples. On fully jointed body. $3,000.00. *Courtesy Frasher Doll Auctions.*

#1310: Open/closed mouth, modeled mustache. 19½" - $19,000.00.

#1338: Open mouth, jointed body. 18" - $1,500.00; 24" - $2,600.00; 28" - $3,200.00.

#1339: (See photos in Series 5, pg. 135; Series 7, pg. 157.) Character face, open mouth. 18" - $1,800.00; 26" - $3,200.00.

#1339, 1358 Black: 16" - $5,800.00; 20" - $7,200.00.

#1345: 15" - $2,900.00; 17" - $4,300.00.

#1388, 1398: Lady Doll. 22" - $18,500.00 up.

#1428: Very character face. Open/closed mouth, glass eyes. 16" - $1,750.00; 22" - $2,600.00.

#1448: Full closed mouth. 17" - $19,000.00 up; 21" - $24,000.00 up.

#1448: Open/closed mouth, laughing, modeled teeth. 16" - $14,000.00 up; 21" - $24,000.00 up.

#1478: 17" - $9,700.00 up.

#1488: Child, closed mouth. 16" - $3,400.00; 20" - $4,700.00; 24" - $5,600.00.

Character Babies: 1909 to 1930s. Wigs or molded hair, painted or sleep eyes, open or open/closed mouth and on five-piece bent limb baby bodies. (Allow more for toddler body.)

#1294: 16" - $675.00; 19" - $825.00; 23" - $1,200.00; 26" - $1,800.00. **With clockwork in head to move eyes:** 25-26" - $3,000.00. **Toddler:** 22" - $1,600.00.

#1299: With open mouth. 10" - $365.00; 16" - $975.00. **Toddler:** 16" - $1,100.00; 18" - $1,300.00.

#1428 Toddler: (See photo in Series 7, pg. 158.) 12" - $1,400.00; 16" - $1,600.00; 20" - $2,000.00; 26" - $2,500.00.

#1428 Baby: 12" - $1,050.00; 15" - $1,250.00; 19" - $1,600.00.

#1488 Toddler: (See photo in Series 6, pg. 175.) 15" - $2,800.00; 18" - $3,700.00; 22" - $5,000.00. **Baby:** 15" - $1,200.00; 18" - $2,500.00; 22" - $3,400.00; 26" - $3,800.00.

#1489 Erika Baby: (See photos in Series 6, pg. 176; Series 7, pg. 159.) 20" - $3,500.00; 22" - $4,200.00; 26" - $4,900.00.

#1498 Toddler: (See photo in Series 6, pg. 175.) 16" - $6,600.00; 20" - $7,600.00. **Baby:** 16" - $6,000.00; 20" - $6,900.00.

#1039 Walker: Key wound. 16" - $1,600.00; 20" - $2,000.00; 23" - $2,400.00. **Walking/Kissing:** 20" - $1,200.00; 24" - $1,600.00.

Edison, Thomas: Metal body with phonograph. Uses S&H head (mold #719, etc.) Open mouth. 18" - $2,600.00 up; 24" - $3,400.00 up.

Miniature Dolls: Tiny dolls with open mouth on jointed body or five-piece body with some having painted-on shoes and socks.

#1078, 1079, etc.: Fully jointed. 7" - $385.00; 10" - $525.00. **Five-piece body:** 7" - $325.00; 10" - $425.00. **Walker:** 10–11" - $625.00.

#1160: "Little Women" type. Closed mouth and fancy wig. 5½–6½" - $400.00; 10–11" - $600.00. **Head only:** 2–3" - $85.00–145.00.

Ladies: Ca. 1910. Open mouth, molded lady-style slim body with slim arms and legs.

#1159, 1179: 12" - $950.00; 15" - $1,500.00; 19" - $1,900.00; 22" - $2,400.00; 26" - $2,900.00.

Ladies: Closed mouth. Ca. 1910. Adult slim limb body.

#1303: 15" - $11,000.00; 17" - $13,000.00.

#1305: Lady. Open/closed mouth, long nose. 18" - $9,600.00 up; 22" - $14,000.00 up.

#1307: Lady, long face. 18" - $15,500.00 up; 24" - $22,500.00 up.

#1308: Man. 13" - $5,700.00; 15" - $6,300.00.

#1398: 18" - $14,000.00 up.

#1468, 1469: Sweet expression. Closed mouth, glass eyes. 14" - $2,800.00; 16" - $3,200.00.

#1527: 18" - $9,500.00 up; 22" - $11,000.00 up.

#152 Lady: 17" - $17,800.00 up; 23" - $29,500.00 up.

12", 7", and 6½" Simon & Halbig mold #1160 dolls called "Little Women." All have glass eyes, original mohair wigs, and closed mouths. 12" - $625.00; 6½–7" - $450.00. *Courtesy Turn of Century Antiques.*

The Société Française de Fabrication de Bébés et Jouets (S.F.B.J.) was formed in 1899 and known members were Jumeau, Bru, Fleischmann & Bloedel, Rabery & Delphieu, Pintel & Godchaux, P.H. Schmitz, A. Bouchet, Jullien, and Danel & Cie. By 1922, S.F.B.J. employed 2,800 people. The Society was dissolved in 1958. There is a vast amount of "dolly-faced" S.F.B.J. dolls, but some are extremely rare and are character molds. Most of the characters are in the 200 mold number series.

Marks:

S.F.B.J.
239
PARIS

S.F.B.J.
301

Child: 1899. Sleep or set eyes, open mouth and on jointed French body. No damage and nicely dressed.
#60: 12" - $500.00; 14" - $575.00; 20" - $900.00; 28" - $1,400.00.
#301: 8" - $400.00; 12" - $625.00; 14" - $750.00; 20" - $950.00; 28" - $1,600.00.
Bleuette: 1930s–1960s. Exclusively made for Gautier-Languereau and their newspaper for children, *La Semaine de Suzette.* (Just as "Betsy McCall" was used by *McCall's* magazine.) Marked "SFBJ" or "71 UNIS FRANCE 149 301" with "1½" at base of neck socket. Body marked "2" and feet marked "1." Sleep eyes, open mouth. (See photo in Series 7, pg. 36.) 10" - $800.00 up.
Jumeau Type: Open mouth. (See photo in Series 7, pg. 163; Series 8, pg. 164; Series 9, pg. 170.) 15" - $1,000.00; 20" - $1,600.00; 24" - $2,000.00; 30" - $2,500.00; 40" - $3,500.00. **Closed mouth:** 17" - $2,300.00; 21" - $3,000.00; 25" - $3,400.00.
Lady #1159: Open mouth, adult body. 24" - $2,800.00.
Character: Sleep or set eyes, wigged, molded hair, jointed body. (Allow more for flocked hair. Usually found on mold #227, 235, 237, 266.) No damage and nicely dressed.
#211: 18" - $6,000.00 up.
#226: Glass eyes: 14" - $1,600.00; 19" - $2,200.00. **Painted eyes:** 16" - $1,300.00.
#227: (See photo in Series 5, pg. 136.) 16" - $2,300.00; 20" - $2,600.00.
#229: 17" - $4,200.00.
#230: 15" - $1,500.00; 18" - $2,000.00; 20" - $2,300.00.
#233: Screamer. 14" - $2,000.00; 17" - $2,900.00.
#234: 17" - $3,000.00; 23" - $3,500.00.
#235: Glass eyes: 14" - $1,550.00; 22" - $2,100.00. **Painted eyes:** 15" - $1,400.00; 22" - $2,100.00.

21" S.F.B.J. #60 with sleep eyes and open mouth. She is a walker. When head turns and legs move, she raises her arm to throw kiss. On jointed French body with S.F.B.J. original label. $2,100.00.
Courtesy Turn of Century Antiques.

18½" on composition jointed adult lady body. Smiling open mouth with four square cut teeth. Original. Marked "S.F.B.J. 1159 Paris." (See Series 7, pg. 162 for lady mold #238.) **$2,500.00.** *Courtesy Frasher Doll Auctions.*

#236, 262 Toddler: 12" - $1,300.00; 16" - $1,400.00; 20" - $1,900.00; 24" - $2,100.00; 26" - $2,400.00. **Baby:** 14" - $700.00; 19" - $1,200.00; 25" - $1,700.00.

#237: (See photo in Series 7, pg. 161.) 15" - $2,000.00; 20" - $2,400.00.

#238: 16" - $3,800.00; 24" - $4,300.00. **Lady:** 22" - $4,400.00.

#239 Poulbot: 16" - $8,500.00 up.

#242: (See photo in Series 5, pg. 137.) 14" - $2,600.00; 16½" - $3,000.00 up.

#247: 16" - $2,400.00; 20" - $2,950.00; 26" - $3,400.00.

#248: Very pouty, glass eyes. 14" - $4,000.00; 19" - $5,600.00.

#251 Toddler: 18"- $1,500.00; 22" - $2,000.00; 26" - $2,400.00. **Baby:**

15" - $1,100.00; 21" - $1,700.00; 25" - $2,000.00.

#252 Toddler: 16" - $5,500.00; 20" - $7,200.00; 26" - $7,900.00. **Baby:** 12" - $1,800.00; 16" - $4,800.00; 22" - $7,200.00; 26" - $8,300.00.

#257: 18" - $2,700.00.

#266: 22" - $4,200.00.

#306: Princess Elizabeth. See Jumeau section.

14" called "Street Urchin." A very rare character doll. Wide spaced eyes with molded eyelids, no lashes or eyebrows. Closed mouth. Original orange-red mohair wig. On five-piece toddler body with straight wrists. Dress and head scarf may be original. Marked "S.F.B.J." 239 Paris/ Poulbot." **$7,600.00.** *Courtesy Frasher Doll Auctions.*

Googly: See Googly section.

Kiss Throwing, Walking Doll: (See photo in Series 5, pg. 138; Series 9, pg. 170.) Composition body with straight legs and walking mechanism. When it walks, arm goes up to throw kiss. Head moves from side to side. Flirty eyes, open mouth. In working condition, no damage to bisque head and nicely dressed. 21–22" - $2,100.00.

SKOOKUMS

Skookums have mask faces with wigs. Wool blankets form the bodies that are stuffed with twigs, leaves, and grass. Wooden dowel rods form the legs and they have wooden feet. They were made from 1920 to 1940s. After 1949, they have plastic feet.

Squaw with baby: 15" - $135.00; 18" - $200.00; 22" - $385.00.

Portrait Chief: 15" - $145.00; 18" - $225.00; 22" - $400.00; 30" - $500.00.

Sitting Squaw: 8" - $100.00; 12" - $145.00.

Plastic feet: 4" - $18.00; 6" - $25.00; 12" - $50.00; 15" - $125.00; 18" - $165.00; 22" - $250.00; 30" - $350.00; 36" - $425.00.

15" Skookum squaw with baby. 1920s. Tagged "Yosemite National Park." $185.00. *Courtesy Kathy Tvrdik.*

Snow babies have fired-on "pebble-textured" clothing and were made in Germany and Japan. German-made babies were made as early as the 1880s and have excellent details. These early ones had no shoes or mittens, and these "stubs" were covered with all-white pebbly "snow." In the 1890s, some snow had a blue-grey appearance. Those babies are of excellent quality but did not remain on the market long.

After 1900, the hands and feet of the snow babies became defined. Early ones had beautiful painted features, but the later ones tended to have high color and poor artist workmanship. Japan reproduced snow babies in 1971 and they are stamped "Japan."

Snow babies can be excellent to poor in quality from both countries. Many are unmarked. Prices are for good quality painted features, rareness of pose, and no damage to the piece.

Single Figure: 1½" - $50.00; 3" - $100.00 – 125.00.

Two Figures: Molded together. 1½" - $100.00 – 125.00; 3" - $150.00 – 195.00.

Three Figures: Molded together. 1½" - $145.00 – 185.00; 3" - $195.00 – 245.00.

One Figure on sled: 2 – 2½" - $185.00. With reindeer: $200.00.

Two Figures on sled: 2 – 2½" - $200.00.

Three Figures on sled: (See photo in Series 6, pg. 180.) 2 – 2½" - $265.00.

Jointed: Shoulders and hips. (See photo in Series 5, pg. 139.) 3¼" - $185.00 up; 5" - $365.00 up; 7" - $465.00 up.

Shoulder head: Cloth body with china limbs. 9" - $385.00; 12" - $450.00.

On sled in glass: "Snow" scene. $225.00 up. **Sled/dogs:** 3 – 4" - $285.00.

With bear: $265.00.

With snowman: 2½" - $145.00.

With musical base: $185.00 up.

Laughing child: 3" - $150.00 up.

Snow bear with Santa: $365.00.

With reindeer: $250.00

Snow Baby riding polar bear: 3" - $225.00.

Snow Angel: White texturing. Pink feathered smooth bisque wings. 3" - $300.00 up.

Three Snow Babies attached to bisque sled by wooden pegs. Larger figure is 4" and smaller ones are 2" tall. Larger one is attached to sled (front of sled broken). Three on sled - $265.00 up; 4" - $185.00 up. *Courtesy Frasher Doll Auctions.*

SNOW BABIES

Igloo: $90.00.
Ice skater: 3" - $200.00 up.
Dog: Pulling sled with one figure.
$250.00.
In airplane: 4½" - $365.00.

Mother: Pushing two babies in red sled carriage. 4½" - $365.00 up.
Rolling snowball: 5" - $225.00.
Pushing carriage with twins: $325.00.

STEIFF

Steiff started business in 1894. This German maker is better known for their plush/stuffed animals than for dolls.

Steiff Dolls: Felt, velvet or plush with seam down middle of face. Button-style eyes, painted features and sewn-on ears. The dolls generally have large feet so they stand alone. Prices are for dolls in excellent condition and with original clothes. Second prices are for dolls that are soiled and may not be original.

Adults: (See photo in Series 7, pg. 165.) 18" - $2,400.00 up; 22" - $2,900.00 up.
Military Men or Uniforms: Policemen, conductors, etc. (See photo in Series 7, pg. 165.) 15" - $4,000.00 up; 17" - $4,400.00 up; 21" - $4,900.00 up.
Children: (See photo in Series 6, pg. 181.) 12" - $1,000.00 up; 15–16" - $1,600.00; 18–19" - $1,900.00 up.
Made in U.S. Zone Germany: Has glass eyes. 12" - $800.00 up; 16" - $1,000.00 up.
Comic Characters: Such as chef, elf, musician, etc. 14" - $2,500.00 up; 16" - $3,300.00 up.
Mickey Mouse: 9–10" - $1,200.00 up.
Minnie Mouse: 9–10" - $1,800.00 up.
Clown: 16" - $2,300.00 up.
Leprechaun or Elf: All felt, straw stuffed, carries felt cloverleaf. Red mohair beard. 12" - $650.00 up; 16" - $725.00.
Max and Moritz: "Bendy" type. Felt costumes. Ca. 1960. Each - $165.00.

Early 16" Steiff dolls with soft felt bodies and wires inside limbs to permit posing. Felt arms with stitched fingers. Felt face with center seam. Applied ears, beard, and brows. Both original. Each - $725.00. *Courtesy Frasher Doll Auctions.*

Jules Nicholas Steiner operated from 1855 to 1892 when the firm was taken over by Amedee LaFosse. In 1895, this firm merged with Henri Alexander, the maker of Phenix Bébé and a partner, May Freres Cie, the maker of Bébé Mascotte. In 1899, Jules Mettais took over the firm and in 1906, the company was sold to Edmond Daspres.

In 1889, the firm registered the girl with a banner and the words "Le Petit Parisien" and in 1892, LaFosse registered "Le Parisien."

Steiner body: All fingers are nearly same length. (See photo in Series 8, pg. 167.)

Marks:

J. STEINER
STE. S.G.D.G.
FIRE A12
PARIS

STE C3
J. STEINER
B. S.G.D.G.

16" Steiner "Le Petit Parisien" with closed mouth and excellent bisque. Steiner jointed body with pull string for "mama/papa" cryer box. Marked with name of store where purchased "Au Bonheur des Enfants–Paris." **$4,900.00.** *Courtesy Turn of Century Antiques.*

"A" Series Child: Closed mouth. (Also see "Le Parisien – "A" Series in this listing.) 1885. Paperweight eyes, jointed body and cardboard pate. No damage and nicely dressed. 8" - $2,800.00; 10" - $3,300.00; 15" - $4,400.00; 22" - $6,500.00; 25" - $7,500.00; 28" - $8,200.00.

"A" Series Child: Open mouth. Otherwise same as previous listing. 14" - $1,500.00; 18" - $2,300.00; 22" - $2,700.00.

"B" Series: Closed mouth. 24" - $5,400.00; 30" - $7,500.00.

"C" Series Child: Ca. 1880. Closed mouth, round face, paperweight eyes. No damage, nicely dressed. (See photo in Series 9, pg. 173.) 18" - $5,400.00; 22" - $7,000.00; 27" - $8,900.00; 30" - $9,200.00. **Open mouth:** Two rows teeth. 22" - $6,200.00.

Bourgoin Steiner: 1870s. With "Bourgoin" incised or in red stamp on head along with the rest of the Steiner mark. Closed mouth. No damage, nicely dressed. 16" - $5,600.00; 20" - $6,700.00; 25" - $8,600.00.

Wire Eye Steiner: Closed mouth, flat glass eyes that open and close by moving wire in back of the head. Jointed body, no damage and nicely dressed. **Bourgoin:** 17" - $5,400.00; 21" - $6,200.00; 26" - $7,600.00. **"A" Series:** 17" - $5,200.00; 21" - $6,100.00; 26" - $7,400.00. **"C" Series:** 17" -

$5,200.00; 21" - $6,100.00; 26" - $7,500.00.

"Le Parisien" - "A" Series: 1892. **Closed mouth:** 8–9" - $2,800.00; 13–14" - $4,100.00; 17" - $5,200.00; 21" - $6,400.00; 24" - $7,300.00; 28" - $8,000.00. **Open mouth:** 16" - $2,400.00; 22" - $2,700.00; 25" - $3,500.00.

Mechanical and Kicking Steiner: See that section.

Bisque Hip Steiner: Bisque head, Motschmann-style body with shoulders, lower arms and legs and bisque torso sections. No damage anywhere. 18" - $7,000.00 up.

Early White Bisque Steiner: Round face, open mouth with two rows of teeth. On jointed Steiner body. Pink wash over eyes. Unmarked. No damage, nicely dressed. (See Series 8, pg. 167; Series 9, pg. 174.) 16" - $4,200.00; 20" - $5,000.00.

Beautiful example of a Steiner with open/closed mouth and heavy painted eyebrows. 17" on Steiner jointed body. Marked "A 34 Paris 8" on head and stamped on body in red "Le Parisien." $5,200.00. *Courtesy Turn of Century Antiques.*

20" doll has lever in back of head that operates sleep eyes. On Steiner body with bisque hands. Closed mouth. Marked "Ste. C.2" on head. $6,800.00. *Courtesy Frasher Doll Auctions.*

Swaine & Co. operated from 1910 into the 1930s.

Babies: Bisque head, composition baby body. **"Lori":** Incised on head. See that section.

DIP: Glass eyes, wig, and closed mouth. 10" - $900.00; 14" - $1,450.00; 16" - $1,600.00.

DV: Molded hair, glass eyes, open/closed mouth. 13" - $1,200.00.

DI: Molded hair, intaglio eyes, open/closed mouth. 13" - $1,200.00; 20" - $2,000.00.

FP: 10" - $685.00.

S & C child with B.P.: Made for Bahr & Proschild. Smiling open/closed mouth. Very character face. 14" - $6,000.00 up; 17" - $7,500.00 up; 21" - $8,700.00 up.

Marked S & C: 7" - $325.00; 14" - $500.00; 17" - $650.00; 22" - $725.00; 25" - $850.00; 30" - $1,150.00; 38" - $2,200.00.

14" made by Franz Schmidt for Swaine & Co. Intaglio eyes with laugh lines. Open/closed smiling mouth with molded teeth. Dress and shoes may be original. Marked "B.P. 4" green stamp "Geschutzt S & C/Germany." $6,000.00 up. *Courtesy Frasher Doll Auctions.*

25" boy with sleep eyes, open mouth, and on German fully jointed body. Made by James Scholly Taft in 1910 and marked "Taft/1910." $725.00. *Courtesy Ellen McCorkell.*

TYNIE BABY

"Tynie Baby" was made for Horsman Doll Co. in 1924. Doll will have sleep eyes, closed pouty mouth and "frown" between eyes. Its cloth body has celluloid or composition hands. Markings will be "1924/E.I. Horsman/Made in Germany." Some will also be incised "Tynie Baby." Doll should have no damage and be nicely dressed.

Bisque head: 11" - $350.00; 13" - $475.00; 16" - $750.00.

Composition head: 15–16" - $295.00.

All bisque: Glass eyes, swivel neck. 6" - $1,000.00; 9" - $1,700.00.

Painted eyes: 6" - $565.00.

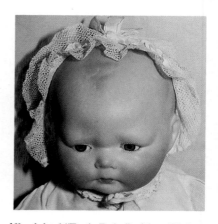

All original "Tynie Baby" with solid dome bisque head, closed pouty mouth, and sleep eyes. Cloth body with celluloid or composition hands. $750.00. *Courtesy Frasher Doll Auctions.*

"UNIS, France" was a type of trade association or a "seal of approval" for trade goods to consumers from the manufacturers. This group of businessmen, who were to watch the quality of French exports, often overlooked guidelines and some poor quality dolls were exported. Many fine quality UNIS marked dolls were also produced.

UNIS began right after World War I and is still in business. Two doll companies are still members, "Poupee Bella and "Petit Colin. Other manufacturers in this group include makers of toys, sewing machines, tile, and pens.

Marks:

#60, 70, 71, 301: Bisque head, composition jointed body. Sleep or set eyes, open mouth. No damage, nicely dressed. (Allow more for flirty eyes.) 8–9" - $400.00; 15" - $565.00; 18" - $700.00; 22" - $850.00; 25" - $975.00. **Closed mouth:** 16" - $2,400.00; 20" - $3,000.00. **Black or brown:** 11–12" - $375.00; 16" - $750.00.

#60, 70, 71, 301: On five-piece body, glass eyes. 6½" - $185.00; 12" - $365.00; 14" - $500.00.

Bleuette: See S.F.B.J section.

Provincial Costume Doll: Bisque head, painted, set or sleep eyes, open mouth (or closed on smaller dolls.) Five-piece body. Original costume, no damage. 6" - $225.00; 12" - $400.00; 14" - $550.00.

Baby #272: Glass eyes, open mouth, cloth body, celluloid hands. 15" - $575.00; 18" - $975.00. **Painted eyes:** Composition hands. 16" - $375.00; 19" - $565.00.

#251 Toddler: 15" - $1,250.00 up; 24" - $2,200.00

Princess Elizabeth: (See photo in Series 6, pg. 185.) 1938. Jointed body, closed mouth. (Allow more for flirty eyes.) 18" - $1,600.00; 23" - $1,900.00; 32" - $3,200.00 up.

Princess Margaret Rose: 1938. Closed mouth. 18" - $1,700.00; 23" - $2,000.00; 32" - $3,400.00.

8" doll on five-piece papier maché body with painted-on boots. Closed mouth, sleep eyes. Original with original paper sticker. Marked "UNIS 60 Paris." $465.00. *Courtesy Frasher Doll Auctions.*

UNIS

20" with open mouth and flirty sleep eyes. French jointed body. Marked "UNIS 301." $850.00.
Courtesy Turn of Century Antiques.

WAGNER & ZETZSCHE

Closed mouth: 16" - $650.00; 21" - $825.00; 24" - $1,000.00; 27" - $1,200.00.
Open mouth: 16" - $400.00; 21" - $500.00; 24" - $600.00; 27" - $800.00.

Beautiful shoulder head doll on kid body with bisque lower arms. Head slightly turned with downcast expression. Closed mouth. Under side of eyebrows painted very straight. $825.00. *Courtesy June Murkins.*

Poured Wax: Cloth body with wax head, limbs and inset glass eyes. Hair is embedded into wax. Nicely dressed or in original clothes, no damage to wax, but wax may be slightly discolored evenly all over. Not rewaxed. (See photos in Series 5, pg. 144; Series 7, pg. 174.) 16" - $1,200.00; 19" - $1,500.00; 22" - $1,700.00; 25" - $2,000.00. **Lady or Man:** 20" - $2,600.00 up; 24" - $3,600.00.

Wax Over Papier Maché or Composition: Cloth body with wax over papier maché or composition head and with wax over composition or wood limbs. Only minor scuffs with no chipped out places, good color and nicely dressed. (See photo in Series 6, pg. 189.)

Early Dolls: 1860 on. **Sleep eyes:** Pull string to move eyes. 16" - $850.00. **Molded hair:** 14" - $285.00; 21" -

16" wax fashion child with sleep eyes, rooted hair, cloth body, and wax limbs. Very pretty face. 12" Fritz Bartenstein two-faced wax doll with one side sleeping and the other side crying. Both have glass eyes. Signed on cloth body. Deeply modeled wax design. 16" - $1,200.00; 12" - $800.00. *Courtesy Turn of Century Antiques.*

$485.00; 24" - $565.00. **Squeeker body:** 14" - $325.00; 17" - $575.00.00.

"Alice:" Headband hairdo: 14" - $475.00; 17" - $550.00. **With wig:** Excellent quality. Heavy wax. 12" - $265.00; 16" - $425.00; 21" - $550.00; 24" - $650.00; 29" - $800.00. **Lever-operated eyes:** 1850s. 17" - $800.00. **Common quality:** Wax worn or gone. 12" - $150.00; 16" - $325.00; 21" - $350.00; 24" - $465.00.

Later Dolls: 12" - $225.00; 16" - $400.00.

Bonnet or Cap: (See photo in Series 6, pg. 190.) **Hat molded on forehead:** 16" - $2,600.00. **Derby-type hat:** 22" - $2,100.00. **Bonnet-style hat:** 20" - $2,250.00. **Round face, poke bonnet:** 22" - $2,450.00. **Baby:** $16" - $1,400.00.

Pumpkin: Hair laced over ridged raised front area. 16" - $425.00; 20" - $525.00.

Slit Head Wax: English, 1830–1860s. Glass eyes, some open and closed by an attached wire. (See photo in Series 6, pg. 189.) 14" - $500.00 up; 18" - $775.00; 21" - $900.00; 25" - $1,200.00 up.

Two-faced Doll: 1880–1890s. Body stamped "Bartenstein" (Fritz). One side laughing, other crying. 15–16" - $950.00.

15" slit head wax doll with glass eyes and closed smiling mouth. Blue leather arms. Pristine condition and all original. Hat added for effect. $675.00. *Courtesy Ricki Small.*

WEBBER, WILLIAM AUGUSTUS

William Augustus Webber of Medford, Massachusetts made the "Webber Singing Doll" for a period of two years, 1892–1894. He advertised two sizes in 1892 — 22" and 30." The dolls had wax over papier maché heads, cloth bodies, and wooden voice box in stomach. A push button on front of the doll activated the singing mechanism. Songs included "America" and several others. In 1893–1894, the dolls came in 22", 24", and 26" sizes and additional songs included "Pop Goes The Weasel" and "God Bless The Prince of Wales." These dolls had wax over composition limbs or leather arms and cloth legs.

Webber Singing Doll: 22" - $1,600.00; 24" - $1,800.00; 30" - $2,900.00.

24" "Webber Singing Doll" with glass eyes, wax over composition lower arms and legs, cloth body, and singing box. Clothes and wig may be original. Doll marked "The Webber Doll" in fancy script on the cloth body. $1,800.00 up. *Courtesy Pat Timmons.*

WELLINGS, NORAH

Norah Wellings' designs were made for her by Victoria Toy Works in Wellington, Shropshire, England. These dolls were made from 1926 into the 1960's. The dolls are velvet as well as other fabrics, especially felt and velour. They will have a tag on the foot "Made in England by Norah Wellings."

Child: All fabric with stitch jointed hips and shoulders. Molded fabric face with oil-painted features. Some faces are papier maché with a stockinette covering. All original felt and cloth clothes, clean condition. **Painted eyes:** 12" - $425.00; 17" - $700.00; 21" - $1,000.00; 23" - $1,400.00. **Glass eyes:** 14" - $600.00; 17" - $800.00; 21" - $1,200.00.

Mounties, Black Islanders, Scots, and Other Characters: These are most commonly found. Must be in same condition as child. 8" - $85.00 up; 12" - $165.00 up; 14" - $200.00 up.

Glass Eyes: White: 14" - $300.00; 17" - $450.00. **Black:** 14" - $250.00; 20" - $400.00; 26" - $650.00.

Babies: Same description as child and same condition. 15" - $565.00; 22" - $950.00.

WELLINGS, NORAH

11" Norah Wellings child doll made of all velvet with oil-painted features and yarn hair. Original cotton dress and felt shoes. $425.00.

WIEGAND, HUGO

This doll was made for Hugo Wiegand of Walterhausen, Thuringia, Germany by Armand Marseille. Has bisque shoulder head with molded bust, slim kid body, cloth lower legs, and bisque lower arms. Open mouth. Wig may be original.

Mark:

H. W & Co.
A   M

16" - $450.00; 20" - $785.00; 24" - $975.00; 28" - $1,400.00; 34" - $1,800.00. *Courtesy Arthur Michnevite.*

The Adolf Wislizenus doll factory was located at Waltershausen, Germany and the heads he used were made by Bahr & Proschild, Ernst Heubach of Koppelsdorf, and Simon & Halbig. The company was in business starting in 1851, but it is not known when they began to make dolls.

Marks:

GERMANY
A. W.

Child: 1890s into 1900s. Bisque head on jointed body, sleep eyes, open mouth. No damage and nicely dressed. 12" - $200.00; 14" - $385.00; 17" - $500.00; 22" - $600.00; 25" - $700.00.

Walker: Open mouth, one-piece legs. Head turns as legs move. 20" - $550.00.

Baby: Bisque head in perfect condition and on five-piece bent limb baby body. No damage and nicely dressed. 16" - $500.00; 19" - $600.00; 25" - $1,000.00.

#110, 115: 16" - $1,100.00. **Glass eyes:** 16" - $3,800.00 up.

English: William & Mary Period, 1690s–1700. Carved wooden head, eyes. Eyebrow and eyelashes are painted with tiny lines. Colored cheeks, human hair or flax wig. Wood body, carved wood hands shaped like forks. Legs are wood and jointed. Upper arms are cloth. In medium to fair condition: 15–18" - $55,000.00 up.

English: Queen Anne Period. Early 1700s. Eyebrows and lashes made of dots. Glass pupiless eyes (some painted). Carved wooden egg-shaped head. Jointed wooden body, cloth upper arms. Back (including hips) was planed flat. Nicely dressed, in overall good condition. 14" - $9,700.00 up; 18" - $19,000.00 up; 24" - $26,000.00 up.

English: Georgian Period, 1750s–1800. Round wooden head with gesso coating, inset glass eyes. Eyelashes and eyebrows made of dots. Human or flax wig. Jointed wood body with pointed torso. Medium to fair condition. 13" - $2,950.00; 16" - $4,600.00; 18" - $5,200.00; 24" - $6,550.00.

English: 1800s–1840s. Gesso coated wooden head, painted eyes. Human hair or flax wig. Original gowns

generally longer than wooden legs. 12–13" - $1,450.00; 15" - $1,950.00; 20" - $2,900.00.

German: 1810s–1850s. Hair is delicately carved and painted with little spit curls around face. Some have decorations carved in hair such as yellow tuck comb. Features are painted. All wood doll with pegged or ball jointed limbs. 7" - $765.00; 12-13" - $1,400.00; 16-17" - $1,700.00. **Exceptional:** All original. 17" - $3,200.00.

German: 1850s–1900. All wood with painted plain hairstyle. Some may have spit curls around face. 5" - $150.00; 8" - $235.00; 12" - $375.00. **Wooden shoulder head:** Same but with more elaborate carved hair such as buns. Wood limbs and cloth body. 9–10" - $400.00; 16–17" - $600.00; 23" - $875.00.

German: After 1900. Turned wood head with carved nose. Hair painted and painted lower legs with black shoes. Peg jointed. 10–11" - $100.00. **Child:** All wood, body is fully jointed. **Glass eyes, open mouth:** 14–15" - $450.00; 18" - $700.00; 23" - $900.00.

Nesting Dolls: Called "Matryoshka." Prices are for the set. **Old:** 1930s and before. 3" - $60.00 up; 6" - $100.00 up; 8" - $150.00 up. **New:** 4" - $10.00; 6" - $20.00. **Political:** Includes Gorbachev, Yeltsin. 4½" - $25.00; 6½" - $40.00.

Swiss: Carved wooden dolls. Dowel jointed all wood bodies. Jointed elbows, hips, and knees. 8" - $500.00.

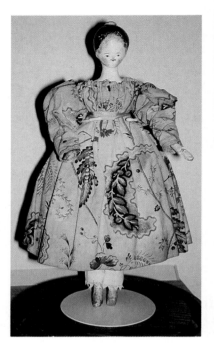

9" German tuck comb wooden doll that is all original. **$925.00.** *Courtesy Ricki Small.*

3½" Mickey Mouse and Pluto that are all wood with the dog having felt ears. Mickey - $400.00 up; Pluto - $350.00 up. *Courtesy Shirley Bertrand.*

Center: 13" "Queen Anne" type wooden doll of mid-1700s. Inset pupilless glass eyes, dotted lashes and brows, nailed on human hair wig. Wooden body with square torso. Original. Left: 32" closed mouth doll by Kestner. Holding 14" Belton-type marionette by Limbach that has clover leaf mark. Right: 16" Franz Schmit toddler marked "F.S. & C. 1267." Shown with French tea set. 13" wooden - $9,600.00 up; 32" - $4,600.00; marionette - $750.00; 16" - $2,600.00; tea set - $650.00. *Courtesy of Frasher Doll Auctions.*

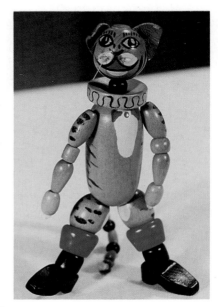

3½" "Puss n' Boots" that is all wood, segmented and painted. Maker unknown. $350.00 up. *Courtesy Shirley Bertrand.*

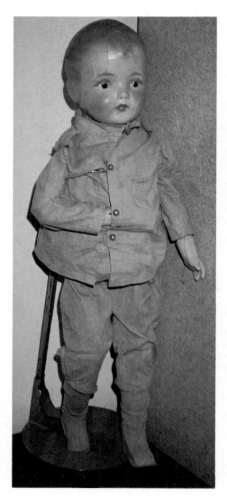

World War I wounded soldier that is a walker. Composition head with painted features and hair. Composition hands and wrists, rest is wood. Made by Wood Toy Co. of New York City, 1919–1920. Some marked "Patented in U.S.A./other patents pend./applied for in all countries." Above average to mint condition - $565.00; fair condition - $200.00. *Courtesy Ellen McCorkell.*

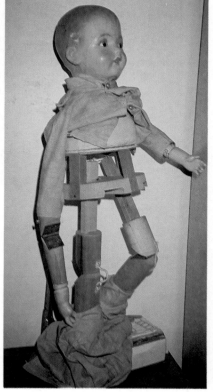

Right: This photo shows construction and arm out of uniform jacket.

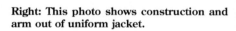

MODERN DOLLS

Effanbee's "Little Lady Majorette" - $425.00; Mattel's "Chatty Cathy," MIB - $125.00; Ideal's "Toni" - $225.00; American Character's "Sweet Sue," no shoes and redressed - $95.00; American Character's 30" "Toodles," MIB - $400.00. *Courtesy Frasher Doll Auctions.*

Large 24" "Baby Of Mine" made by Acme Doll Co. of New York and Chicago, 1908–1930s. Tin sleep eyes and open mouth with two upper teeth. Happy smile and dimples. Cloth body with composition head and limbs. This doll was made in 1932. Mint condition - $350.00; Fair condition - $145.00. *Courtesy Jeannie Mauldin.*

MADAME ALEXANDER – ALEXANDER-KINS

The author's separate price guide covering over 1,000 Madame Alexander dolls is available from book dealers or Collector Books.

1953–1954: 7½–8" straight leg non-walker. Heavy hard plastic. **Party Dress:** Mint, all correct - $550.00 up. Soiled, dirty hair, mussed, or parts of clothing missing - $95.00. **Ballgown:** Mint and correct - $1,000.00 up. Soiled, dirty, bad face color, not original - $150.00. **Nude:** Clean, good face color. $200.00. Dirty, bad face color - $40.00.

1955: 8" straight leg walker. **Party Dress:** Mint, all correct - $425.00 up. Soiled, dirty, parts of clothes missing - $65.00. **Ballgown:** Mint, all correct - $985.00 up. Dirty, part of clothing missing, etc. - $95.00. **Basic sleeveless dress:** Mint - $250.00. Dirty - $40.00. **Nude:** Clean, good face color - $200.00. Dirty, not original, faded face color - $35.00.

1956–1965: Bend knee walker. **Party Dress:** Mint, all correct - $325.00 up. Dirty, part of clothes missing, etc. - $50.00. **Ballgown:** Mint, correct - $1,000.00 up. Soiled, dirty, parts missing, etc. - $150.00. **Nude:** Clean, good face color - $200.00. Dirty, faded face color - $40.00. **Basic sleeveless dress:** Mint - $225.00. Dirty, faded face color - $40.00. **Internationals:** $125.00–300.00. Dirty, parts missing - $50.00.

1965–1972: Bend knee non-walker. **Party Dress:** Mint, original - $225.00 up. Dirty, missing parts - $40.00. **Internationals:** Clean, mint - $95.00. Dirty or soiled - $25.00. **Nude:** Clean, good face color - $100.00. Dirty, faded face color - $25.00.

1973–1976: "Rosies." Straight leg non-walker. Rosy cheeks. Marked "Alex." $60.00. **Bride or Ballerina:** Bend knee walker - $225.00 up. Bend knee only - $200.00. Straight leg -

$50.00. **Internationals:** $50.00. **Storybook:** $60.00.

1977–1981: Straight leg non-walker. Marked "Alexander." **Ballerina or Bride:** $40.00–50.00. **International:** $50.00–60.00. **Storybook:** $45.00–55.00.

1982–1987: Straight leg non-walker. Deep indentation over upper lip that casts a shadow, makes doll look like it has mustache. **Bride or ballerina:** $45.00–55.00. **International:** $45.00–55.00. **Storybook:** $45.00–55.00.

1988–1989: Straight leg, non-walker with new face. Looks more like older dolls but still marked with full name "Alexander." **Bride or ballerina:** $45.00–55.00. **International:** $45.00–55.00. **Storybook:** $50.00–60.00.

Left: Rare 8" "Rose Ballerina" from 1955. Bend knee walker. Right: 8" "Alexander-kin" bend knee walker that is mint in box. Dressed in an outfit called "Calls on School Friend" from 1956. Ballerina - $450.00 up; Alexander-kin, MIB - $400.00 up. *Courtesy Frasher Doll Auctions.*

MADAME ALEXANDER – BABIES

Prices are for mint condition dolls.

Baby Brother or Sister: 1977–1982. 14" - $65.00; 20" - $80.00.

Baby Ellen: 1965–1972. 14" - $85.00.

Baby Lynn: (Black "Sweet Tears") 1973–1975. 20" - $90.00.

Baby McGuffey: Composition. 22" - $185.00. Soiled - $45.00.

Bonnie: 1954–1955. Vinyl. 19" - $65.00. Soiled - $20.00.

Genius, Little: Composition. 18" - $125.00. Soiled - $40.00.

Genius, Little: Vinyl. May have flirty eyes. 21" - $85.00. Soiled - $30.00.

Genius, Little: 8" - $245.00 up. Soiled - $30.00.

Happy: 1970 only. Vinyl. 20" - $260.00. Soiled - $80.00.

Honeybun: 1951. Vinyl. 19" - $120.00. Soiled - $30.00.

Huggums, Big: 1963–1979. 25" - $85.00. **Lively:** 1963. 25" - $125.00.

Kathy: Vinyl. 19" - $95.00; 26" - $125.00. Soiled: 19" - $30.00; 26" - $45.00.

Kitten, Littlest: Vinyl. 8" - $250.00 up. Soiled - $50.00.

Mary Cassatt: 1969–1970. 14" - $135.00; 20" - $200.00.

Mary Mine: 14" - $60.00. Soiled - $25.00.

Pinky: Composition. 23" - $185.00. Soiled - $75.00.

Precious: Composition. 12" - $135.00. Soiled - $45.00.

Princess Alexandria: Composition. 24" - $200.00. Soiled - $75.00.

Pussy Cat: Vinyl. 14" - $75.00. Soiled - 20.00. **Black:** 14" - $95.00. Soiled - $25.00.

Rusty: Vinyl. 20" - $300.00. Soiled - $85.00.

Slumbermate: Composition. 21" - $500.00. Soiled - $185.00.

Sweet Tears: 9" - $45.00. Soiled - $15.00. **With layette:** $135.00.

Victoria: 20" - $50.00. Soiled - $20.00.

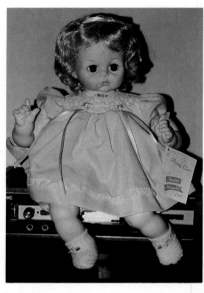

Large **"Pussy Cat"** that is vinyl and cloth with sleep eyes, rooted hair. Original. **20–21" - $45.00.** *Courtesy Gloria Anderson.*

MADAME ALEXANDER – CISSETTE

This 10–11" doll with high heel feet was made from 1957 to 1963, but the mold was used for other dolls later. She is made of hard plastic, and clothes will be tagged "Cissette."

First prices are for mint condition dolls; second prices are for soiled, dirty or faded clothes, tags missing and hair messy.

Street Dresses: $225.00, $75.00
Ballgowns: $450.00, $150.00.
Ballerina: $325.00, $100.00.
Gibson Girl: $800.00, $250.00.
Jacqueline: $425.00 up, $125.00.
Margot: $400.00 up, $150.00.
Portrette: $450.00, $160.00.
Wigged in case: $1,200.00 up, $500.00.

Pretty 10½" "Cissette" ballerina #735 from 1963. Also came dressed in pink tutu. $325.00 up.

"Cissy" was made 1955–1959 and had hard plastic with vinyl over the arms, jointed at elbows, and high heel feet. Clothes are tagged "Cissy." Prices are for excellent face color and clean dolls.

Street Dress: $265.00.
Ballgown: $650.00 up.
Bride: $475.00 up.
Queen: $825.00.
Portrait: "Godey," etc. 21" - $1,200.00 up.
Scarlett: $1,300.00.
Flora McFlimsey: Vinyl head, inset eyes. 15" - $600.00.

20" original "Cissy" shown with extra boxed outfits and hat that could be purchased for the doll. Doll - $450.00 up; boxed outfits - $80.00 up. *Courtesy Turn of Century Antiques.*

The Alexander Company made cloth/plush dolls and animals and oil cloth baby animals in the 1930s, 1940s and early 1950s. In the 1960s, only a few were made.

First prices are for mint condition dolls; second prices are for ones in poor condition, dirty, not original, played with or untagged.

Animals: $300.00 up, $85.00.

Dogs: $265.00, $95.00.

Alice in Wonderland: $800.00, $250.00.

Clarabelle The Clown: 19" - $350.00, $100.00.

David Copperfield or other boys: $600.00 up.

Funny: $55.00, $15.00.

Little Shaver: 7" - $350.00 up; 10" - $400.00.

Little Women: Each - $575.00 up, $150.00.

Muffin: 14" - $55.00, $25.00.

So Lite Baby or Toddler: 20" - $300.0 up, $100.00.

Susie Q: $675.00, $250.00.

Tiny Tim: $675.00, $250.00.

Teeny Twinkle: Has disc floating eyes. $500.00 up, $150.00.

18" "Tippie Toe" inspired by Eugene Fields's poem. Has glass flirty sleep eyes. Mask face painted in oils. Floss style hair. Cloth body and tagged pinafore dress. 1932–1933. $550.00 up. *Courtesy Jane Carlisle.*

16½" all cloth "Meg" of Little Women set with oil-painted features, mohair wig, and original clothes. Shown with rare Cissette "Gibson Girl" that is all original. "Meg" - $600.00; "Gibson Girl" - $900.00 up. *Courtesy Turn of Century Antiques.*

First prices are for mint condition dolls; second prices are for dolls that are crazed, cracked, dirty, soiled clothes or not original.

Alice in Wonderland: 9" - $325.00, $85.00; 14" - $450.00, $100.00; 21" - $950.00, $200.00.

Babs Skater: 1948. 18" - $550.00, $125.00.

Baby Jane: 16" - $875.00, $300.00.

Brides or Bridesmaids: 7" - $225.00, $60.00; 9" - $250.00, $75.00; 15" - $325.00, $80.00; 21" - $525.00, $150.00.

Dionne Quints: 8" - $160.00, $50.00. Set of five - $1,200.00. 11" - $300.00, $100.00. Set of five - $2,000.00. **Cloth Baby:** 14" - $800.00, $175.00; 16" - $800.00, $200.00.

Dr. DeFoe: 14–15" - $1,200.00 up, $500.00.

Fairy Princess: 1939. 15" - $650.00; 21" - $950.00 up.

Flora McFlimsey: Has freckles. Marked "Princess Elizabeth." 15" - $550.00, $150.00; 22" - $700.00, $200.00.

Flower Girl: 1939–1947. Marked "Princess Elizabeth." 16" - $500.00, $125.00; 20" - $650.00, $175.00; 24" - $800.00, $300.00.

Internationals/Storybook: 7" - $200.00, $50.00; 9" - $265.00, $75.00.

Jane Withers: 13" - $1,000.00 up, $400.00; 18" - $1,300.00, $500.00.

Kate Greenaway: Very yellow blonde wig. Marked "Princess Elizabeth." 14" - $500.00, $125.00; 18" - $800.00, $250.00.

Two sets of Dionne Quints. 8¼" toddlers seated in original chair. Wigged and original. Standing are toddlers with molded hair, one lacking shoes and another her bonnet. Quints in chair, set - $1,200.00; Standing quints, set - $1,100.00. *Courtesy Turn of Century Antiques.*

Little Colonel: 9" - $450.00, $150.00; 13" - $600.00, $185.00; 23" - $825.00, $300.00.

Madelaine DuBain: 1937–1944. 14" - $550.00, $150.00; 17" - $675.00, $250.00.

Margaret O'Brien: 15" - $750.00, $300.00; 18" - $900.00, $285.00; 21" - $1,000.00, $450.00.

Marionettes by Tony Sarg: 12" - $285.00, $95.00. **Disney:** $350.00, $165.00. **Others:** 12" - $245.00, $95.00.

McGuffey Ana: Marked "Princess Elizabeth." 13" - $600.00, $185.00; 20" - $800.00, $350.00.

Military Dolls: 1943–1944. 14" - $750.00, $300.00.

Nurse: 1936–1940. 14–15" - $475.00 up.

Portrait Dolls: 1939–1941, 1946. 21" - $2,300.00 up, $950.00.

Princess Elizabeth: Closed mouth. 13" - $500.00, $175.00; 18" - $700.00, $250.00; 24" - $850.00, $350.00.

21" original "Margaret O'Brien" made of all composition. Mint condition. **$1,000.00.** *Courtesy Kris Lundquist.*

15" all composition dolls with sleep eyes and open mouths. Both have original clothes and human hair wigs. Both in played with condition. Marked "Princess Elizabeth." Played with condition, each - $265.00; mint condition, each - $600.00. *Courtesy Turn of Century Antiques.*

Scarlett: 9" - $450.00, $165.00; 14" - $650.00, $175.00; 18" - $1,100.00, $500.00; 21" - $1,500.00, $650.00.

Snow White: 1939–1942. Marked "Princess Elizabeth." 13" - $400.00, $135.00; 18" - $625.00, $200.00.

Sonja Henie: 17" - $950.00, $350.00; 20" - $1,100.00, $450.00. **Jointed waist:** 14" - $700.00, $250.00.

Wendy Ann: 11" - $450.00, $150.00; 15" - $500.00, $150.00; 18" - $600.00, $200.00.

MADAME ALEXANDER – HARD PLASTIC

First prices are for mint condition dolls; second prices are for dolls that are dirty, played with, soiled clothes or not original.

Alice in Wonderland: 14" - $550.00, $200.00; 17" - $625.00, $250.00; 23" - $750.00, $300.00.

Annabelle: 15" - $475.00, $175.00; 18" - $600.00, $200.00; 23" - $700.00, $275.00.

Babs: 20" - $650.00, $200.00.

Babs Skater: 18" - $550.00, $150.00; 21" - $575.00, $200.00.

Ballerina: 14" - $450.00, $175.00.

Brenda Starr: 1964 only. **Dress:** 12" - $225.00. **Gown:** $300.00 up. **Bride**: $250.00.

Binnie Walker: 15" - $165.00, $60.00; 25" - $400.00, $150.00.

Cinderella, in ballgown: 14" - $750.00, $250.00. **"Poor" outfit:** 14" - $625.00, $175.00.

12" "Cinderella" using the "Lissy" doll. All hard plastic with jointed elbows and knees. Medium high heel feet. All original. $1,200.00. *Courtesy Kris Lundquist.*

Cynthia: Black doll. 15" - $1,000.00, $400.00; 18" - $1,200.00, $500.00; 23" - $1,500.00, $600.00.

Elise in street dress: 16½" - $250.00, $80.00. **Ballgown:** $400.00 up, $150.00.

Bride: 16" - $325.00, $165.00.

Fairy Queen: 14½" - $725.00,

Godey Lady: 14" - $1,100.00, $400.00.

Man/Groom: 14" - $1,050.00, $400.00.

Kathy: 15" - $750.00, $250.00.

Kelly: 12" - $450.00, $150.00.

Lissy: Street dress: 12" - $300.00, $150.00. **Bride:** $350.00, $150.00. **Ballerina:** $350.00, $165.00.

Little Women: 8" - $135.00, $60.00. Set of five with bend knees - $700.00; Set of five with straight legs - $350.00. **Using Lissy doll:** 12" -

$300.00, $100.00. Set of five - $1,500.00. 14" - $425.00. Set of five - $1,500.00.

Laurie: Bend knee. 8" - $145.00 up, $60.00; 12" - $350.00, $150.00.

Madeline: 1950-1953. Jointed knees and elbows. 18" - $950.00 up, $300.00.

Maggie: 15" - $525.00, $200.00; 17" - $685.00, $250.00; 23" - $800.00, $350.00.

Maggie Mixup: 8" - $450.00 up, $150.00; 16½" - $400.00, $165.00. **Angel:** 8" - $975.00, $250.00.

Margaret O'Brien: 14½" - $900.00, $400.00; 18" - $1,100.00, $500.00; 21" - $1,350.00, $600.00.

Marybel: 16" - $365.00, $125.00.

Mary Martin: Sailor suit or ballgown. 14" - $850.00 up, $450.00; 17" - $1,000.00, $450.00.

McGuffey Ana: 1948-1950. Hard plastic/vinyl. 21" - $900.00, $450.00.

Peter Pan: 15" - $950.00 up, $425.00.

Polly Pigtails: 14" - $700.00, $300.00; 17" - $900.00, $400.00.

Prince Charming: 14" - $800.00, $375.00; 18" - $950.00, $400.00.

Queen: 18" - $1,200.00, $600.00.

Shari Lewis: 14" - $400.00, $165.00; 21" - $600.00, $250.00.

Sleeping Beauty: 16½" - $550.00, $150.00; 21" - $950.00, $425.00.

Wendy (Peter Pan Set): 14" - $800.00, $400.00.

Wendy Ann: 14½" - $725.00, $250.00; 17" - $875.00, $400.00; 22" - $925.00, $425.00.

Winnie Walker: 15" - $165.00, $60.00; 18" - $250.00, $80.00; 23" - $350.00, $95.00.

18" "Mary Martin" using the "Margaret" doll. Made of all hard plastic. Lamb's wool wig. Shown in one of the original outfits made for her. Has "Mary Martin" written on front of sailor shirt. $1,100.00.
Courtesy Sandra McDowell.

First prices are for mint condition dolls; second prices are for dolls that are played with, soiled, dirty and missing original clothes.

Bellows' Anne: 1987 only. 14" - $80.00.

Bonnie Blue: 1989 only. 14" - $100.00.

Bride: 1982–1987. 17" - $145.00.

Caroline: 15" - $300.00, $100.00.

Cinderella: Pink: 1970–1981. **Blue:** 1983–1986. 14" - $70.00.

Edith The Lonely Doll: 1958–1959. 16" - $375.00; 22" - $450.00.

Elise: Street dress: Made in 1966. 17" - $225.00. **Formal:** 1966, 1976–1977. $250.00. **Bride:** 1966–1986. $145.00.

First Ladies: First set of six - $850.00. Second set of six - $625.00. Third set of six - $575.00. Fourth set of six - $550.00. Fifth set of six - $475.00. Sixth set of six - $600.00.

Grandma Jane/Granny, Little: 1970–1972. 14" - $285.00, $95.00.

Ingres: 1987 only. 14" - $70.00.

Isolde: 1985 only. 14" - $90.00.

Jacqueline: Street Dress: 21" - $550.00, $250.00. **Ballgown:** $650.00 up, $350.00. **Riding Habit:** $600.00, $250.00.

Janie: 12" - $300.00, $125.00.

Joanie: 36" - $375.00, $180.00.

Leslie: Black doll. **Ballgown:** 17" - $485.00, $225.00. **Ballerina:** $375.00, $100.00. **Street dress:** $400.00, $185.00.

Little Shaver: 1963 only, vinyl. 12" - $225.00, $90.00.

Nancy Drew: 1967 only. 12" - $400.00, $135.00.

Napoleon: 1980–1986. 12" - $70.00.

Marybel: 16" - $250.00, $90.00. **In case:** $350.00 up; $175.00.

Mary Ellen: 31" - $650.00 up, $275.00.

14" "Jenny Lind" made in 1970 only. Uses the "Marybel" doll. Mint and original. A very difficult doll to find in this condition. $425.00.

Melinda: 14" - $275.00, $125.00; 16" - $325.00, $150.00.

Michael with bear: Peter Pan set. 11" - $475.00, $185.00.

Peter Pan: 14" - $400.00, $125.00.

Polly: 17" - $375.00, $145.00.

Renoir Girl: 14" - $100.00 – 50.00. With watering can: 1986 – 1987. $85.00 – 35.00. With hoop: 1986 – 1987. $85.00 – 35.00.

Scarlett: White gown, green ribbon. 1969 – 1986. 14" - $145.00, 70.00.

Smarty: 12" - $365.00, $145.00.

Sound of Music: Small set: $1,400.00. Large set: $1,700.00. **Liesl:** 10" - $200.00, $95.00; 14" - $225.00, $95.00. **Louisa:** 10" - $265.00, $125.00; 14" - $300.00, $145.00. **Brigitta:** 10" - $225.00, $95.00; 14" - $225.00, $95.00. **Maria:** 12" - $350.00, $150.00; 17" - $375.00, $160.00; **Marta:** 8" - $225.00, $75.00; 11" - $200.00, $145.00. **Gretl:** 8" - $225.00, $95.00; 11" - $200.00, $145.00. **Friedrich:** 8" - $225.00, $95.00; 11" - $200.00, $100.00.

Wendy: Peter Pan set. 14" - $325.00, $145.00.

Prices are for mint condition dolls. There are many 21" Portrait dolls and all use the Jacqueline face. The early ones have jointed elbows; later dolls have one-piece arms. All will be marked "1961" on head.

Agatha: 1967–1980. $550.00.

Bride: 1965. $900.00 up.

Coco: 1966. **Portrait:** 21" - $2,300.00. **Street Dress:** $2,400.00. **Ballgown:** Other than portrait series. $2,300.00.

Cornelia: 1972–1978. $325.00 – 600.00.

Gainsborough: 1968 –1978. $425.00 –650.00.

Godey: 1965, 1967–1977. $675.00, $350.00–600.00.

Jenny Lind: 1969. $1,700.00.

Lady Hamilton: 1968: $575.00.

Madame Pompadour: 1970. $1,300.00.

Magnolia: 1977: $475.00. **1988:** $300.00.

Manet: 1982–1983. $300.00.

Melanie: 1967–1989. $350.00– 600.00.

Mimi: 1971. $650.00.

Monet: 1984. $325.00.

21" Portraits "Melanie," "Agatha," and "Scarlett." All are original. "Melanie" - **$375.00;** "Agatha" - **$295.00;** "Scarlett" - **$400.00.** *Courtesy Turn of Century Antiques.*

Morisot: 1985–1986. $375.00.
Queen: 1965. $900.00 up.
Renoir: 1965–1973. $650.00 – 850.00.

Scarlett: 1965–1989. $325.00 – 1,200.00 up.
Toulouse-Lautrec: 1986–1987. $265.00.

ALLIED DOLL CO.

21" "Bonnie Miss" with high heel feet, stuffed vinyl body and legs. Made by Allied Doll Co. All original with tag. Marked "14 R" on head and "A" on back. Dolls like this one, marked "14 R" and with silver grey and brunette hair, were purchased by Ideal for "Mother of the Bride." Mint condition - $95.00 up; played with condition - $45.00.

21" "Mother of The Bride" was made by Allied Doll Co. for Ideal's "Miss Revlon Bride." Doll was not very successful on the market and very few were sold. Allied also marketed the doll as "Aunty Kate" in 1959 only. Doll is marked "14 R" on head. Has silver grey and brunette hair and heavier eye make-up. Mint - $200.00; played with - $85.00.

All American Character dolls are very collectible and all are above average in quality of doll material and clothes. Dolls marked "American Doll and Toy Co." are also made by American Character, and this name was used from 1959 until 1968 when the firm went out of business. Early dolls will be marked "Petite." Many will be marked "A.C."

First prices are for mint dolls; second prices are for dolls that have been played with, dirty, with soiled clothes or not original.

"A.C." marked child: Composition. 14" - $160.00, $50.00; 20" - $250.00, $95.00.

Annie Oakley: 1955, original, hard plastic. 17" - $425.00, $160.00.

Betsy McCall: See Betsy McCall section.

Butterball: 1961. 19" - $135.00, $65.00.

19" "Butterball" with large round sleep eyes and short fingers. Plastic and vinyl. Marked "American Character 1961." $135.00. *Courtesy Jeannie Mauldin.*

Carol Ann Berry: Daughter of Wallace Berry. All composition, sleep eyes, closed mouth. Mohair wig with braid over top of head. Marked "Petite Sally" or "Petite." 13" - $500.00; 16½" - $725.00; 19½" - $975.00.

Cartwrights: Ben, Hoss, Little Joe: 1966. 8" - $100.00, $45.00.

Chuckles: 1961. 23" - $175.00, $75.00. **Baby:** 18" - $135.00, $40.00.

Composition Babies: 1930's – 1940s. Cloth bodies, marked "A.C." 14" - $85.00, $30.00. 22" - $165.00, $70.00. **Marked "Petite":** 1920s–1930s. 14" - $175.00, $80.00; 22" - $250.00, $100.00.

Cricket: 1964. 9" - $40.00, $15.00. **Growing hair:** $40.00, $20.00.

Eloise: 1950s. Cloth character with yarn hair and crooked smile. (See photo in Series 7, pg. 212.) 14–15" - $285.00; 21" - $400.00.

Freckles: 1966. Face changes. 13" - $40.00, $15.00.

Hedda-Get-Betta: 1960. 21" - $95.00, $45.00.

Miss Echo, Little: Talker, 1964. (See photo in Series 8, pg. 190.) 30" - $225.00, $100.00.

"Petite" marked child: Composition. 16" - $200.00, $85.00; 20" - $265.00, $100.00; 24-25" - $345.00, $165.00.

Preteen: 14" child. Marked "AM. Char. 63." (1963) **Grow hair:** $30.00, $15.00.

Puggy: All composition, painted eyes, frown. Marked "Petite." 12–13" - $500.00, $165.00.

Ricky, Jr.: 1955–1956. 13" - $70.00, $35.00; 20" - $135.00, $50.00.

Sally: 1929–1935. Composition, molded hair in "Patsy" style. 12" - $185.00, $60.00; 14" - $225.00, $80.00. 16" - $300.00, $85.00; 18" - $325.00, $145.00.

Sally Says: 1965. Talker, plastic/vinyl. 19" - $80.00, $40.00.

Sweet Sue/Toni: 1949–1960. Hard plastic, some walkers, some with extra joints at knees, elbows and/or ankles, some combination hard plastic and vinyl. Marked "A.C. Amer. Char. Doll," or "American Character" in circle. *Must have excellent face color and be original.* **Ballgown:** 1958. 10½" - $175.00, $75.00; 15" - $285.00, $85.00; 18" - $365.00, $125.00. **Street dress:** 1958. 10½" - $150.00, $60.00; 15" - $225.00, $70.00; 18" - $325.00, $125.00; 22" - $385.00, $145.00; 24" - $450.00, $165.00; 30" - $565.00, $200.00. **Vinyl:** 10½" - $160.00, $50.00; 17" - $275.00, $60.00; 21" - $375.00, $100.00; 25" - $465.00, $175.00; 30" - $550.00 up, $200.00. **Groom:** 20" - $450.00, $150.00. **Mint in box:** 14" - $450.00 up; 17–18" - $600.00 up.

18" "Sweet Sue Walker" is all hard plastic and original. $365.00 up. *Courtesy Kris Lundquist.*

14" "Sweet Sue" is all hard plastic and original. $285.00. *Courtesy Sharon McDowell.*

20" "Sweet Sue Sophisticate." All vinyl with sleep eyes and high heel feet. All original. $375.00. *Courtesy Charmaine Shields.*

Talking Marie: 1963. Record player in body, battery operated. Vinyl/plastic. 18" - $95.00, $40.00.

Tiny Tears: 1955–1962. **Hard plastic/vinyl:** 8" - $50.00, $20.00; 13" - $125.00, $45.00; 17" - $185.00, $90.00. **All vinyl:** 1963. 8" - $45.00, $15.00; 12" - $50.00, $25.00; 16" - $60.00, $30.00. **Mint in box:** 13" - $300.00 up.

Toodles: 1956–1960. **Baby:** 14" - $135.00, $50.00. **Tiny:** 10½" - $165.00, $50.00. **Toddler:** With "follow me eyes." 22" - $225.00, $80.00; 28" - $300.00, $130.00; 30" - $325.00, $165.00.

Toodle-Loo: 1961. 18" - $185.00, $80.00.

Tressy: 12½". **Grow Hair:** 1963–1964. (#1 heavy makeup). $55.00, $20.00. **#2 Mary/Magic Makeup:** 1965–1966. Pale face, no lashes, bend knees. $35.00, $15.00.

Whimette/Little People: 1963. 7½" - $25.00, $10.00.

Whimsey: 1960. 19" - $95.00, $40.00.

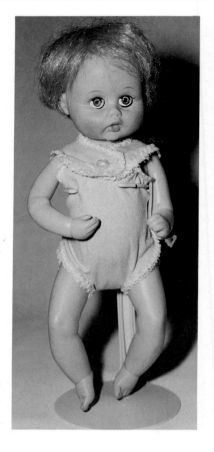

8½" all vinyl "Teeny Tiny Tears." Made by American Character in 1964. Sleep eyes, open mouth, rooted hair. Marked on head. $45.00. *Courtesy Kathy Tvrdik.*

30" "Peek-A-Boo Toodles" is made of plastic/vinyl with toddler body. Sleep eyes that seem to follow you around the room. Open/closed mouth with modeled teeth. Original romper suit and "glasses." In original box - $325.00 up. Mint, as this one - $485.00. *Courtesy Jeannie Mauldin.*

10½" "Toni" by American Character. Shown in the "American Beauty" gown from 1959. All vinyl, sleep eyes, and rooted hair. Mint and unplayed with. $175.00 up. *Courtesy Peggy Pergande.*

ANNALEE MOBILITEE DOLLS

The first Annalee tags were red woven lettering on white linen tape. Second tags were made of white rayon with red embroidered lettering. The third tags, around 1969, were red printing on white satin tape. The fourth tags, about 1976, had red printing on gauze-type cloth. The hair on dolls from 1934–1963 was made of yarn. From 1960–1963, it was made of orange or yellow chicken feathers. Since 1963, the hair has been made of synthetic fur.

Animals became part of the line in 1964. On the oldest models, tails were made of the same materials as the body. During the mid-1970s, cotton bias tape was used and the ones made during the 1980s are made of cotton flannel.

Child: 1950s: 10" - $2,000.00 up. **1960s:** 10" - $1,200.00 up. **1970s:** 10" - $300.00 up. **1980s:** $150.00.

Adults: 1950s: 10" - $3,000.00 up. **1970s:** 7" - $1,800.00.

Babies: Usually angels. **1960s:** 7–8" - $325.00. **1970s:** 7" - $275.00. **1980s:** 7" - $200.00.

Skiers: 1960s: 7" - $350.00 up. **1970s:** 7" - $200.00. **1980s:** 7" - $75.00 up.

Elf/Gnome: 1970s: 7" - $200.00; 12" - $300.00. **1980s:** 7" - $50.00; 12" - $85.00; 16" - $125.00; 22" - $165.00.

Monks: 1970s: 8" - $75.00 up.

Indians: 1970s: 7" - $200.00. **1980s:** 8" - $150.00 up; 18" - $250.00 up.

Santa/Mrs. Claus: 1970s: 7" to 26" - $75.00-200.00. **1980s:** 7 to 26" - $45.00-175.00.

Bears: 1970s: 7" - $150.00 up; 10" - $185.00 up; 18" - $265.00 up. **1980s:** 7" - $80.00 up; 10" - $150.00 up; 18" - $175.00 up.

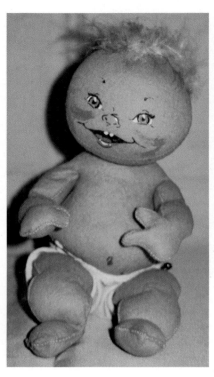

18" Bear with bee on his nose, holding honey pot. All felt and original. Only 938 made in 1986. $200.00 up. *Courtesy Bette Todd.*

10" "Baby Angel" from 1956. Wears diaper. Number made unknown, but is very rare. $600.00 up. *Courtesy Bette Todd.*

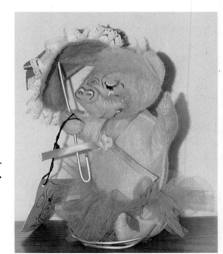

8" "Ballerina Pig" of 1981–1982. Flesh-colored body, blue tutu, and parasol. $145.00 up. *Courtesy Bette Todd.*

Large 18" "Santa Fox" of 1981. Brownish red felt and red Santa jacket and hat. **$295.00 up.** *Courtesy Bette Todd.*

12" all felt monkey with banana and trapeze from 1981. Only 1,031 were made. $225.00 up. *Courtesy Bette Todd.*

ARRANBEE DOLL COMPANY

The Arranbee Doll Company began making dolls in 1922 and was purchased by the Vogue Doll Company in 1959. Vogue used the Arranbee marked molds until 1961. Arranbee used the initials "R & B."

First prices are for mint condition dolls; second prices are for dolls that have been played with, are cracked, crazed, dirty or do not have original clothes.

Angeline: 1951–1952. Hard plastic, mohair wig. 14" - $225.00; 18" - $285.00.

Babies: Bisque heads. See Armand Marseille section.

Babies: Original. 1930s–1940s. Composition/cloth bodies. 16" - $125.00, $50.00; 22" - $150.00, $60.00.

Bottletot: 1932–1935. Has celluloid bottle molded to celluloid hand. 18" - $225.00, $90.00.

Debu-Teen: 1940. Composition girl with cloth body. 14" - $185.00, $65.00; 18" - $265.00, $95.00; 21" - $325.00, $125.00.

Dream Baby, My: (See Armand Marseille section for bisque heads.) **Composition:** 1934–1944. 14" - $265.00 up, $100.00; 16" - $375.00 up; 19" - $500.00 up. **Vinyl/cloth:** 1950. 16" - $75.00, $35.00; 23" - $150.00, $60.00.

Francine: Hard plastic, waist length saran wig, 1955. 14" - $250.00; 18" - $300.00.

Kewty: 1934–1936. Original. Composition "Patsy" style molded hair. 10" - $145.00, $45.00; 16" - $225.00, $85.00.

Littlest Angel: 1956. All hard plastic. 10" - $45.00, $10.00. **Vinyl head:** 10" - $30.00, $10.00. **Red hair/freckles:** 1960. 10" - $65.00, $30.00.

Miss Coty: 1958. Vinyl, marked "Ⓟ." ("Ⓟ" dolls also dressed and marketed by Belle Doll Co.) 10" - $100.00, $30.00.

My Angel: 1961. Plastic/vinyl. 17" - $45.00, $20.00; 22" - $75.00, $40.00; 36"-$185.00, $90.00. **Walker:** 1957–1959. 30" - $200.00. **Oil cloth body/vinyl:** 1959. 22" - $65.00.

Nancy: 1936–1940. Composition, molded hair or wig. 12" - $185.00, $65.00; 17" - $350.00, $140.00; 19" - $450.00, $165.00. **Hard plastic with vinyl arms/head:** 1951–1952 only. **Wig:** 14" - $135.00, $70.00; 18" - $185.00, $90.00. **Walker:** 24" - $250.00, $100.00.

Nancy Lee: 1939. **Composition:** 14" - $245.00, $100.00; 17" - $350.00, $150.00; 20" - $450.00, $165.00. **Hard plastic:** 1950–1959. 14" - $265.00, $100.00; 20" - $465.00, $150.00.

16" "Crying Baby" with open/closed mouth, molded tongue, and sleep eyes. Stuffed vinyl one-piece body and limbs. $80.00. *Courtesy Kathy Tvrdik.*

18" "Deb-U-Teen" dolls that have cloth bodies and composition limbs. Sleep eyes, human hair wigs. Both are original and in mint condition. Mint - $265.00 up; played with - $95.00 up. *Courtesy Turn of Century Antiques.*

Nancy Lee: 1954. Unusual eyebrows/vinyl. 15" - $175.00, $90.00.

Nancy Lee: 1952. Baby, painted eyes, "crying" look. 15" - $145.00, $70.00.

Nancy Lee: 1934–1939. Baby with composition head and limbs, open mouth with upper and lower teeth. 25" - $250.00, $95.00.

Nanette: 1949–1959. Hard plastic. 14" - $200.00, $85.00; 17" - $300.00, $100.00; 21" - $350.00 up, $150.00; 23" - $450.00, $165.00. **Walker:** 1957–1959. Jointed knees. 18" - $325.00, $125.00; 25" - $500.00, $200.00. **Plastic/vinyl walker:** 1955–1956. 30" - $195.00, $95.00. **Hard plastic:** Mint in box. 17" - $500.00 up.

14" all hard plastic "Nanette Skater" with cap and skates added. Mohair wig and sleep eyes. **$250.00 up.** *Courtesy Sharon McDowell.*

Sonja Skater: 1945. Composition. 14" - $265.00, $95.00; 17" - $300.00, $100.00; 21" - $400.00, $150.00.

Storybook Dolls: 1930–1936. All composition. Molded hair, painted eyes. 9–10" - $165.00, $45.00. **Mint in box:** $265.00.

Taffy: 1956. Looks like Alexander's "Cissy." 23" - $75.00, $40.00.

Beautiful 18" all composition "Nancy Lee." Mohair wig and sleep eyes. Dress may be original. Marked "R.B." on head. **$365.00 up.** *Courtesy Kris Lundquist.*

25" doll from 1957. Sold as "Marlene," "Stunning," or "Sweet Judy." Good quality vinyl and rigid vinyl. Jointed waist, sleep eyes, and poodle cut hairdo. Original clothes, high heel feet.

Mark:

(See doll in different dress in Series 6, pg. 218.) $80.00. *Courtesy Kathy Tvrdik.*

20" "Raving Beauty" made by the Artisan Novelty Co. in 1953. All hard plastic and unmarked. Original cowgirl outfit, even has guns in the holsters. Large brown sleep eyes and open smile mouth. (See variation of cowgirl outfit in Series 9, pg. 202.) 20" - $275.00 up; 19–20" walker - $365.00 up. *Courtesy Chris McWilliams.*

First prices are for mint dolls; second prices are for dolls in average condition, dirty, soiled, or not original.

Alfred E. Newman: Vinyl head. 20" - $225.00, $150.00.

Captain Kangaroo: 19" - $145.00, $80.00; 24" - $225.00, $95.00.

Christopher Robin: 18" - $165.00, $75.00.

Daisy Mae: 14" - $200.00, $55.00; 21" - $285.00, $100.00.

Emmet Kelly (Willie the Clown): 15" - $165.00, $45.00; 24" - $250.00, $85.00.

Lil' Abner: 14" - $200.00, $55.00; 21" - $285.00, $100.00.

Mammy Yokum: 1957. **Molded hair:** 14" - $200.00, $100.00; 21" - $300.00, $125.00. **Yarn hair:** 14" - $250.00, $100.00; 21" - $350.00, $135.00. **Nose lights up:** 23" - $400.00, $150.00.

Pappy Yokum: 1957. 14" - $150.00; 21" - $300.00, $125.00. **Nose lights up:** 23" - $400.00, $150.00.

24" and 14½" "Emmett Kelly" dolls. Both are original and tagged. Larger one is cloth and vinyl. Smaller has magic skin body and limbs. 24" - $250.00; 14½" - $165.00. *Courtesy Patricia Woods.*

BANISTER

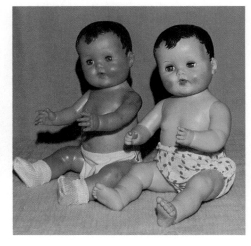

Constance Banister was a famous child photographer, and these 17" dolls were fashioned after one of her subjects. They were made by The Sun Rubber Co. They have sleep eyes and molded hair. On left is an early "lastic-plastic" doll. On right is a heavy vinyl doll made after 1955. Note difference in hands. Dolls marked "Constance Banister, New York, N.Y." Left - $75.00; right - $85.00. *Courtesy Phyllis Teague.*

See related dolls, such as "Midge," "Ken," etc. in Mattel section. Prices are for mint dolls with accessories.

1958–1959: #1, holes in feet for metal cylinders on stand. Iris of eyes are white. **In box:** $3,000.00. **Doll only:** Mint. $1,700.00 up. **Very good:** $1,200.00.

1960: #3, curved eyebrows, marked 1959 body. **In box:** $550.00 up. **Doll only:** $265.00.

1961: #4, marked "Pat. Pend. 1961." $275.00. **Bubble cut:** $195.00 up.

1963: Fashion Queen with three wigs. $475.00 up. **Gift sets:** $500.00 up.

1964: Ponytail with swirl bangs. No curly bangs. $200.00 up. **In box:** $350.00 up.

1965: Color 'n Curl with two heads and accessories. Dutch boy style hair, full bangs. (First bend knee Barbie.) $425.00 up.

1967: Twist 'n Turn: $95.00.

1968: Spanish Talking: $450.00 up.

1969: Twist 'n Turn: Wears pink swimsuit fashioned with a fan blade design. $85.00 up.

Back row: Four #3 Barbie dolls from 1960–1961 and Barbie with swirl bangs. Front row: Two #4 Barbie dolls from 1961. All are original. $200.00–300.00. *Courtesy Turn of Century Antiques.*

1970: Standard Barbie: Pink/green vertical striped swimsuit. $65.00.

1971: Growing Pretty Hair: $325.00 up. New Living: $65.00 up. Live Action: $70.00.

1972: Ward's Anniversary: $500.00. Busy Barbie: Has long hair. $100.00. Growing Pretty Hair: Long gown, blue top, and red print skirt. $225.00. Walk Lively: $90.00.

1973: Quick Curl: $95.00.

1974: Sweet Sixteen: $85.00. Newport: $45.00. Sun Valley: $80.00.

1975: Free Moving: $70.00. Funtime: $70.00. Gold Medal Skater: $60.00. Winter Sports: $40.00. Olympic Sports: $45.00. Hawaiian: $90.00.

1976: Ballerina: $60.00. Deluxe Quick Curl: $60.00. Free Moving: $70.00. Beautiful Bride: $90.00. Gold Medal Skier: $60.00.

Barbie Astronaut of 1986. $95.00 up.
Courtesy Kathy Tvrdik.

1977: Super Star: $75.00.

1978: Super Size Barbie: 18" - $125.00 up. Super Size Christie: 18" - $125.00. Fashion Photo: $50.00. In The Spotlight: $95.00.

1979: Pretty Changes: $70.00. Kissing: $50.00. Sunlovin' Malibu: $30.00 up.

1980: Beauty Secrets: $40.00; Black Barbie: $45.00. Roller Skater: $30.00.

1981: Western: $35.00.

1982: Pink & Pretty: $35.00. Magic Curl: $50.00. Fashion Jeans: $30.00. All Stars: $40.00.

1983: Twirly Curls: White - $35.00; Black or Hispanic - $75.00. Happy Birthday: $35.00.

1983: My First Barbie: $20.00. My First Barbie: Short dress. Second issue. $25.00.

1983: Horse Lovin': $40.00. Golden Dream: Department store. $60.00. Dream Date: $30.00. Angel Face: $30.00.

1984: Lovin' You: $20.00. Sun Gold Malibu: $20.00. Great Shape: $35.00. Crystal: $30.00.

1985: Peaches & Cream: $45.00. Dreamtime: $30.00. Day to Night: $40.00.

1986: Dream Glow: $30.00. Rockers: $45.00 up. Gift Giving: $25.00. Tropical: $20.00. Astronaut: Red/silver suit. $95.00. Magic Moves: $25.00. Super Hair: $25.00.

Holiday Specials: 1988: Red gown. $325.00 up. **1989:** White gown/marabou trim. $150.00 up.

Bob Mackie: 1990. Gold sequin gown in case. $175.00 up.

International, Specials:

1981: Royal, Parisian, Italian. $90.00–150.00.

1982: Scottish: $165.00. Oriental: $95.00.

1983: Hawaiian: $80.00. Eskimo: $95.00. India: $95.00.

1984: Spanish: $150.00. Swedish: $100.00. Japanese: $210.00.

1985: Swiss, Irish: $100.00. Billyboy™ Barbie: (See photo in Series 8, pg. 263.) $95.00–265.00. Nouveau Theatre de la Mode: $250.00.

1986: Japanese: $100.00. Greek: $48.00. Peruvian: $45.00. German: $35.00. Canadian: $35.00. Korean: $40.00. Hispanic: $65.00. Iceland: $85.00.

1987: Doctor Barbie: $35.00. Sears Star Dream: $45.00. Perfume Pretty: $35.00. Mardi Gras: $35.00.

1988: Show 'N Ride: $55.00. Skating Star: $75.00.

1989: Peach Pretty: $35.00. Sweet Roses: $35.00. Party Lace: $25.00. UNICEF: $18.00. Ice Capades: $28.00.

Porcelain: Blue Rhapsody: $695.00. Bride: $450.00. Gay Parisienne: $160.00. Benefit Performance: $350.00. Solo In Spotlight: $150.00. Plantation Belle: $200.00.

Barbie Gift Sets:

Olympic Gymnast: $85.00 up. Fur Collection: $400.00 up. Malibu Beach Party: $250.00 up. Ice Breaker: Boxed. $600.00 up. Career Girl: Boxed. $550.00 up. Mix 'n Match Set: 1962. $700.00 up. Sparkling Pink: 1963. $800.00 up. Round The Clock Wedding Party: 1964. $850.00 up. On Parade: Majorettes. $1,000.00 up.

Barbie Items: Travel Trailer: $45.00. Silver-vette: $55.00. Cycle: $30.00. Roadster: $200.00 up. Sports Car: $175.00 up. Speed Boat: $175.00 up. Dune Buggy: $90.00 up. Clock: $30.00 up. Family House: $165.00. Watches: $20.00–45.00. Small dial

Porcelain "Plantation Belle" Barbie made for Walt Disney World in 1964. Limited edition of 300. $400.00. *Courtesy Turn of Century Antiques.*

Mardi Gras Barbie of 1987. Made in Taiwan. $35.00. *Courtesy Kathy Tvridk.*

watch: $50.00. Airplane: $1,000.00 up. Horse "Dancer": Brown. $200.00. First Barbie stand: Round, two pronged. $200.00. Heirloom Service: $100.00. Record Tote: $25.00. Photo Album: $40.00. Diary: 1963. $30.00. Autograph book: 1962. $30.00.

Barbie Clothes:

1958: #900 series. Easter Parade: $900.00. Gay Parisienne: $900.00. Roman Holiday: $900.00. Solo In Spotlight: $900.00. Enchanted Evening: Pink gown. $300.00. Plantation Belle: $350.00. Picnic Set: $250.00. Commuter set: $200.00.

1963: Drum Majorette: $150.00. Cheerleader: $150.00. Little Theatre outfits: $85.00–200.00. Travel outfits: $40.00–80.00. Masquerade: $150.00. Sophisticated Lady: Pink gown, red cape with high collar. $300.00. Midnight Blue gown and cape: $350.00.

1964: Astronaut: $250.00 up. Holiday Dance: $85.00. Campus Sweetheart: $100.00. Junior Prom: $85.00. Skin Diver: $55.00.

1965: Golden Glory: $70.00. Benefit Performance: $250.00. Debutante Ball: $200.00. Riding In Park: $100.00. Reception Line: $100.00. Garden Wedding: $150.00.

1966: Patio Party: $100.00. Evening Enchantment: $300.00 up. Tropicana: $125.00. Floating Gardens: $185.00 up.

50th Anniversary Ice Capades Barbie from 1989. Made in China. $28.00. *Courtesy Kathy Tvrdik.*

Show 'N Ride Barbie of 1988. $55.00. *Courtesy Kathy Tvrdik.*

First prices are for mint condition dolls; second prices are for played with, dirty, soiled or not original dolls.

8": All hard plastic, jointed knees. Made by American Character Doll Company in 1958. **Street Dress:** $175.00, $70.00. **Ballgown:** $225.00 up, $90.00. **Bathing Suit or Romper:** $125.00, $40.00. **Ballerina:** $185.00; $65.00. **Riding Habit:** $200.00, $80.00.

11½": Vinyl/plastic with brown sleep eyes, and reddish rooted hair. Original. Made by Uneeda but unmarked. $145.00, $60.00.

13": Made by Horsman in 1975, but doll is marked "Horsman Dolls, Inc. 1967" on head. $65.00, $35.00.

14": Vinyl with rooted hair, medium high heels, and round sleep eyes. Made by American Character Doll Company in 1961. Marked "McCall 1958." $265.00, $95.00.

8" "Betsy McCall" in very hard to find formal. Mint and original. In this gown - $300.00. *Courtesy Leslie Robinson.*

8" "Betsy McCall" in "School Girl" outfit. $175.00 up. *Courtesy Peggy Pergande.*

14" American Character "Betsy McCall" in 1958 "Birthday Party" dress. $265.00 up. *Courtesy Peggy Pergande.*

14": Vinyl head, hard plastic body and limbs. Rooted hair. Marked "P-90" body. Made by Ideal Doll Company. $295.00, $90.00.

22": Extra joints at waist, ankles, wrists and above knees. Unmarked. Made by American Character Doll Company. $265.00, $90.00.

20": Vinyl with rooted hair and slender limbs. Made by American Character Doll Company. (Allow more for flirty eyes.) $300.00, $100.00.

22": Vinyl/plastic with extra joints. Made by Ideal Doll Company. $325.00, $125.00.

29-30": All vinyl with rooted hair. Made by American Character Doll Company. $400.00, $165.00.

29": Extra joints at ankles, knees, waist and wrists. Made by American Character Doll Company. Marked "McCall 1961." $450.00 up, $140.00.

20" flirty eye "Betsy McCall" from 1959 with rare ponytail hairstyle. All original in black velvet, organdy, and straw hat. **$375.00 up.** *Courtesy Leslie Robinson.*

29": Marked "B.M.C. Horsman 1971." $175.00, $60.00.

36": All vinyl with rooted hair. Made by American Character Doll Company. $650.00 up, $300.00.

36": Made by Ideal Doll Company. Marked "McCall 1959." $550.00 up, $225.00.

39": Boy called "Sandy McCall." Made by Ideal Doll Company. Marked "McCall 1959." $700.00 up, $350.00.

29" "Betsy McCall" with extra joints at ankles, knees, waist, and wrists. Dressed in black leotards and original jumper outfit. Made by American Character Doll Company. Marked "McCall 1961." $450.00.

"Buddy Lee" dolls were made in composition to 1949, then changed to hard plastic and discontinued in 1962–1963. "Buddy Lee" came dressed in two Coca-Cola® uniforms. The tan with green stripe outfit matched the uniforms worn by delivery drivers while the white with green stripe uniforms matched those of plant workers. (Among Coca-Cola employees the white uniform became more popular and in warmer regions of the country, the white outfit was also worn by outside workers.)

"Buddy Lee" came in many different outfits.

Engineer: $300.00 up.

Gas Station attendant: $250.00 up.

Cowboy: $350.00 up.

Coca-Cola uniform: White with green stripe - $450.00 up. Tan with green stripe - $500.00 up.

Other soft drink companies uniforms: $285.00 up.

Hard Plastic: Original clothes. $350.00 up.

Rare all hard plastic Coca-Cola uniformed "Buddy Lee." Shown with 18" "Saralee" by Ideal. Made of cloth and vinyl. In front is "Doc" from the Seven Dwarfs. Made by Ideal. Glasses are missing. "Buddy Lee" - $450.00 up; "Saralee" - $285.00; "Doc" - $750.00.
Courtesy Turn of Century Antiques.

Babyland General Hospital: Cleveland, Georgia. Original dolls. (See photos in Series 5, pg. 173; Series 6, pg. 222; Series 7, pg. 203.)

"A" Blue Edition: Made in 1978. $1,500.00 up.

"B" Red Edition: Made in 1978. $1,200.00 up.

"C" Burgundy Edition: Made in 1979. $900.00 up.

"D" Purple Edition: Made in 1979. $800.00 up.

"X" Christmas Edition: Made in 1979. $1,200.00 up.

"E" Bronze Edition: Made in 1979. $600.00 up.

Preemie Edition: Made in 1980. $650.00 up.

Celebrity Edition: Made in 1980. $500.00 up.

Christmas Edition: Made in 1980. $600.00 up.

Two original Babyland General Cabbage Patch dolls. Turquoise editions. Each - $175.00. *Courtesy Frasher Doll Auctions.*

Grand Edition: Made in 1980. $750.00 up.

New Ears Edition: Made in 1981. $125.00.

Ears Edition: Made in 1982. $150.00 up.

Green Edition: Made in 1983. $400.00 up.

"KP" Dark Green Edition: Made in 1983. $550.00 up.

"KPR" Red Edition: Made in 1983. $550.00.

"KPB" Burgundy Edition: Made in 1983. $200.00.

Oriental Edition: Made in 1983. $850.00.

Indian Edition: Made in 1983. $850.00.

Hispanic Edition: Made in 1983. $750.00.

"KPZ" Edition: Made in 1983–1984. $175.00.

Champagne Edition: Made in 1983–1984. $900.00.

Left: Rare small-eyed #2 Coleco "Cabbage Patch Kid" with freckles and single auburn ponytail. Right: 1985 freckled tennis player with gold colored braids. Sitting: 1983 #2 baby with small eyes, freckles, and bald head. Wearing rare blue/white sleeper outfit. 1983, auburn ponytail - $200.00; 1985 - $95.00; 1983, bald baby - $160.00. *Courtesy Betty Chapman.*

Standing: 1984 Coleco "Couture Kid" with fur coat and rose red corduroy snowsuit. Sitting: 1986 #5 black girl with single tooth. Wearing rare burgundy twin outfit. 1984 - $125.00; 1986 - $50.00. *Courtesy Betty Chapman.*

19" "Cabbage Patch Circus Kids" clown from 1986. Also came in orange pants and lined multi-striped jacket. Green polka dot bowtie and small red hat. Marked "China" on foot. $75.00. *Courtesy Kathy Tvrdik.*

"KPP" Purple Edition: Made in 1984. $250.00.

Sweetheart Edition: Made in 1984. $250.00.

Bavarian Edition: Made in 1984. $250.00.

World Class Edition: Made in 1984. $175.00 up.

"KPF," "KPG," "KPH," "KPI," "KPJ" Editions: Made in 1984–1985. $100.00–150.00 up.

Emerald Edition: Made in 1985. $100.00 up.

Coleco Cabbage Patch Dolls:

1983: Have powder scent and black signature stamp. **Boys or girls:** $95.00. **Bald babies:** $100.00 up. **With pacifiers:** $50.00–175.00. **With freckles:** $100.00 up. **Black boys or girls with freckles:** $175.00 up. Without freckles - $75.00 up. **Red hair boys:** Fuzzy hair. $175.00 up.

1984–1985: Green signature stamp in 1984; blue signature stamp in 1985. Only a few dolls of these years are worth more than retail prices. **Single tooth:** Brunette with ponytail. $165.00 up. **Popcorn hairdos:** Rare. $200.00. **Gray-eyed girls:** $165.00 up. **Freckled girl with gold hair:** $95.00 up.

Valued from retail to $65.00: From collectible years. Includes baldies, popcorn curl with pacifier, red popcorn curls with single tooth, and freckled girls with gold braided hair.

Valued slightly higher than retail: There are many various types and molds that are collected due to personal preferences. These include ringmaster, clown, baseball player, astronaut, travelers, twins, babies, talking Preemie, Splash Kid, Cornsilk Kid, etc. The value for these dolls is not more than $30.00–50.00. These dolls and others are easily attainable for collectors.

Annie Rooney, Little: 1926. All composition, legs painted black, molded shoes. 12" - $400.00 up; 17" - $700.00 up.

Baby Bo Kaye: 1925. Bisque head, open mouth. 16" - $2,550.00; 19–21" - $3,100.00. **All bisque:** 4½" - $1,300.00; 6½" - $1,700.00. **Celluloid head:** 12" - $375.00; 15" - $685.00. **Composition head:** Mint: 14" - $600.00. Light craze: Not original. 14" - $150.00.

Baby Mine: 1962–1964. Vinyl/cloth, sleep eyes. **Mint:** 16" - $135.00; 19" - $165.00. **Slightly soiled:** Not original. 16" - $60.00; 19" - $75.00.

Bandy: Wood/composition. Ad doll for General Electric. Large ears. Painted-on majorette uniform. Non-removable tall hat. 17" - $500.00 up.

Betty Boop: 1932. Composition head, wood jointed body. **Mint:** 12" - $625.00. **Light craze:** A few paint chips. 12" - $300.00.

Champ: 1942. Composition with freckles. **Mint:** 16" - $600.00. **Light craze:** Not original. 16" - $300.00.

Giggles: 1946. Composition with molded loop for ribbon. **Mint:** 11" - $325.00; 14" - $600.00. **Light craze:** 11" - $145.00; 14" - $200.00.

Ho-Ho: 1940. **Plaster:** Excellent condition. 4" - $55.00. **Vinyl:** Excellent condition: 4" - $12.00.

Joy: 1932. Composition with wood jointed body. **Mint:** 10" - $275.00; 15" - $425.00. **Slight craze:** 10" - $145.00; 15" - $200.00.

Kewpie: See Kewpie section.

Margie: 1935. **Composition:** Mint condition. 6" - $185.00; 10" - $285.00. **Slight craze:** Not original. 6" - $90.00; 10" - $125.00. **Segmented wood/composition:** 1929. 9½" - $325.00, 145.00.

Two 16" molded hair "Baby Mine" dolls with open nurser mouths and sleep eyes. All vinyl construction. Both are original. Each - $60.00 up. *Courtesy Jeannie Mauldin.*

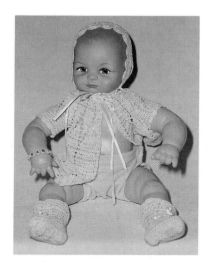

15" "Miss Peep" with inset eyes. All vinyl with hinge jointed arms and regular jointed legs. Marked "Cameo" on head. $45.00.
Courtesy Kathy Tvrdik.

Miss Peep: 1957 and 1970s. Pin-jointed shoulders and hips. **Vinyl:** Mint condition and original. 1960s. 15" - $45.00; 18" - $60.00. **Black:** 18" - $75.00. Slightly soiled, not original. 18" - $28.00. **Black, from 1972:** 18" - $35.00. **Ball-jointed shoulders and hips:** 1970s–1980s. 17" - $55.00; 21" - $90.00.

Miss Peep, Newborn: 1962. Vinyl and plastic. **Mint:** Original. 18" - $40.00. **Slight soil:** Not original. 18" - $22.00.

Peanut, Affectionately: 1958. Vinyl. **Mint:** Original. 18½" - $85.00. **Slight soil:** Not original. 18½" - $35.00.

Pete the Pup: 1930–1935. Composition with wood jointed body. **Mint:** 9" - $250.00. **Slight craze:** Few paint chips. 9" - $100.00.

Pinkie: 1930–1935. **Composition:** Mint: Original. 10" - $285.00. Slight craze: 10" - $145.00. **Wood jointed body:** 10" - $375.00. **Vinyl/plastic:** 1950s. Mint condition: 10–11" - $150.00. Slight soil: Not original. 10–11" - $75.00.

Plum: 1952–1954. Body hinged like "Miss Peep." Has dimples. 18" - $55.00; 23" - $85.00.

Scootles: 1925, 1930s. **Composition:** Mint condition: Original. 8" - $400.00 up; 12" - $450.00 up; 15" - $525.00 up; 20" - $675.00; 22–23" - $725.00 up. Light craze: Not original. 8" - $100.00; 12" - $225.00; 15" - $285.00; 20" - $350.00; 22" - $385.00. **Composition/sleep eyes:** Mint condition: 15" - $600.00; 21" - $800.00 up. Slight craze: 15" - $350.00; 21" - $385.00. **Black, composition:** Mint: 15" - $775.00. Slight craze: 15" - $300.00. **Vinyl:** 1964. Mint: Original. 14" - $185.00 up; 19" - $350.00 up; 27" - $500.00 up. Lightly soiled: Not original. 14" - $80.00; 19" - $125.00; 27" - $200.00. **All Bisque:** See that section.

"Skootles" with hard plastic head. Has sleep eyes and one-piece "magic skin" body and limbs which has turned dark brown with age. Original, made in 1954. Shown with composition "Kewpie" that is jointed at neck, hips, and shoulders. Has painted features. In front is a 12" Schoenhut baby with bent limbs and painted features. "Skootles" - $195.00 up; "Kewpie" - $250.00 up; 12" baby - $425.00. *Courtesy Turn of Century Antiques.*

Pretty Bettsie: Composition one-piece body and limbs. Separate wooden neck joint. Has molded hair. and smile mouth. Molded-on yellow, pink, or blue short dress with white ruffles at hem. Painted-on shoes and socks. Chest paper label marked "Pretty Bettsie/Copyright J. Kallus." 9" - $200.00; 14" - $285.00 up.

CEE, FRANCINE

16" "Campbell Kids" from the "American Kids Series." All vinyl construction. Original. Made in a limited edition in 1992. Authorized by Campbell; designed and marketed by Francine Cee of Scotsdale, Arizona. Each - $57.00. *Courtesy Claudia's Collectibles.*

27" all cloth Lucille Ball doll from the "I Love Lucy" TV show. Plastic face mask, orange yarn hair, and painted features. Apron marked "I Love Lucy/Desi 1953." Mint condition - $150.00; played with - $50.00–80.00. *Courtesy Ellyn McCorkell.*

20" cloth dolls from early 1930s to mid 1940s. Maker unknown. Girl doll has oil-painted features and mitt style hands. Boy doll has painted features on oil cloth head and stitched fingers. $185.00 up. *Courtesy Marjorie Uhl.*

17" Lenci-type doll made of all felt except back of head. Glass eyes to the side, mohair wig, free standing thumbs, and stitched fingers. Jointed shoulders and hips only. All original felt clothes. May have been made in England. $350.00.

23" all felt doll with mohair wig, oil-painted features, and long inset lashes. Formed legs and calfs. Slightly individual fingers. Right arm bent at elbow. Metal/wooden pin joints. Excelsior filled. Clothes possibly original. American made but maker unknown. Excellent quality, ca. 1930–1935. $265.00.

7" "Rambo" figures and 7" "Trautman" from *Rambo* movies. Molded-on clothes. Extra joints at knees. Made for Coleco in 1985. Rambo, each - $16.00; Trautman - $18.00.
Courtesy Don Tvrdik.

20" "Beauty" made of porcelain and cloth with glass eyes. Original. Made by Danbury Mint in 1990. $175.00 up.

17" "Bubbles, The Circus Clown" by Danbury Mint. Porcelain and cloth. Glass eyes, modeled tongue, and glazed hands. Original, made in 1990. $85.00 up.

10" porcelain baby entitled "Brave and Free." Dressed to represent the Blackfoot tribe. Designed by famous artist Gregory Perillo. Created by Artaffects, Ltc. for the Danbury Mint in 1992. $125.00. *Courtesy Danbury Mint.*

10" child entitled "Bedtime Prayer" was made by Danbury Mint in 1990. Porcelain and cloth. Glass eyes with modeled half-closed eyelids. Molded in kneeling position. 4½" doll has pink bow painted on top of solid dome head. Wooden bed. Set - $125.00 up.

DELUXE TOPPER, READING, PREMIUM

This company also used the names Topper Toys and Topper Corp. They were well known for making dolls that did things and were battery operated during the 1960s and 1970s. These dolls have become highly collectible as they were well played with and not many dolls survived.

Penny Brite: 8" child. Mint - $30.00. Played with - $10.00 up.

Susie Cute: 1964. 7" - $20.00.

Baby Boo: Battery operated, 1965. 21" - $40.00.

Baby Magic: 1966. 18" - $50.00.

Baby Tickle Tears: 14" - $40.00.

Party Time: Battery operated, 1967. 18" - $45.00.

Lil' Miss Fussy: Battery operated. 18" - $40.00.

Baby Catch A Ball: Battery operated, 1969. 18" - $60.00.

Baby Peek 'N Play: Battery operated, 1969. 18" - $40.00.

Smarty Pants: Battery operated, 1971. 19" - $35.00.

Dawn: 6". Mint - $20.00. In original box - $27.00. Played with - $6.00 up.

Dawn Model Agency Dolls: Mint - $35.00. In box - $45.00. Played with - $18.00.

Boys of Dawn Series: Mint - $28.00. In box - $35.00. Played with - $15.00.

8" "Penny Brite" in original box and in mint condition. All vinyl with painted features. Bendable arms and legs. Marked on head "A9/Deluxe Reading Corp. 1963." $30.00. *Courtesy Kathy Tvrdik.*

6½" "Tomboy" is one of the "Go Go" set. Eight dolls in set. Made by Topper Toys in 1966. Painted features and black eye. Removable clothes. Fully bendable body. $35.00.

7" "Suzy Cute" by Deluxe Reading. Original with inset glass eyes. Move arms and face changes expressions. Marked "Pat. Pend." on body. $20.00 up. *Courtesy Kathy Tvrdik.*

21" "Pretty Betty Bride" made of plastic and vinyl. Has lever in lower back that activates arms to throw flowers. Original. Marked "Hong Kong" on head; "Deluxe Reading/Pat. Pend." on body. $45.00 up. *Courtesy Kathy Tvrdik.*

DOLL ARTIST

Bell, Yolanda: Napoleon - $1,200.00; Alexandria - $1,000.00; Jason - $900.00; Nina - $350.00; Tai Ling - $500.00; Hanna - $600.00; Rashta - $600.00.

Himstedt, Annette: Lisa - $850.00; Bastian - $800.00; Ayoka - $700.00; Janka - $750.00; Michiko - $950.00.

Ashton-Drake: Chen - $150.00; Jack Horner - $125.00; Mary Had A Lamb - $140.00; Natasha - $70.00; Jessica - $80.00.

Gorham: Ashley - $750.00; Amy - $650.00; Joy - $500.00; Cassie - $500.00; Amanda - $650.00; Veronica - $500.00; Colette - $600.00; Victoria - $400.00.

Jerri: Rebecca (1979) - $650.00; Angela (12") - $275.00; Gigi (8") - $210.00; Chelsea - $425.00; Sunny - $190.00; Buffy - $190.00; Emily (rare) - $2,000.00; Scottie (rare) - $1,000.00; Becky - $500.00.

Lawton, Wendy: Crystal Winter - $375.00; Girl's Day (Japan) - $425.00; Nideko - $700.00; Baa, Baa - $975.00; Blessing - $950.00; Black Sambo - $800.00; Marigold Garden - $475.00; Summer Rose - $375.00; Peter and Wolf - $525.00; Patricia and Her Patsy - $625.00; Walks In Beauty - $675.00; Wee Bit of Woe - $500.00.

Dunham Arts: "La Mode" - $725.00; Empress Josephine - $750.00; Modern Venus - $725.00; Christy - $525.00; Yupik, Eskimo Child - $525.00; California Girl - $1,100.00; Empress Theodora - $1,500.00; West African Dogon - $1,200.00; My Little Dumplin - $1,100.00; Dimples - $950.00; Happi - $975.00; The Other Guy - $1,000.00; Jenny Ford - $900.00.

16½" "Princess" and "Prince - Protector of the Realm" are hand-carved wooden figures by artist/designer Paul Spencer. Both are jointed at elbows, wrists, waist, knees, and ankles. (She has extra joints at neck, shoulders, and hips.) Carved hair, painted features. Prince has open/closed mouth with missing front tooth. Each - $950.00 up.

14" "King Troll" is a hand-carved wooden figure by Paul Spencer. Amazingly, Paul does not know what he is going to carve until he starts. He selects a piece of wood, and when he begins to carve, the figure emerges and he "finds" his creation. $1,200.00.

20" "Miss Unity" doll of the United Federation of Doll Clubs (U.F.D.C.). Made just like 1920s Chase dolls with oil-painted features. Very unique face and hairdo. Designed by Kathy Tvdrik. $250.00 up.

Beautiful 28" Indian child made of porcelain and cloth. Made in Denmark and sold through a TV shopping network. $500.00.

"Spring Blossom" is the fourth and final edition in Wendy Lawton's Season Collection. Made in 1991. Limited to 500 dolls. Has green glass eyes. $800.00.

12" "He Won't Bite" designed by Bessie Peece Gutmann and made for the Hamilton Collection. Porcelain and cloth, painted eyes. Comes with oversized hat, dog, and umbrella. $185.00.

15" "Pepper" from the "Sugar 'N Spice Collection" by Linda Mason for Georgetown Collections. Porcelain and cloth. Wires in pigtail braids gives the appearance of movement as she jumps rope. $190.00.

EEGEE DOLL COMPANY

The "Eegee" name was made up from the name of company founder, E.G. Goldberger. Founded in 1917, the early dolls were marked "E.G.", then E. Goldberger." Now the marks "Eegee" and "Goldberger" are used.

Andy: Teen type. 12" - $40.00.

Annette: Teen type. 11½" - $50.00.

1966: Marked "20/25M/13." 25" - $70.00; 28" - $85.00; 36" - $125.00.

Walker: 1966. Plastic/vinyl. 25" - $50.00; 28" - $75.00; 36" - $100.00.

Baby Luv: 1973. Cloth/vinyl. Marked "B.T. Eegee." 14" - $40.00.

Baby Susan: 1958. Name marked on head. 8½" - $18.00.

Baby Tandy Talks: 1960. Pull string talker. Foam body/vinyl. $65.00.

Babette: 1962. Barbie look-alike. 11½" - $70.00 up.

Ballerina: 1958. Hard plastic/vinyl head. 20" - $45.00.

Ballerina: 1964. Hard plastic/vinyl head. 31" - $100.00.

Ballerina: 1967. Foam body and limbs, vinyl head. 18" - $30.00.

Boy Dolls: Molded hair, rest vinyl. 13" - $35.00; 21" - $35.00 up.

Composition: Open mouth girls. Sleep eyes. 14" - $150.00 up; 18" - $200.00 up. **Babies:** Cloth/composition. 16" - $85.00 up; 20" - $125.00 up.

Debutante: 1958. Vinyl head, rest hard plastic. Jointed knees. 28" - $100.00.

Dolly Parton: 1980. 12" - $30.00; 18" - $60.00.

Flowerkins: 1963. Plastic/vinyl. Marked "F-2" on head. Seven in set. 16", in box - $90.00. Played with, no box - $30.00.

Gemmette: 1963. Teen type. (See photo in Series 8, pg. 216.) 14" - $45.00 up.

Georgie or Georgette: 1971. Red-headed twins. Cloth/vinyl. 22–23" - $50.00.

Gigi Perreaux: 1951. Hard plastic, early vinyl head. 17" - $350.00 up.

Granny: Old lady modeling. Grey rooted hair, painted or sleep eyes. From "Beverly Hillbillies." 14" - $75.00.

Miss Charming: 1936. All composition Shirley Temple look-alike. 19" - $425.00 up. Pin - $35.00.

Miss Sunbeam: 1968. Plastic/vinyl, dimples. 17" - $35.00.

Musical Baby: 1967. Key wind music box in cloth body. 17" - $25.00.

My Fair Lady: 1956. Adult type. All vinyl, jointed waist. 10½" - $45.00; 19" - $75.00.

Posey Playmate: 1969. Foam and vinyl. 18" - $25.00.

Puppetrina: 1963. 22" - $35.00.

Shelly: 1964. "Tammy" type. Grow hair. 12" - $20.00.

Sniffles: 1963. Plastic/vinyl nurser. Marked "13/14 AA-EEGEE." 12" - $20.00.

Susan Stroller: 1955. Hard plastic with vinyl head. 15" - $45.00; 20" - $50.00; 23" - $60.00; 26" - $70.00.

Tandy Talks: 1961. Pull string talker. Plastic with vinyl head and freckles. 20" - $65.00.

22" Eegee twins "Georgette" and "Georgie." Cloth body, green sleep eyes, and freckles. One arm bent at elbow. Made in 1971. Marked "17 RNG Eegee Co." Each - $50.00. *Courtesy Jeannie Mauldin.*

EEGEE DOLL COMPANY

19" all composition "Miss Charming" is a Shirley Temple look-alike. Had pin stating name and company. Mint and original. $425.00 up. *Courtesy David Spurgeon.*

"Susan Stroller" with rooted hair and sleep eyes. Doll came in various sizes. Earlier models were made of hard plastic. Similar to Ideal's "Saucy Walker." Original. This doll is from 1962. 20" - $45.00.

EFFANBEE DOLL COMPANY

First prices are for mint condition dolls; second prices for dolls that are played with, soiled, dirty, cracked or crazed or not original. Dolls marked with full name or "F & B."

Alyssia: 1958. Hard plastic walker. Vinyl head. 20" - 225.00, $90.00.

American Children: (See photo in Series 8, pgs. 217–218.) 1938. All composition. Painted or sleep eyes. Marked with that name. Some have "Anne Shirley" marked bodies; others are unmarked. **Closed Mouth Girls:** 19–21" - $1,100.00. **Closed Mouth Boy:** 15" - $900.00; 17" - $1,100.00. **Open Mouth Girl:** Barbara Joan: 15" - $650.00. Barbara Ann: 17" - $700.00. Barbara Lou: 21" - $900.00 up.

Anne Shirley: 1936–1940. All composition. Marked with name. 15" - $275.00; 17" - $300.00; 21" - $400.00; 27" - $500.00.

Armstrong, Louis: 1984–1985 only. 15½" - $70.00.

Babyette: 1946. Sleeping baby. Cloth/composition. 12" - $265.00, $125.00; 16" - $350.00; $175.00.

Babykin: 1940. **All composition:** 9–12" - $175.00, $85.00. **All vinyl:** 10" - $30.00.

Baby Cuddleup: 1953. Oil cloth body. Vinyl head/limbs. Two lower teeth. 20" - $50.00, $20.00; 23" - $85.00, $40.00.

Baby Dainty: 1912–1922. Cloth/composition. Marked with name. 15" - $265.00, $95.00; 17" - $300.00, $125.00.

Baby Evelyn: 1925. Composition/cloth. Marked with name. 17" - $300.00, $125.00.

15" "Baby Face" with sleep eyes to side. Plastic and vinyl. Marked "Effanbee/1967/2500." Mint and original. $65.00. In child's dress - $45.00.

Baby Grumpy: See Grumpy.

Baby Tinyette: 1933–1936. Composition. 7–8" - $245.00, $100.00. **Toddler:** 7–8" - $265.00; $100.00.

Betty Brite: 1933. All composition. Fur wig, sleep eyes. Marked with name. 16–17" - $300.00, $100.00.

Bright Eyes: 1938, 1940's. Same doll as Tommy Tucker and Mickey. Composition/cloth, flirty eyes. 16" - $300.00; 18" - $350.00; 22–23" - $400.00.

Brother or Sister: 1943. Composition head and hands, rest cloth. Yarn hair, painted eyes. 12" - $175.00, $70.00; 16" - $200.00, $80.00.

Bubbles: 1924. Composition/cloth. Marked with name. 15" - $265.00, $125.00; 19" - $345.00, $145.00; 22" - $400.00, $175.00; 25" - $475.00, $175.00. **Black:** 16" - $550.00; 20" - $865.00.

Button Nose: 1936–1943. (See photo in Series 8, pg. 218.) **Composition:** 8–9" - $185.00, $75.00. **Vinyl/cloth:** 1968. 18" - $45.00, $25.00.

Candy Kid: 1946. All composition. 12" - $250.00, $95.00. **Black:** 12" - $325.00, $95.00.

Churchill, Sir Winston: 1984. $70.00.

Charlie McCarthy: Composition/cloth. 15" - $285.00; 19–20" - $450.00, $175.00.

Coquette: Composition with molded hair. Some have loop for hair ribbon. Painted eyes, smile. 10" - $225.00; 14" - $285.00.

Composition Dolls: 1930s. All composition. Jointed neck, shoulders and hips. Molded hair. Painted or sleep eyes. Open or closed mouth. Original clothes. Marked "Effanbee." Perfect condition. 9" - $150.00, $85.00; 15" - $200.00, $100.00; 18" - $250.00, $100.00; 21" - $325.00, $125.00.

Composition Dolls: 1920s. Composition head/limbs with cloth body. Open or closed mouth. Sleep eyes. Original clothes. Marked "Effanbee."

Perfect condition. 18" - $165.00, $80.00; 22" - $200.00, $100.00; 25" - $300.00, $125.00; 27–28" - $375.00, $145.00.

Currier & Ives: Plastic/vinyl. 12" - $40.00, $10.00.

Disney Dolls: 1977–1978. Snow White, Cinderella, Alice in Wonderland and Sleeping Beauty. 14" - $175.00, $85.00.

Dydee Baby: 1933 on. Hard rubber head, rubber body. Later versions had hard plastic head. Perfect condition. 14" - $125.00, $30.00.

Dydee Baby: 1950 on. Hard plastic/vinyl. 15" - $125.00, $40.00; 20" - $200.00, $100.00.

Emily Ann: 1937. Composition puppet. 13" - $145.00, $35.00.

Fields, W.C.: 1938. Composition/cloth. 22" - $500.00, $150.00. **Plastic/vinyl:** See Legend Series.

8" all vinyl "Fluffy" dolls dressed in Brownie and Girl Scout uniforms. Sleep eyes and rooted hair. Made from 1957 into 1960s. (Brownie's shoes not original.) Each - $45.00. *Courtesy Kathy Tvrdik.*

Fluffy: 1954. All vinyl. 10" - $35.00, $15.00. **Girl Scout:** 10" - $45.00, $15.00. **Black:** 10" - $45.00, $15.00. **Katie:** 1957. Molded hair. 8½" - $45.00, $20.00.

Gumdrop: 1962 on. Plastic/vinyl. 16" - $35.00, $20.00.

Grumpy: 1912–1938. Frowns. Cloth/composition. Painted features. 12" - $200.00, $100.00; 14" - $275.00, $100.00. **Black:** 12" - $325.00, $165.00; 14–15" - $400.00, $175.00.

Hagara, Jan: Designer. **Laurel:** 1984. 15" - $135.00. **Cristina:** 1984 only. $185.00. **Larry:** 1985. 15" - $85.00. **Lesley:** 1985. $80.00. **Originals:** George Washington, Uncle Sam, Amish, etc. 12" - $200.00 up.

Half Pint: 1966 on. Plastic/vinyl. 10" - $35.00, $15.00.

Happy Boy: 1960. All vinyl. Molded tooth and freckles. 10½" - $45.00, $20.00.

20" "Dolly Dumplin" from 1918. Cloth body and composition head/limbs. Painted eyes, open/closed mouth, and molded hair. Marked "Effanbee" on shoulder plate. Mint - $250.00. In this condition - $125.00.

Hibel, Edna: Designer. 1984 only. **Flower girl:** $150.00. **Contessa:** $175.00.

Historical Dolls: 1939. All composition. Original. 14" - $600.00, $250.00; 21" - $1,200.00, $700.00.

Honey: All composition. 14" - $225.00, $95.00; 20" - $350.00, $150.00; 27" - $500.00, $200.00.

Honey: 1949–1955. All hard plastic, closed mouth. Must have excellent face color. (Add more for unusual, original clothes.) 14" - $300.00, $90.00; 18" - $400.00, $150.00; 21" - $550.00, $175.00.

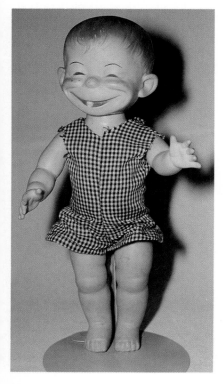

10½" all vinyl "Happy Boy" with painted tooth and open/closed mouth. Laughing closed painted eyes and freckles. Marked "1960 Effanbee." $45.00 up. *Courtesy Kathy Tvrdik.*

Honey: 1947–1948. Composition, flirty eyes: 21" - $450.00, $125.00. **Walker:** 14" - $245.00, 19" - $345.00. **Jointed knees:** 19" - $365.00.

Howdy Doody: 1947: Composition/cloth. String operated mouth. 16–17" - $185.00. **Puppet on string:** Composition head/limbs. 17" - $145.00; 20" - $185.00. **1947–1949:** Composition/cloth, puppet mouth formed but not moveable. 18" - $250.00. **1950s:** Hard plastic/cloth doll. 18" - $185.00.

Humpty Dumpty: 1985. $75.00 up.

Ice Queen: 1937. Skater outfit. Composition with open mouth. 17" - $750.00, $200.00.

Lamkins: 1930. Composition/cloth. 15" - $365.00 up; 18" - $500.00 up; 22" - $650.00.

Legend Series:
1980: W.C. Fields - $265.00. **1981:** John Wayne as soldier. $185.00. **1982:** John Wayne as cowboy. $185.00. **1982:** Mae West - $95.00. **1983:** Groucho Marx - $85.00. **1984:** Judy Garland dressed as "Dorothy" from *Wizard of Oz.* $80.00. **1985:** Lucille Ball. $70.00. **1986:** Liberace - $75.00. **1987:** James Cagney - $60.00.

Lil Sweetie: 1967. Nurser with no lashes or brow. 16" - $55.00, $25.00.

Limited Edition Club:
1975: Precious Baby - $550.00. **1976:** Patsy - $375.00. **1977:** Dewees Cochran - $200.00. **1978**: Crowning Glory - $165.00. **1979:** Skippy - $350.00. **1980:** Susan B. Anthony - $165.00. **1981:** Girl with watering can - $165.00. **1982:** Princess Diana - $125.00. **1983:** Sherlock Holmes - $185.00. **1984:** Bubbles - $125.00. **1985:** Red Boy - $125.00. **1986:** China head - $125.00.

Little Lady: 1939–1947. All composition. (Add more for original clothes.) 15" - $325.00, $90.00; 17" - $450.00, $125.00; 21" - $500.00, $165.00; 27" - $650.00, $225.00.

18" "Little Lady" in her South American dancing dress. (As shown in 1942 Montgomery Ward's catalog.) All composition with sleep eyes and mohair wig. Mint and original. $550.00 up.
Courtesy Chris McWilliams.

Little Lady: 1943. **Cloth body:** Yarn hair. 21" - $365.00 up. **Pink cloth body:** Wig. 17" - $285.00 up. **Magnets in hands:** 15" doll only - $350.00. Doll/accessories - $450.00.

Lovums: 1928. Composition/cloth. Open smiling mouth. Marked with name. 15" - $235.00, $100.00. 20" - $300.00, $150.00; 23" - $350.00.

Mae Starr: Record player in torso. Composition/cloth. Marked with name. 30" - $465.00, $200.00.

Marionettes: Composition/wood. 14" - $145.00 up.

Martha and George Washington: 1976. 11", pair - $125.00.

Mary Ann or Lee: 1928–1937. Open smile mouth. Composition and cloth or all composition. Marked with name. 16" - $265.00, $95.00; 18" - $285.00, $125.00; 20" - $325.00, $150.00; 24" - $425.00, $175.00.

Marilee: 1920s. Composition/cloth. Open mouth. Marked with name. 13" - $250.00, $100.00; 16" - $300.00, $125.00; 23" - $365.00, $150.00; 28" - $475.00; $200.00.

Mary Jane: 1960. Plastic/vinyl walker with freckles. 31" - $265.00, $100.00.

Mary Jane: 1917–1920. Composition. Jointed body or cloth. "Mama" type. 20–22" - $275.00.

Mickey: 1946. Composition/cloth with flirty eyes. (Also Tommy Tucker and Bright Eyes.) 16" - $300.00; 18" -

27" "Melodie" is a walker with legs jointed at the knees. Hard plastic with vinyl head. Rooted hair and sleep eyes. Made from 1953–1956. All original. $200.00 up. *Courtesy Jeannie Mauldin.*

$350.00, $100.00; 22–23" - $400.00, $125.00.

Mickey: 1956. All vinyl. (Some have molded-on hats.) 11" - $85.00, $25.00.

Miss Chips: 1965 on. Plastic/vinyl. **White:** 18" - $35.00. **Black:** 18" - $45.00.

Pat-O-Pat: Composition/cloth with painted eyes. Press stomach and hands pats together. 13–14" - $175.00, $80.00.

Patricia: 1932–1936. All composition. 14" - $385.00, $145.00. Original: $450.00 up.

Patricia-kin: 1929–1930s. 11" - $325.00, $125.00.

Patsy: 1927–1930s. **All composition:** 14" - $365.00, $150.00. **Composition/cloth:** 14" - $375.00, $175.00. Original: $425.00 up.

16" all composition "Patsy Joan" with sleep eyes and original "Patsy" pin. Her dress came in several other colors. All original. $450.00 up. *Courtesy Gloria Anderson.*

Patsy Babyette: 1930s, 1940s. 9" - $245.00, $90.00. Original: $300.00 up.

Patsyette: 1930s. 9" - $265.00, $100.00. Original: $350.00 up.

Patsy Ann: 1930s. 19" - $465.00, $165.00. Original: $525.00 up. **Vinyl:** 1959. 15" - $165.00, $60.00. Original: $200.00 up.

Patsy Joan: 1927–1930. Reissued 1946–1949. 16" - $450.00, $175.00. Original: $500.00 up. **Black:** 16" - $750.00 up, $225.00. Original: $550.00 up.

Patsy, Jr.: 11" - $285.00, $100.00. Original: $350.00 up.

26" "Mommy's Baby" from 1952. Plastic shoulder plate with hard plastic swivel head. Cloth body and stuffed vinyl limbs. Sleep eyes, wig, and open mouth. Not original. $160.00. *Courtesy Jeannie Mauldin.*

Patsy Lou: 1929–1930s. 22" - $485.00, $175.00. Original: $575.00 up.

Patsy Mae: 1932. 30" - $785.00, $325.00. Original: $865.00 up.

Patsy Ruth: 1935. 26–27" - $765.00, $325.00. Original: $850.00 up.

Patsy, Wee: 1930s. 5–6" - $300.00, $125.00. Original: $365.00 up.

Polka Dottie: 1953. 21" - $175.00, $60.00.

Portrait Dolls: 1940. All composition. 12" - $200.00, $80.00.

Presidents: 1984. **Lincoln:** 18" - $50.00. **Washington:** 16" - $50.00. **Teddy Roosevelt:** 17" - $60.00. **F.D. Roosevelt:** 1985. $55.00.

Prince Charming or Cinderella: All hard plastic. 16" - $450.00 up, $165.00.

Pum'kin: 1966 on. All vinyl with freckles. 10½" - $30.00, $15.00.

Rootie Kazootie: 1953. 21" - $175.00, $60.00.

Roosevelt, Eleanor: 1985. 14½" - $55.00.

Rosemary: 1925 on. Composition/cloth. Marked with name. 13" - $250.00, $125.00; 16" - $300.00, $150.00; 23" - $365.00, $150.00; 28" - $475.00, $200.00.

Santa Claus: 19" composition with molded beard and hat. (See photo in Series 8, pg. 223.) $1,200.00 up.

Skippy: 1929, 1940s. All composition. 14" - $445.00, $165.00. **Soldier:** $500.00. **Sailor:** $565.00.

Suzanne: 1940. All composition. Marked with name. 14" - $275.00, $125.00.

Suzie Sunshine: 1961 on. Has freckles. 17–18" - $45.00-20.00. **Black:** 17–18" - $65.00, $35.00.

22" "Precious Baby" with sleep eyes and open mouth/nurser. Oil cloth body, vinyl head and limbs. Has baby bracelet and tag with her name. All original and mint. $85.00. *Courtesy Jeannie Mauldin.*

Suzette: 1939. Marked with name. All composition. 12" - $245.00, $100.00.

Sweetie Pie: 1938–1940s. Composition/cloth. 14" - $165.00, $50.00; 19" - $265.00, $90.00; 24" - $365.00, $125.00.

Tommy Tucker: 1946. Composition/cloth with flirty eyes. (Also Mickey and Bright Eyes.) 16" - $300.00, 18" - $350.00, 22–23" - $400.00, $125.00.

Twain, Mark: 1984. 16" - $60.00.

Witch: Designed by Faith Wick. 18" - $95.00 up.

16" "Sweetie Pie" has cloth body and composition head/limbs. Lamb's wool wig and sleep, flirty eyes. (Also sold as "Bright Eyes," "Tommy Tucker," and "Mickey.") Original. $300.00 up. *Courtesy Sharon McDowell.*

ELLANEE

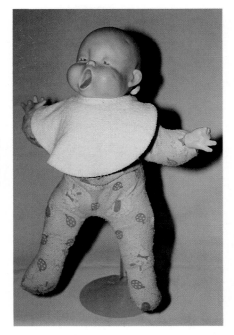

15" "Baby Yawn" is made of cloth and vinyl with painted yawning mouth. Pajamas form body, arms, and legs. Marked "Ellanee Doll/1975" on head. $35.00. *Courtesy Kathy Tvrdik.*

EPPY

12" "Color Me Doll" that is all plastic. Child could use crayons and color the doll, then wash it off. Marked "Eppy U.S.A. 1964 Pat. Pending." $30.00. *Courtesy Kathy Tvrdik.*

FORTUNE TOYS

8" "Ninette" is made of all hard plastic. Sleep eyes and mohair wig. Doll unmarked. Box marked "A Michele Cartier Original 'School Outfit.' Made by Fortune Toys, Brooklyn, N.Y." In box - $65.00; doll only - $25.00 up. *Courtesy Nanette Ringler.*

1987: Gibson Bride - $425.00.

1988: Swan Lake - $300.00; Queen Galadril - $300.00; Scarlett & Rhett - $200.00 each; Amy (Little Women) - $200.00; Christmas Angel - $285.00.

1989: Mary, Mary - $200.00; Cinderella - $300.00; Snow White (marked 1988) - $300.00; Bo Peep - $200.00.

1990: Snow Queen - $465.00; Rapunzel - $285.00; Jewels of Month Dolls - $185.00; Country Store figures - $225.00; Glinda, The Good Witch - $225.00; Victorian Bride - $600.00; Baby (Days of Week) - $200.00; Marilyn Monroe - $245.00; Promenade (Mother & Child) - $300.00.

1991: Gibson Girl - $285.00; Disney Cinderella - $300.00; Rose Princess - $325.00; John Wayne - $265.00; Evil Witch of Oz - $285.00; Cyrena/Atlantis - $385.00; Scarlett/ case - $500.00.

20" "Cyrena, Princess of Atlantis" designed by artist Lynn Lupetti for the Franklin Mint in 1991. $385.00.

Cute cloth and bisque cats dressed as different occupations. Author has seen 12 different ones, but there may be more. Made for the Franklin Mint, date unknown. Each - $75.00.

GERBER BABY

1936: 8" all printed cloth doll. Holds can of baby food and toy dog. Rare. $400.00.

1954: 12" rubber doll made by Sun Rubber Co. Mint - $95.00 up; Mint in box - $225.00 up.

1966: 14" soft vinyl doll made by Arrow Industries. Has lopsided smile. $65.00 up.

1972: 10" plastic/vinyl doll made by Uneeda Doll Co. $45.00 up.

11" all rubber "Gerber Baby" with inset eyes. Marked "Gerber Baby/Gerber Products Co." on head; "Mfd by/The Sun Rubber Co./Barbarton, Oh./U.S.A. 1954" on body. In excellent condition. Mint - $95.00; Mint in box - $225.00. *Courtesy David Spurgeon.*

GIBBS, RUTH

12" #229 "Mrs. Fitzgerald's Visiting Dress" in original box. China glazed head and limbs with pink cloth body. Made by Ruth Gibbs, 1940s to 1952. Marked "R.G." on shoulder. (For more information see Series 7, pg. 233.) In box - $200.00; doll only - $150.00.
Courtesy Christine Green and Ellyn McCorkell.

Hartland Industries made many figures with horses during the mid to late 1950s. These are extremely collectible as they are rare, especially when the horses have saddles. Most came from the Warner Brothers television productions. The figures included:

James Arness as "Matt Dillon" on *Gunsmoke*. (Sept. 1955 to Sept. 1975)

James Garner as "Bret Maverik" on *Maverik*. (See photo Series 8, pg. 228.)

John Lupton as "Tom Jefords" on *Broken Arrow*. (Sept. 1956 - Sept. 1960)

Gail Davis as "Annie Oakley." (April 1953 – Dec. 1956)

Hugh O'Brien as "Wyatt Earp." (Sept. 1955 – Sept. 1961)

Dale Robertson as "Jim Hardie" on *Wells Fargo*. (March 1957 – Sept. 1962)

Pat Conway as "Clay Hollister" on *Tombstone Territory*. (Oct. 1957 – Oct. 1959)

Wayde Preston as "Capt. Chris Colt" on *Colt 45*. (Oct. 1957 – Sept. 1960)

Richard Boone as "Paladin" on *Have Gun Will Travel*. (Sept. 1957 – Sept. 1963)

John Payne as "Vint Bonner" on *The Restless Gun*. (Sept. 1957 – Sept. 1959)

Clint Walker as "Cheyenne" (Sept. 1955 – Sept. 1963)

Ward Bond as "Major Seth Adams" on *Wagon Train*. (Sept. 1957 – Sept. 1965)

Chief Thunderbird with his horse "Northwind."

Robert E. Lee with his horse "Traveler."

General George Custer and his horse "Bugler."

Brave Eagle with his horse "White Cloud."

General George Washington with his horse "Ajax."

7½" **"Lone Ranger" with horse "Silver." Plastic figure molded in one piece. Made by Hartland Industries. $250.00.** *Courtesy Shirley Bertrand.*

"Lone Ranger" with his horse "Silver."

"Tonto" with his horse "Scout."

Jim Bowie with his horse "Blaze."

"Sgt. Preston of the Yukon" with his horse.

Roy Rogers with his horse "Trigger."

Dale Evans with her horse "Buttercup."

Cochise with pinto horse.

Buffalo Bill with horse.

Other figures made by the company include baseball notables Mickey Mantle, Ted Williams, Stan Musial, Henry Aaron, Ed Mathews, and George "Babe" Ruth.

Figure and horse: $250.00 up.

Figure in box with horse and accessories: $425.00.

Figure alone: $125.00.

Horse alone: $175.00.

Baseball figure: $325.00 up.

All prices are for mint condition dolls.

Adam: 1971. Boy for World of Love series. 9" - $18.00.

Aimee: 1972. Plastic/vinyl. 18" - $55.00.

Charlie's Angels: 1977. 8½" Jill, Kelly or Sabrina. $18.00 each.

1964 "G.I. Joe" that is original and one of the first on the market. Molded hair. $90.00. *Courtesy Don Tvrdik.*

Defender: 1974. One-piece arms and legs. 11½" - $65.00 up.

Dolly Darling: 1965. 4½" - $10.00.

Flying Nun: Plastic/vinyl, 1967. 5" - $45.00.

(Add $50.00 more in mint in box on G.I. Joe's.)

G.I. Joe, #1: 12" marked "G.I. Joe Copyright 1964 by Hasbro Patent Pending Made in U.S.A." **1964–1966:** (4 models.) White only. Scar, molded hair, no beard. #1 marking. $90.00 up. **1965–1966:** (5 models.) **Black:** #1 marking. $90.00 up. **1966–1967:** No scar on face. $135.00 up. **1966:** Russian, German, Japanese, British, Australian. Each - $275.00 up. In box, each - $400.00.

G.I. Joe, #2: 1967–1974. 12" marked "G.I. Joe Copyright 1964 by Hasbro Pat. No. 3,277,602 Made in U.S.A." **1967:** (6 models) #2 marking. Design same as #1. **Talking Commander:** No scar, blonde, brown eyes. $165.00 up.

G.I. Joe, #3: 1975. 12" with body marked same as #2 model. Head marked "Hasbro Ind. Inc. 1975 Made in Hong Kong." **1968:** Same style (6 models). Scar on face. #2 marking. $90.00 up.

G.I. Joe, #4: 1975. 12" marked in small of back "Hasbro Pat. Pend. Par. R.I." Talking 1975 version has #2 marked body. **1970:** (9 models.) Flocked hair and/or beard. Black and white. **Land Adventurer:** $225.00 up. **Sea Adventurer:** $245.00 up. **Air Adventurer:** $265.00 up. **Astronaut:** $275.00 up. **Talking:** $350.00 up.

G.I. Joe, #5: 1974. (8 models.) #2 and #3 markings. Has Kung Fu grip. $200.00 up.

G.I. Joe, #6: 1975. (7 models.) #3 and #4 markings. White. **Mike Powers, Atomic Man:** $80.00 up. **Eagle Eye:** $85.00. **Fire Fighter:** $185.00 up. **West Point:** $250.00 up.

12" "Duke - A Hall of Fame G.I. Joe" sold through Target Stores. Numbered collectors edition made in 1991 only. Fully poseable. Wearing official battle uniform and dog tags. Has electronic light and sound weapon. There are other Hall of Fame G.I. Joes on the market, but this first one had a very limited edition. Hasbro tested the market with this action figure. $85.00 up.

Military Police: $200.00 up. **Ski Patrol:** $450.00 up. **Secret Agent:** Unusual face, mustache. $300.00 up. **Foreign:** (See photo in Series 7, page 235.) $275.00 up. **Green Beret:** $150.00 up. **Negro Adventurer:** No beard. $350.00 up. **Frogman:** 1973. With 17" sled. $300.00 up. **G.I. Joe Nurse:** In box - $1,000.00 up.

G.I. Joe Accessories:
   Armored Car: 20" - $125.00 up. **Motorcycle and side car:** By Irwin. $145.00 up. **Desert Jeep:** Tan. $250.00 up. **Turbo Swamp Craft:** $85.00 up. **Space Capsule:** $225.00 up. **Foot Locker:** $30.00 up. **Sea Sled:** $85.00

up. **Tank:** $175.00 up. **Jeep:** Olive green. $145.00 up. **Helicopter:** $275.00 up. **All Terrain Vehicle:** $165.00 up.
   G.I. Joe Boxed Uniforms and Accessories:
   Boxed figure in uniform: $250.00 up. **Adventure Team outfit:** $300.00 up. **Diver:** "Eight Ropes of Danger." $400.00 up. **Scuba Diver:** "Jaws of Death." $300.00 up. **Safari:** "White Tiger Hunt." $300.00 up. **Test Pilot:** $650.00 up. **Jungle Explorer:** "Mouth of Doom." $450.00 up. **Secret**

12" figure from "Jem" doll set. Green painted eyes and purple tinsel hair mixed with regular rooted hair. Original. Marked "1985 Hasbro, Inc./China." $35.00 up.

Agent: "Secret Mission To Spy Island." $600.00 up. **Space Man:** "Space Walk Mystery." $450.00 up. "The Hidden Missle" $450.00 up. **Polar Explorer:** "Fight For Survival." $465.00 up. **Shark's Surprise:** $350.00 up.

Leggie: 1972. 10" - $25.00. **Black:** $35.00.

Little Miss No Name: 1965. 15" - $90.00.

9" "Miss Breck" advertising doll for Breck products. Painted eyes with lashes. Rooted hair is parted in center. Original gown tagged "Beautiful Bonnie Breck." Doll marked "4/Hasbro/U.S. Pat. Pend." $45.00 up. *Courtesy Kathy Tvrdik.*

Mamas and Papas: 1967. (See photo in Series 8, pg. 230.) $45.00 each.

Monkees: Set of four. 4" - $95.00 up.

Show Biz Babies: 1967. $40.00 each. Mama Cass: $50.00.

Storybooks: 1967. 3" - $45.00 – 65.00 in boxes.

Sweet Cookie: 1972. 18" - $40.00.

That Kid: 1967. 21" - $85.00.

World of Love Dolls: 1971. **White:** 9" - $15.00. **Black:** 9" - $20.00.

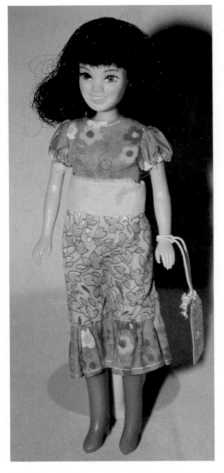

9" "Music" from the 1971 "World of Love" group of dolls. Painted eyes with inset lashes. All vinyl with bendable knees. Marked "33/Hong Kong/Hasbro /U.S. Pat Pend." $15.00.

The founder of Hollywood Dolls was Dominick Ippolite. They made dolls from 1941 to 1956. In a span of 15 years, he put on the market more dolls than any other manufacturer during that period. The dolls are well marked, but if they are undressed, it is next to impossible to distinguish which character they represent.

Dolls are made of painted bisque, composition, and hard plastic. They are marked "Hollywood Doll" and some will also have a star. Add more for mint in box dolls.

Composition or Painted Bisque: Jointed at hips and shoulders only. Painted features and mohair wig. Painted-on shoes and socks. Excellent, original: 9" - $45.00. Played with: 9" - $18.00.

Hard Plastic: Jointed shoulders and hips. Sleep eyes and mohair wig. Painted-on shoes and socks. Excellent, original: 5½–6" - $30.00. Played with: 5½–6" - $12.00.

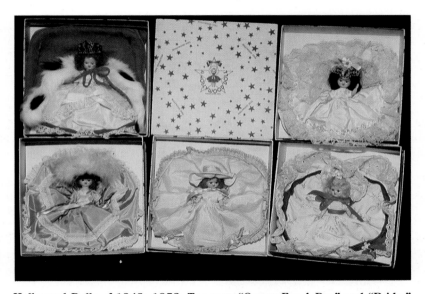

Hollywood Dolls of 1949–1952. Top row: "Queen For A Day" and "Bride." Bottom: "Lady Guinevere," "Little Girl Where Have You Been?" and "Lady Elaine." Each - $30.00 up. *Courtesy Sharon Hamilton.*

HORSMAN DOLL COMPANY

First prices are for mint condition dolls; second prices for ones that have been played with, are dirty and soiled or not original. Marked "Horsman" or "E.I.H."

Angelove: 1974. Plastic/vinyl. Made for Hallmark. 12" - $30.00.

Answer Doll: 1966. Button in back moves head. 10" - $20.00, $10.00.

Billiken: 1909. Composition head, slant eyes, plush or velvet body. 12" - $345.00, $125.00; 16" - $425.00.

Baby Bumps: 1910. Composition/cloth. 12" - $165.00, $65.00; 14" - $225.00, $95.00. **Black:** 11" - $200.00, $90.00; 15" - $300.00, $125.00.

Baby First Tooth: 1966. Cloth/vinyl. Cry mouth with one tooth. Tears on cheeks. 16" - $45.00, $18.00.

16" doll that is one of the "American Kid" series of 1914. Tight stuffed cloth with "Can't Break 'Em" composition arms. Composition shoulder head with painted features. Molded hair parted on side. Original clothes. Marked "E.I.H." Mint - $160.00. In this condition - $70.00.

Baby Tweaks: 1967. Cloth/vinyl, inset eyes. 20" - $30.00, $15.00.

Ballerina: 1957. Vinyl, one-piece body and legs, jointed elbows. 18" - $65.00.

Betty: All composition. 16" - $225.00, $90.00. All vinyl: 1951. One-piece body and limbs: 14" - $60.00. Plastic/vinyl: 16" - $25.00, $15.00.

Betty Jo: All composition. 16" - $225.00, $90.00. Plastic/vinyl: 1962. 16" - $25.00, $15.00.

Betty Ann: (Add more for original clothes.) All composition: 19" - $275.00, $125.00. Plastic/vinyl: 19" - $60.00, $25.00.

Betty Jane: All composition. 25" - $350.00, $150.00. Plastic/vinyl: 25" - $75.00, $40.00.

Blink: (Also called "Happy.") 1916 Gene Carr designed character. Cloth body, composition head and limbs. Painted eyes are almost closed. Watermelon-style open/closed mouth with one lower tooth. Very prominent ears, painted hair. 14–15" - $345.00 up.

Bye-Lo Baby: 1972. Made for 100th anniversary for Wards. Cloth/vinyl. 14" - $50.00. Reissued: 1980–1990s. 14" - $25.00.

Body Twist: 1929–1930. All composition. Top of body fits down into torso. 11" - $185.00, $75.00.

Bright Star: 1937–1946. (See photo in Series 8, pg. 233.) All composition: 18–19" - $350.00, $125.00. All hard plastic: 1952. 15" - $250.00, $95.00.

Brother: Composition/cloth. 22" - $265.00 up, $100.00. Vinyl: 13" - $50.00, $20.00.

Campbell Kids: Ca. 1911. Cloth/composition with painted features. Marked "E.I.H." 14" - $425.00 up. "Dolly Dingle" style face: 1930–1940s. All composition. 13" - $350.00 up.

Celeste Portrait Doll: In frame. Eyes painted to side. 12" - $30.00, $15.00.

Christopher Robin: 11" - $30.00, $10.00.

Child Dolls: 1930–1940s. All composition: 14" - $145.00, $60.00; 16" - $200.00, $80.00; 18" - $265.00, $95.00. All hard plastic: 14" - $125.00, $50.00; 18" - $225.00 up, $100.00. **Toddler:** All composition, very chubby. 14" - $135.00, $50.00; 17" - $185.00, $85.00.

Cindy: 1950s. Marked "170." All hard plastic: 15" - $125.00 up, $40.00; 17" - $165.00 up, $80.00. All early vinyl: 1953. 18" - $50.00, $15.00. Lady type with jointed waist: 1959. 19" - $85.00, $40 00.

Cindy Kay: 1950–on. All vinyl child with long legs. 15" - $85.00, $40.00; 20" - $125.00; 27" - $225.00.

Cinderella: 1965. Plastic/vinyl. Painted eyes to side. 11½" - $35.00, $15.00.

Composition Dolls: 1910s–1920s. "Can't Break 'Em" composition/cloth body. Marked "E.I.H." 12" - $165.00, $60.00; 16" - $195.00, $100.00. 1930's: 16" - $160.00, $70.00; 18" - $225.00, $90.00; 22" - $285.00, $125.00.

Crawling Baby: 1967. Vinyl. 14" - $20.00, $10.00.

Dimples: 1928–1933. Composition/cloth. 16" - $225.00, $90.00; 20" - $325.00, $125.00; 24" - $350.00, $145.00. **Toddler:** 20" - $365.00, $145.00; 24" - $400.00, $165.00. **Laughing:** Painted teeth. 22" - $400.00, $185.00.

Disney Exclusives: "Cinderella," "Snow White," "Mary Poppins," "Alice in Wonderland." 1981. 8" - $40.00 each.

Gold Medal Doll: 1930s. Composition/cloth. Upper & lower teeth. 21" - $200.00, $90.00. Vinyl/molded hair: 1953. 26" - $185.00, $85.00. Vinyl Boy: 1954. 15" - $75.00, $30.00.

Ella Cinders: 1925. Comic character. Composition/cloth. 14" - $425.00; 18" - $700.00.

Elizabeth Taylor: 1976. 11½" - $45.00, $20.00.

Horsman's "Wee Three" set with 20" "Cindy," 11" "Peggy Ann," and 6½" "Softee." Made of plastic and vinyl. Made in 1958. Boxed set - $325.00. *Courtesy Belinda Morse-Carpenter.*

Floppy: 1965. Foam body and legs/vinyl. 18" - $20.00.

Flying Nun: (Sally Field) 1965. Original. 12" - $50.00, $15.00.

Hansel & Gretel: 1963. Sleep eyes, unusual faces. (See photo in Series 7, pg. 238.) Each - $200.00.

Hebee-Shebee: All composition. 10½" - $465.00, $200.00

Jackie Coogan: 1921. Composition/cloth, painted eyes. 14" - $465.00, $165.00.

Jackie Kennedy: 1961. Marked "Horsman J.K." Adult body, plastic/vinyl. 25" - $145.00, $70.00.

Jeanie Horsman: 1937. All composition: 14" - $225.00, $90.00. Composition/cloth: 16" - $185.00, $80.00.

Jojo: 1937. All composition. 12" - $175.00, $75.00. 16" - $225.00, $100.00.

Life-size Baby: Plastic/vinyl. 26" - $250.00, $100.00.

Lullabye Baby: 1964, 1967. Cloth/vinyl. Music box in body. 12" - $20.00, $8.00. All vinyl: 12" - $15.00, $5.00.

Mary Poppins: 1964: 12" - $35.00, $15.00; 16" - $70.00, $30.00; 26" (1966) - $200.00, $100.00; 36" - $350.00, $175.00. In box with "Michael" and "Wendy": 12" and 8" - $150.00.

Mama Style Babies: 1920s–1930s. Composition/cloth. Marked "E.I.H" or "Horsman." 14" - $165.00, $85.00; 18" - $225.00, $100.00. **Girl Dolls:** 14" - $250.00, $90.00; 18" - $300.00, $125.00; 24" - $385.00, $165.00. **Hard plastic/cloth:** 16" - $75.00; $35.00; 22" - $90.00, $40.00. **Vinyl/cloth:** 16" - $20.00, $8.00; 22" - $30.00, $15.00.

Michael: (Mary Poppins) 1965. 8" - $30.00, $15.00.

Mousketeer: 1971. Boy or girl. 8" - $30.00, $15.00.

Patty Duke: 1965. Posable arms. 12" - $45.00, $18.00.

Peek-A-Boo: Designed by Grace Drayton. Cloth and composition. 7½–8" - $145.00 up.

Peggy: 1957. All vinyl child. One-piece body and legs. 25" - $85.00, $40.00.

16" "Miss Top Knot" by Horsman. Plastic and vinyl with sleep eyes. All original. Marked "Horsman 1964." (Also sold as "Peggy" and "Peggy Ann.") $40.00.

13" "Perthy" made of vinyl with rooted hair, glass eyes, and smile. Made in 1961. Mint and all original. Marked "14-Horsman" on body. Mint/original with tag - $50.00; played with - $22.00. *Courtesy Jeannie Mauldin.*

Peggy Pen Pal: 1970. Multi-jointed arms. Plastic/vinyl. 18" - $40.00, $20.00.

Pippi Longstocking: 1972. Vinyl/cloth. 1972. 18" - $35.00, $15.00.

Polly & Pete: 1957. All vinyl Black dolls with molded hair. 13" - $245.00, $60.00.

Poor Pitiful Pearl: 1963, 1976. 12" - $50.00, $25.00; 17" - $100.00, $50.00.

Peterkin: 1915–1930. All composition. Painted googly-style eyes. 12" - $300.00, $115.00.

Pudgie Baby: Plastic/vinyl. 1978: 12" - $35.00, $15.00. 1980: 24" - $50.00, $30.00.

Pudgy: 1974. All vinyl, very large painted eyes. 12½" - $35.00, $15.00.

Roberta: 1928: All composition. 1937: Molded hair or wigs. 14" - $250.00, $90.00; 20" - $325.00, $125.00. 24" - $325.00, $150.00.

Rosebud: 1928. Composition/cloth. Dimples and smile. Sleep eyes and wig. Marked with name. 14" - $250.00, $90.00; 18" - $300.00, $125.00. 24" - $385.00, $165.00.

Ruthie: 1958–1966. All vinyl or plastic/vinyl. 14" - $22.00, $8.00; 20" - $38.00, $12.00.

Sleepy Baby: 1965. Vinyl/cloth. Eyes molded closed. 24" - $50.00, $25.00.

Tuffie: 1966. All vinyl. Upper lip molded over lower. 16" - $50.00, $20.00.

Tynie Baby: See that section.

12" girl is one of the "Pip Squeeks" - a singing group composed of two girls and two boys. Plastic and vinyl with freckles, molded tongue, and painted features. Original. Marked "Horsman Dolls, Inc./1967/0712-A." $25.00. *Courtesy Kathy Tvrdik.*

HOYER, MARY

The Mary Hoyer Doll Mfg. Co. operated in Reading, Pa. from 1925. The dolls were made in all composition, all hard plastic, and last ones produced were in plastic and vinyl. Older dolls are marked in a circle on back "Original Mary Hoyer Doll" or "The Mary Hoyer Doll" embossed on lower back.

First price is for perfect doll in tagged factory clothes. Second price for perfect doll in outfits made from Mary Hoyer patterns and third price is for redressed doll in good condition with only light craze to composition or slight soil to others.

Composition: 14" - $475.00, $385.00 up, $165.00.

Hard Plastic: 14" - $425.00 up, $400.00, $195.00; 17" - $565.00 up, $500.00, $250.00.

Plastic/Vinyl: 14–15" (Margie). Marked "AE23." 12" - $145.00, $70.00, $15.00; 14" - $200.00, $95.00; $30.00.

14" hard plastic Mary Hoyer girl and boy. Mint with original boxes. Outfits are made from Hoyer patterns. Mint in box, each - $575.00 up. *Courtesy Peggy Pergarde.*

All of these Mary Hoyer dolls are made of hard plastic or composition and are original. Mint condition. Each - $425.00–800.00. *Courtesy Patricia Wood.*

First prices are for mint condition dolls. Second prices are for cracked, crazed, dirty, soiled or not original dolls.

April Showers: 1968. Battery operated. Splashes with hands and head turns. (See photo in Series 7, pg. 242.) 14" - $28.00, $15.00.

Baby Belly Button: 1970. Plastic/vinyl. **White:** 9" - $18.00, $7.00. **Black:** 9" - $25.00, $12.00.

Baby Crissy: 1973–1975. Pull string to make hair grow. **White:** 24" - $85.00, $35.00. **Black:** 24" - $100.00, $45.00. Re-issued in 1981: No grow hair. 24" - $40.00, $15.00.

Baby Snooks (Fannie Brice) and other Flexies: Wire and composition. 12" - $285.00 up, $100.00.

Bam-Bam: 1963. Plastic/vinyl or all vinyl. 12" - $18.00, $8.00; 16" - $28.00, $10.00.

Batgirl and other Female Super Heroes: Vinyl. (See photo in Series 7, pg. 243.) 12" - $150.00, $60.00.

Betsy McCall: See that section.

Betsy Wetsy: 1937 on. Composition head. Excellent rubber body. 13" - $95.00, $20.00; 16" - $125.00, $35.00. **Hard plastic/vinyl:** 12" - $75.00, $20.00; 14" - $90.00, $35.00. **All vinyl:** 12" - $25.00, $9.00; 18" - $55.00, $20.00.

Betty Big Girl: 1968. Plastic/vinyl. 30" - $245.00, $95.00.

Betty Jane: 1930s–1944. Shirley Temple type. All composition, sleep eyes, open mouth. 14" - $185.00, $90.00; 16" - $265.00, $100.00; 24" - $300.00, $145.00.

Blessed Event: 1951. Called "Kiss Me." Cloth body with plunger in back to make doll cry or pout. Vinyl head with eyes almost squinted closed. 21" - $165.00, $50.00.

Bonnie Braids: 1951. Hard plastic/vinyl head. (See photo in Series 7, pg. 245.) 13" - $65.00, $25.00. **Baby:** 13" - $55.00; $15.00.

30" "Betty Big Girl" of 1968. A happy and beautiful smiling child. Plastic and vinyl with sleep eyes and rooted hair. Artistic detailed hands. $245.00 up. *Courtesy Jeannie Mauldin.*

Bonnie Walker: 1956. Hard plastic. Pin-jointed hips. Open mouth, flirty eyes. Marked "Ideal W-25." 23" - $85.00, $35.00.

Brandi: 1972. Of Crissy family. 18" - $50.00, $20.00.

Brother/Baby Coos: 1951. Cloth/composition with hard plastic head. 25" - $100.00, $60.00. Composition head/latex: 24" - $35.00, $10.00. Hard plastic head/vinyl: 24" - $65.00, $20.00.

Busy Lizy: 1971. 17" - $25.00, $15.00.

Bye Bye Baby: 1960. Lifelike modeling. 12" - $150.00, $35.00; 25" - $350.00, $150.00.

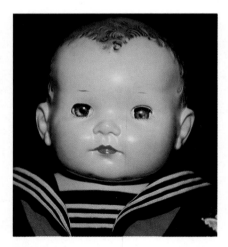

30" "Brother Coos" from 1950. Also called "Magic Squeezums." Hard plastic head and shoulder plate with cloth body and composition limbs. Sleep eyes. $85.00 up. *Courtesy Jeannie Mauldin.*

Captain Action: 1966. Extra joints. (Add $50.00 if mint in box.) 11½" - $75.00 up. As Batman, etc.: $95.00 up.

Cinnamon: 1971. Of Crissy family. 12" - $45.00, $20.00. **Black:** $60.00, $30.00. **Hair Doodler:** $35.00. **Curly Ribbons:** $40.00.

Composition Child: All composition girl with sleep eyes, some flirty. Open mouth. Original clothes. Excellent condition. Marked "Ideal" and a number or "Ideal" in a diamond. 14" - $165.00, $70.00; 18" - $250.00, $90.00; 22" - $300.00, $100.00. **Cloth body:** With straight composition legs. 14" - $125.00, $45.00; 18" - $185.00, $70.00; 22" - $200.00, $80.00.

Composition Baby: 1930s–1940s. (Also see "Mama Dolls.") Composition head and limbs with cloth body. Closed mouth. Sleep eyes, allow more for flirty eyes. Original. In excellent condition. 16" - $200.00, $85.00; 18" - $225.00, $90.00; 22" - $285.00, $125.00; 25" - $365.00, $150.00. **Flirty eyes:** 16" - $225.00, $90.00; 18" - $285.00, $100.00.

Cricket: 1970–1971. Of Crissy family. 18" - $40.00, $15.00. **Black:** $50.00, $20.00. **Look-a-round:** $45.00, $20.00.

Crissy: 1968–1971. 18" - $45.00, $15.00. **Black:** $60.00, $30.00. **Look-a-round:** 1972. $40.00, $20.00. **Talking:** 1971. $50.00, $30.00. **Floor length hair:** First issue in 1968. $145.00, $60.00. **Moving:** $45.00, $20.00. **Swirls Curler:** 1973. $40.00, $20.00. **Twirly Beads:** 1974. $35.00, $15.00. **Hair Magic:** 1977. No ponytail. $35.00, $15.00.

Daddy's Girl: 1961–1962. 42" - $850.00 up, $300.00 up.

Deanna Durbin: 1939. All composition. 14" - $500.00, $200.00; 17" - $600.00, $200.00; 21" - $725.00, $300.00; 24" - $800.00, $325.00; 27" - $1,000.00 up, $400.00.

Diana Ross: Plastic/vinyl. 18" - $150.00, $70.00.

Dina: 1972. Of Crissy family. 15" - $50.00, $20.00.

Doctor Evil: 1965. Multi-jointed. Came with face masks. 11" - $55.00 up, $15.00.

Dodi: 1964. Of Tammy family. Marked "1964-Ideal-D0-9E." 9" - $40.00, $10.00.

Dorothy Hammill: 1977. 11½" - $25.00, $8.00.

Electro-Man: 1977. Switch sets off alarm. Activated by beam of light. 16" - $200.00.

Eric: 1976. Tuesday Taylor's boyfriend. 12½" - $35.00, $15.00.

Flatsy: 1968–1970. Set of nine in frames. 5" - $15.00 each, $5.00 each. **Fashion:** 1969. 8" - $15.00 each, $6.00 each.

Flexies: 1940s. Composition and wire. Soldier, children, Fanny Brice, etc. 12" - $285.00 up, $100.00.

Flossie Flirt: 1938–1945. Cloth/composition. **Flirty eyes:** 20" - $265.00, $95.00; 24" - $350.00, $125.00. **Black:** $400.00, $150.00.

21" "Deanna Durbin" made of all composition. Sleep eyes and open mouth. Mint and all original. Mint - $725.00 up; played with - $300.00. *Courtesy Martha Sweeney.*

Note condition of the doll's eyes. These eyes, manufactured in the 1930s, crazed over time.

Giggles: Plastic/vinyl. 16" - $45.00, $20.00; 18" - $65.00, $35.00. **Black:** 18" - $125.00, $75.00. **Baby:** 16" - $40.00, $20.00.

Goody Two Shoes: 1965. 18" - $165.00, $45.00. **Walking/talking:** 27" - $225.00, $70.00.

Harmony: 1971. Battery operated. 21" - $50.00, $35.00.

Harriet Hubbard Ayer: 1953. Hard plastic/vinyl. 15" - $200.00 up, $70.00; 17" - $300.00 up, $125.00.

Honey Moon: 1965. From "Dick Tracy." White yarn hair, magic skin body. 15" - $50.00, 10.00. **Cloth/vinyl:** $65.00, $30.00.

22" "Harmony" made by Ideal. Extra joints at elbows, wrists, waist. Legs are molded with knees in slightly bent position. Battery operated, strums guitar. All original. $50.00.

Howdy Doody: 1940s. Composition head. Composition/cloth body. Floating disc eyes. Mouth moves by string in back of head. Original cowboy clothes. (See photo in Series 8, pg. 240.) 20" - $225.00 up.

Joan Palooka: 1952. 14" - $90.00, $45.00.

Joey Stivic (Baby): 1976. One-piece body and limbs. Sexed boy. 15" - $40.00, $20.00.

Jiminy Cricket: 1939–1940. Composition/wood. 9" - $275.00, $125.00.

Judy Garland: 1939. All composition. 14" - $1,000.00, $400.00; 18" - $1,400.00 up, $500.00. Marked with backward "21": From 1941. 21" - $625.00, $225.00.

Judy Splinters: 1951. Cloth/vinyl/latex. Yarn hair, painted eyes. 18" - $165.00, $45.00; 22" - $235.00, $75.00; 36" - $400.00, $125.00.

Katie Kachoo: 1968. Raise arm and she sneezes. $35.00; $15.00.

Kerry: 1971. Of Crissy family. 18" - $45.00, $15.00.

King Little: 1940. Composition/wood. 14" - $325.00, $100.00.

Kiss Me: 1951. See "Blessed Event."

Kissy: 22" - $50.00, $35.00. **Black:** $100.00, $40.00. **Cuddly:** 1964. Cloth/vinyl. 17" - $40.00, $20.00.

Kissy, Tiny: 1962. 16" - $40.00, $15.00. **Black:** $75.00, $30.00. **Baby:** 1966. Kisses when stomach is pressed. 12" - $30.00, $10.00.

Liberty Boy: 1918. 12" - $300.00, $85.00.

Little Lost Baby: 1968. Three-faced doll. (See photo in Series 7, pg. 249.) 22" - $75.00, $45.00.

Magic Lips: 1955. Vinyl coated cloth/vinyl. Lower teeth. 24" - $65.00, $35.00.

Mama Style Dolls: 1920–1930s. **Composition/cloth:** 16" - $200.00, $85.00; 18" - $285.00, $95.00; 24" -

$325.00, $125.00. **Hard plastic/cloth:** 18" - $85.00, $35.00; 23" - $125.00, $45.00.

Mary Hartline: 1952 on. All hard plastic. (See photo in Series 8, pg. 241.) 15" - $400.00, $100.00; 21–23": $650.00 up, $250.00.

Mary Jane or Betty Jane: All composition, sleep and/or flirty eyes, open mouth. Marked "Ideal 18": 18" - $250.00 up, $100.00. 21" - $325.00, $175.00.

Mia: 1970. Of Crissy family. 15½" - $45.00, $20.00.

Mini Monsters: (Dracky, Franky, etc.) 8½" - $20.00, $15.00.

Miss Clairol (Glamour Misty): 1965. Marked "W-12-3." 12" - $45.00, $20.00.

Miss Curity: 1952 on. **Hard plastic:** 14" - $300.00 up, $100.00. **Composition:** 21" - $450.00, $125.00.

Miss Ideal: 1961. Multi-jointed. 25" - $375.00 up, $100.00; 28" - $425.00, $165.00.

Miss Revlon: 1956–on. 10½" - $85.00, $35.00; 17" - $165.00 up, $65.00. 20" - $200.00, $95.00. **In box or trunk:** 20" - $450.00; $125.00.

Mitzi: 1960. Teen. 12" - $75.00 up, $40.00.

Mortimer Snerd and Other Flexie Dolls: 1939. Composition and wire. 12" - $285.00 up, $100.00.

Patti Playpal: 1960–on. 30" - $185.00, $100.00; 36" - $285.00, $135.00. **Black:** 30" - $300.00, $125.00; 36" - $425.00, $185.00.

Pebbles: 1963. Plastic/vinyl and all vinyl. 8" - $18.00, $8.00; 12" - $30.00, $15.00; 15" - $45.00, $25.00.

Penny Playpal: 1959. 32" - $150.00, $75.00.

Pepper: 1964. Freckles. Marked "Ideal - P9-3." 9" - $40.00, $25.00.

Pete: 1964. Freckles. Marked "Ideal - P8." 7½" - $40.00, $25.00.

Peter Playpal: 1961. 36-38" - $425.00, $200.00.

28" "Miss Ideal" has extra joints at wrist, waist, and above knees. Made in 1961. Shown with original box. Mint, unplayed with - $425.00 up. Played with - $165.00.
Courtesy Jeannie Mauldin.

15½" "Patti Playpal" with cloth body and vinyl head and limbs. Sleep eyes and wide open mouth with two teeth. Plastic circle and handle attached to head to move mouth. Marked "1970 Ideal Toy Corp./ 16/H/162." $45.00 up. *Courtesy Kathy Tvrdik.*

Pinocchio: 1938–1941. Composition/wood. (See photo in Series 8, pg. 243.) Mint condition: 10" - $300.00; 12" - $385.00. Near mint: 10" - $225.00; 12" - $300.00, $100.00; 21" - $650.00, $200.00.

Pixie: 1967. Foam body. 16" - $20.00, $10.00.

Posey (Posie): 1953–1956. Hard plastic with vinyl head. Jointed knees. Marked "Ideal VP-17." 17" - $85.00, $35.00.

Real Live Baby: 1965. Head bobs. 20" - $30.00, $15.00.

Sally-Sallykins: 1934. Composition/cloth. Flirty eyes, two upper and lower teeth. 14" - $150.00, $75.00; 19" - $225.00, $95.00; 25" - $300.00, $125.00.

Samantha The Witch: 1965. Green eyes. Marked "M-12-E-2." 12" - $125.00, $45.00.

Sandy McCall: See Betsy McCall section.

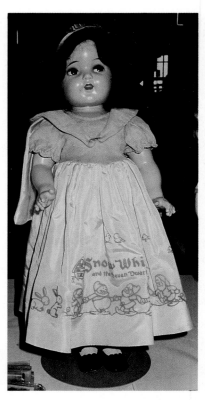

22" all composition "Snow White" from 1937. Flirty sleep eyes/lashes and open mouth. Original. On marked Shirley Temple body. Near mint condition - **$625.00.** *Courtesy Martha Sweeney.*

"Smokey" with vinyl face and plush body. Inset eyes. Cloth stuffed legs sewn on. Shovel included. Note on box: "By the makers of the world's first Teddy Bear." In box - **$250.00**; played with - **$75.00 up.** *Courtesy Shirley Bertrand.*

Sara Ann: 1952 on. Hard plastic. Marked "P-90." (See photo in Series 7, pg. 248.) Saran wig: 14" - $185.00 up, $75.00. Marked "P-93": 21" - $350.00 up, $125.00.

Saralee: 1950. Cloth/vinyl. **Black:** 18" - $285.00, $145.00.

Sara Stimson: (Little Miss Marker) 1980. Marked "1979." $25.00, $10.00.

Saucy Walker: 1951 on. 16" - $85.00, $30.00; 17" - $100.00, $40.00; 20" - $145.00, $45.00. **Black:** 18" - $185.00, $75.00.

Seven Dwarfs: Composition: 12" - $425.00 each; 16" - $575.00 each. Cloth body, composition head: 16" - $625.00 each; 18–20" - $750.00 each. Puppet: Cloth/composition. Pull string operates mouth. 20" - $485.00.

Shirley Temple: See that section.

Snoozie: 1933. Composition/cloth. Molded hair, sleep eyes, open yawning mouth. Marked "B Lipfert." 13" - $175.00, $50.00; 16" - $245.00, $100.00; 20" - $365.00, $150.00.

Snow White: 1937 on. All composition. Black wig. Sleep and/or flirty eyes. On marked Shirley Temple body. 12" - $475.00, $200.00; 18" - $545.00, $225.00. **Molded hair:** 1939. Eyes painted to side. 14" - $185.00, $85.00; 18" - $450.00, $145.00.

Sparkle Plenty: 1947. 15" - $40.00, $20.00.

Suzy Playpal: 1960–1961. Chubby vinyl body and limbs. Marked "Ideal O.E.B. 24-3." 24" - $125.00, $50.00.

Tabitha: 1966. Cloth/vinyl. Eyes painted to side. Marked "Tat-14-H-62" or "82." 15" - $50.00, $30.00.

Tara: 1976. Black doll with grows hair. 16" - $35.00, $15.00.

Tammy: 1962. 12" - $50.00, $20.00. **Black:** $60.00, $25.00. **Grown-up:** 1965. 12" - $45.00, $20.00.

Tammy's Mom: 1963. Eyes to side. Marked: "Ideal W-18-L." 12" - $60.00, $35.00.

Ted: 1963. Tammy's brother. Molded hair. Marked "Ideal B-12-U-2." 1963. 12½" - $50.00, $25.00.

Thumbelina: 1962 on. **Kissing:** 10½" - $20.00, $8.00. **Tearful:** 15" - $30.00, $12.00. **Wake Up:** 17" - $45.00, $20.00. **Black:** 10½" - $50.00, $20.00.

Tickletoes: 1930s. Composition/ cloth. 15" - $150.00, $85.00; 21" - $225.00, $100.00. **Magic Skin body:** 1948. Hard plastic head. 15" - $60.00, $15.00.

Tiffany Taylor: 1973. Top of head swivels to change hair color. 18" - $45.00, $15.00. **Black:** 18" - $60.00, $30.00.

Tippy or Timmy Tumbles: 16" - $30.00, $15.00. **Black:** $30.00, $20.00.

Toni: 1949–on. 14" P-90: 14" - $325.00 up, $85.00. P-91: 15" - $375.00 up, $95.00. P-92: 17–18" - $475.00 up, $100.00. P-93: 21" - $500.00 up, $165.00. P-94: 23" - $650.00 up, $200.00. **Walker:** $300.00 up, $75.00.

Tressy: Of Crissy family. 18" - $45.00, $20.00. **Black:** $60.00, $30.00.

Tribly: 1940s. Composition: Mint/ original. 15" - $295.00. **Three-faced baby:** 1951. Cloth/vinyl. 20" - $50.00, $25.00.

14" all hard plastic "Toni" with red nylon wig. All original with tagged dress. Marked "P-90." $325.00 up. *Courtesy Peggy Millhouse.*

Tubsy: 1966. Plastic/vinyl. Battery operated. 18" - $35.00, $15.00.

Tuesday Taylor: 1977. 11½–12" - $40.00, $10.00.

Uneeda Kid: 1914–1919. Looks like Schoenhut doll. Cloth body, composition head/limbs. Bent right arm. Painted eyes and hair. Yellow rain slicker and hat. Molded-on black boots. (See photo in Series 9, pg. 251.) 16" - $450.00, $150.00.

Upsy Dazy: 1972. Foam body. Stands on head. 15" - $25.00, $10.00.

Velvet: 1970–1971. Of Crissy family. 16" - $45.00, $15.00. **Black:** $85.00, $30.00. **Look-a-round:** $50.00, $20.00. **Talking:** $50.00, $30.00. **Moving:** $45.00, $15.00. **Beauty Braider:** 1973. $40.00, $15.00. **Surely Daisy:** 1974. $40.00, $15.00.

Wingy: Hard plastic body, vinyl head. From Dick Tracy comics. (See photo in Series 8, pg. 247.) 14" - $135.00 up.

IMCO

18" all hard plastic doll that is an Ideal "Saucy Walker" copy. Sleep eyes, open mouth, and pin-jointed hips. Marked "IMCO." $30.00. *Courtesy Kathy Tvrdik.*

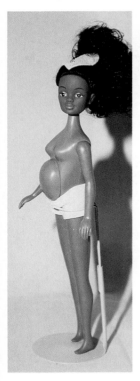 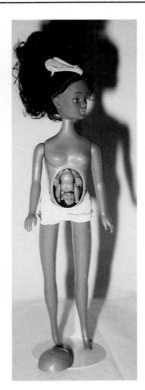 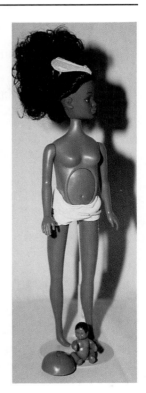

11½" "Mommy-To-Be" doll named "Judy" by the Judith Corp. of Glenview, IL. Was advertised by this corporation in 1992 and then for a short time they signed exclusively with FAO Schwarz. There is a father doll named "Charlie" that was also available. The buyer does not know if they will get a boy or a girl baby until stomach is removed. Plastic and vinyl doll comes in black and white versions. White doll is smiling. $20.00.

KENNER

First prices are for mint condition dolls; second prices are for played with, dirty or missing clothing and accessories.

Baby Bundles: 16"-$20.00, $10.00. **Black:** $28.00, $15.00.

Baby Yawnie: 1974. Cloth/vinyl. 15" - $25.00, $10.00.

Big Foot: All rigid vinyl. (See photo in Series 7, pg. 253.) 13" - $20.00, $9.00.

Butch Cassidy or Sundance Kid: 4" - $18.00, $9.00 each.

Blythe: 1972. Pull string to change the color of eyes. 11½" - $40.00, $10.00.

Charlie Chaplin: 1973. All cloth with walking mechanism. 14" - $75.00, $35.00.

Cover Girls: (Darci, Erica, Dana, etc.) 12½", white. $35.00, $12.00. **Black:** $40.00, $15.00.

Crumpet: 1970. Plastic/vinyl. 18" - $35.00, $20.00.

Dana: 1978. Black doll. 12½" - $35.00, $10.00.

Darci: 1978. Blonde. 12½" - $30.00, $10.00.

Dusty: 12". $25.00, $10.00.

Erica: 1978. Red hair. 12½" - $30.00, $10.00.

Gabbigale: 1972. 18" - $40.00, $15.00. **Black:** $45.00, $20.00.

Garden Gals: 1972. Hand bent to hold watering can. 6½" - $10.00, $4.00.

Hardy Boys: 1978. Shaun Cassidy and Parker Stevenson. 12" - $18.00, $6.00.

International Velvet: 1976. Tatum O'Neill. 11½" - $20.00, $9.00.

Jenny Jones and Baby: 1973. All vinyl. 9" Jenny and 2½" baby. $15.00, $6.00. Set - $25.00, $8.00.

Skye: Black doll. 12" - $25.00, $10.00.

Star Wars: 1974–1978. Large size figures. **R2-D2:** 7½" - $150.00 up, $40.00. **C-3PO:** 12" - $150.00 up, $50.00. **Darth Vader:** 15" - $175.00 up, $25.00. **Boba Fett:** 13" - $250.00 up, $50.00. **Jawa:** 8½" - $65.00, $20.00. **IG-88:** 15" - $375.00 up, $65.00. **Stormtrooper:** 12" - $200.00 up, $40.00. **Leia:** 11½" - $145.00 up, $25.00. **Han Solo:** 12" - $145.00, $25.00. **Luke Skywalker:** 13½" - $195.00, $25.00. **Chewbacca:** 15" - $125.00 up, $40.00. **Obi Wan Kenobi:** 12" - $195.00, $45.00. **Yoda:** 9" - $90.00 up. **Star Wars Characters, MIB:** Sealed box. Any of above - $595.00 up.

Strawberry Shortcake: 1980s. 4½–5". Each - $12.00 up. **Sleep eyes:** Each - $25.00. **Sour Grapes, etc.:** 9" characters. $15.00. **Mint in box:** 4½–5". Each - $18.00.

Steve Scout: 1974. 9" - $18.00, $8.00. **Black:** $25.00, $10.00.

Sweet Cookie: 1972. 18" - $30.00, $12.00.

12" **"Erica Cover Girl" with bendable knees and elbows. Jointed wrists. Original. Marked "Kenner 1978/Made in Hong Kong." $30.00.** *Courtesy Kathy Tvrdik.*

6" **"Super Ninja" with face mask and 6" "Chuck Norris" as Kung Fu Training G.I. is part of the "Karate Kommandos" by Kenner. Made in 1986. Each - $22.00.** *Courtesy Don Tvrdik.*

13" "IG-88" and 12" "Boba Fett" from *Star Wars* movie. "IG-88" is missing his weapons; "Boba Fett" is missing his cape. Both marked "G.M.F.G.I. 1978 Kenner." "IG-88" complete set - $375.00 up; "Boba Fett" complete set - $250.00 up. *Courtesy Don Tvrdik.*

15" "Darth Vader" and 13" "Stormtrooper" from *Star Wars* movie. Both marked "Kenner." "Darth Vader" complete set with weapons - $175.00. "Stormtrooper" complete set with weapons - $250.00. *Courtesy Don Tvrdik.*

8¼" "Jawa" and 9" "Yoda" from *Star Wars.* Jawa is marked "Kenner." "Yoda" is marked "Lucas Films Ltd. 1981/ Made in Hong Kong." "Jawa" - $65.00; "Yoda" - $90.00. *Courtesy Don Tvrdik.*

First prices are for mint condition dolls; second prices are for dolls played with, crazed or cracked, dirty, soiled or not original.

Bisque Kewpies: See antique Kewpie section.

All Composition: Jointed shoulder only. 9" - $165.00, $70.00; 14" - $250.00, $100.00. **Jointed hips, neck and shoulder:** 9" - $250.00, $100.00; 14" - $375.00, $150.00. **Black:** 12" - $400.00.

Talcum powder container: 7-8" - $165.00.

Celluloid: (See photo in Series 8, pg. 253.) 2" - $35.00; 5" - $75.00; 9" - $125.00. **Black:** 5" - $150.00.

Bean bag body: Must be clean. 10" - $40.00, $15.00.

13" all composition "Kewpie" dolls dressed in original outfits. (One missing shoes and socks.) Jointed at neck, shoulders, and hips. One on left in fair condition. One on right is near mint. **$100.00–250.00.** *Courtesy Frasher Doll Auctions.*

Cloth Body: Vinyl head and limbs. 16" - $200.00, $95.00. **Composition head:** $465.00 up.

Kewpie Gal: With molded hair/ribbon. 8" - $45.00, $15.00.

Hard Plastic: 1950s. One-piece body and head. 8" - $95.00, $25.00; 12" - $225.00, $95.00; 16" - $350.00, $145.00. Fully jointed at shoulder, neck and hips: 12–13" - $385.00, $175.00; 16" - $500.00, $225.00.

Ragsy: 1964. Vinyl. One-piece molded-on clothes with heart on chest. 8" - $40.00, $20.00. Without heart: 1971. 8" - $20.00, $10.00.

Thinker: 1971. One-piece vinyl. Sitting down. 4" - $20.00, $8.00.

Kewpie: Vinyl. **Jointed at shoulder only:** 9" - $45.00, $15.00; 12" - $75.00, $20.00; 14" - $90.00, $30.00.

"Kewpie Gal" from 1950. All vinyl with velvet ribbon through head. Original. $45.00.

Jointed at neck, shoulders and hips: 9" - $80.00, $25.00; 12" - $135.00, $35.00; 14" - $185.00, $50.00; 27" - $350.00, $165.00. Not jointed at all: 9" - $25.00, $10.00; 12" - $45.00, $15.00; 14" - $60.00, $20.00. Black: 9" - $50.00, $15.00; 12" - $75.00, $25.00; 14" - $125.00, $45.00. Bean bag type body: 1970s. Vinyl head. 10" - $40.00, $15.00.

Ward's Anniversary: 1972. 8" - $60.00, $20.00.

All Cloth: Made by Kreuger. All one-piece: Including clothing. 12" - $185.00, $90.00; 16" - $350.00, $100.00;

20" - $485.00, $175.00. Removable dress and bonnet: 12" - $265.00, $85.00; 16" - $400.00, $145.00; 20" - $600.00, $200.00; 25" - $1,200.00, $500.00.

Kewpie Baby: 1960s. With hinged joints. 15" - $195.00, $80.00; 18" - $265.00, $95.00.

Kewpie Baby: One-piece stuffed body and limbs. 15" - $165.00, $80.00; 18" - $185.00, $70.00.

Plush: 1960s. Usually red body with vinyl face mask. Made by Knickerbocker. 6" - $35.00, $15.00; 10" - $50.00, $20.00.

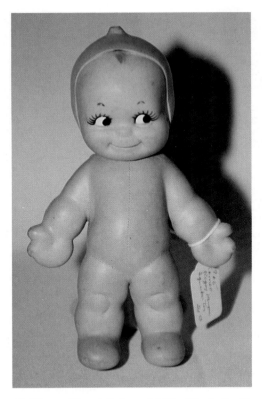

7" "Ragsy Kewpie" from 1965. All vinyl with jointed neck only. Marked "Cameo '64." $40.00.

KLUMPE

Two Klumpe figures made of felt and cloth with oil-painted features. Made in Spain. Left: 11" early 1960s fisherman. Tagged "Klumpe No. 22AA." Right: 11" early 1960s balladeer with felt ears and mohair wig. Tagged "Klumpe No. 10BB." Prices are for both dolls. 1960s - $125.00; 1970s - $95.00; 1980s - $90.00.

KNICKERBOCKER TOY COMPANY

First prices are for mint condition dolls; second prices are for dolls played with, crazed or cracked, dirty, soiled or not original.

Alexander: Comic character from "Blondie." All composition, painted hair and features. 9" - $350.00 up, $125.00.

Bozo Clown: 14" - $30.00; 24" - $80.00.

Cinderella: With two heads - one is sad; the other with tiara. 16" - $25.00.

Clown: Cloth. 17" - $20.00.

Composition Child: 1938–on. Bent right arm at elbow. 15" - $245.00 up.

Daddy Warbucks: 1982. 7" - $18.00, $9.00.

Dagwood: Composition, painted hair and features. 14" - $650.00, $275.00.

Flintstones: 17" - $35.00 each.

Kewpie: See Kewpie section.

Levi Rag Doll: All cloth. 15" - $12.00.

Little House on the Prairie: 1978. 12" - $22.00 each.

Little Orphan Annie: 1982. 6" - $18.00, $6.00.

Lord of Rings: 5" - $10.00 each.

Mickey Mouse: 1930–1940s. 18" - $1,200.00 up.

Miss Hannigan: 7" - $15.00, $9.00.

Molly: 5½" - $15.00, $7.00.

Pinocchio: All plush and cloth. 13" - $185.00 up. All composition: 13" - $350.00 up.

Punjab: 7" - $20.00, $9.00.

Scarecrow: Made of cloth. 23½" - $200.00 up.

Seven Dwarfs: 10" all composition. Each - $265.00 up. All cloth: 14" - $300.00 each.

Sleeping Beauty: 1939. All composition. Bent right arm. 15" - $325.00 up; 18" - $465.00.

Snow White: 1937. All composition. Bent right arm. Black wig. 15" - $350.00 up; 20" - $465.00 up. Molded hair and ribbon: 13" - $285.00.

Soupy Sales: 1966. Vinyl and cloth. Non-removeable clothes. 13" - $125.00.

Two-headed Dolls: 1960s. Vinyl face masks - one crying, one smiling. 12" - $20.00.

"Snow White and Seven Dwarfs" made by Knickerbocker. Made of all composition. All original. 15" "Snow White" has joints at hips, neck, and shoulders. Molded hair ribbon and painted features. "Dwarfs" are jointed at shoulders only and have painted features. Shown with 18" Madame Alexander "Snow White" from 1952. 15" - $285.00; Dwarfs, each - $265.00; 18" - $800.00. *Courtesy Frasher Doll Auctions.*

MATTEL

First prices are for mint condition dolls; second prices are for dolls that have been played with, are dirty, soiled, not original and/or do not have accessories.

Allan: 12" - $60.00. In box - $150.00 up.

Baby First Step: 1964. 18" - $30.00, $15.00. Talking: $35.00, $15.00.

Baby Go Bye Bye: 1968. 12" - $16.00, $8.00.

Baby's Hungry: 1966. 17" - $30.00, $15.00.

Baby Love Light: 1970. Battery operated. 16" - $20.00, $10.00.

Baby Pataburp: 13" - $35.00, $15.00.

Baby Play-A-Lot: 1971. 16" - $25.00, $10.00.

Baby Say 'n See: 1965. 17" - $25.00, $10.00.

Baby Secret: 1965. 18" - $40.00, $15.00.

Baby Small Talk: 1967. 11" - $20.00, $8.00. **Cinderella:** $25.00, $10.00. **Black:** $35.00, $15.00.

Baby Tenderlove: 1969. **Newborn:** 13" - $15.00, $5.00. **Talking:** 1969. 16" - $20.00, $10.00. **Living:** 1970. 20" - $30.00. **Molded hair piece:** 1972. 11½" - $35.00. **Brother:** 1972. Sexed. 13" - $40.00.

Baby Teenie Talk: 1965. 17" - $35.00, $12.00.

Baby Walk 'n Play: 1968. 11" - $20.00, $8.00.

Baby Walk 'n See: 18" - $25.00, $15.00.

Barbie: See that section.

20" "Chatty Cathy" in mint condition with original box. Pull string talker. Mint - $185.00 up; played with - $60.00.
Courtesy Peggy Pergande.

11" "Tiny Baby Tenderlove" with vinyl hair piece attached to vinyl head. One-piece body and limbs. Painted eyes, open/closed laughing mouth. Original. Marked "1971 Mattel, Inc. Mexico." $20.00.
Courtesy Kathy Tvrdik.

Bozo: 18" - $35.00, $15.00.

Brad: 1971. Bend knees. $90.00. **Talking:** 1970. $85.00.

Bucky Love Notes: 1974. Press body parts for tunes. 12" - $18.00.

Buffie: 1967. With Mrs. Beasley. 6" - $50.00, $15.00; 10" - $60.00, $20.00.

Capt. Lazer: 1967. (See photo in Series 9, pg. 259.) 12½" - $250.00 up, $50.00.

Cara: Free Movin': 1975. Black doll. $70.00.

Casey: 1975. 11½" - $95.00 up.

Casper The Ghost: 1964: 16" - $35.00, $15.00. 1971: 5" - $20.00, $7.00.

Charlie's Angels: 1978. Marked "1966." 11½" - $20.00, $8.00.

Charmin' Chatty: 1961. 25" - $135.00, $50.00.

Chatty Brother, Tiny: 1963. 15" - $35.00, $10.00. **Baby:** 1962. $30.00, $10.00. **Black:** $45.00, $20.00.

Chatty Cathy: 1962 on. 20" - $60.00, $30.00. **Brunette:** Brown eyes. $85.00, $35.00. **Black:** $200.00, $55.00.

Cheerleader: 1965. 13" - $25.00, $9.00.

Cheerful Tearful: 1965. 13" - $25.00, $8.00. **Tiny:** 1966. 6½" - $15.00, $6.00.

Christie: 1968. Black doll. 11½" - $75.00 up. **Talking:** 1969. $90.00 up. **Super Star:** 1976. $50.00 up. **Kissing:** 1979. $40.00. **Golden Dream:** 1980. $35.00.

Curtis: Free Movin': 1976. $65.00.

Cynthia: 1971. 20" - $50.00, $25.00.

Dancerina: 1968. 24" - $45.00, $20.00. **Black:** $70.00, $30.00. **Baby: Not battery operated:** $35.00, $15.00. **Black:** $50.00, $25.00.

Debbie Boone: 1978. (See photo in Series 9, pg. 261.) 11½" - $22.00, $9.00.

Dick Van Dyke: 25" - $90.00, $45.00.

Donny Osmond: 1978. Marked "1968." 12" - $18.00, $9.00.

Drowsy: 1966. Pull string talker. 15" - $20.00, $8.00.

Dr. Doolittle: 1967. Talker. **Cloth/ vinyl:** 22½" - $65.00, $25.00. **All vinyl:** 6" - $25.00, $7.00.

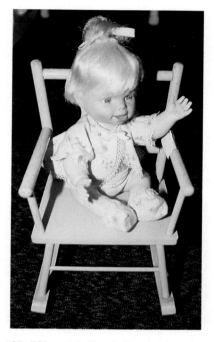

13" "Cheerful Tearful" changes her expression when her arm is rotated. Has painted eyes. Mint and all original. From 1965. $25.00. *Courtesy Jeannie Mauldin.*

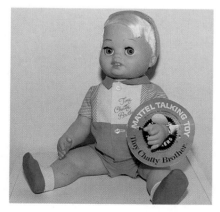

15" "Tiny Chatty Baby" and "Tiny Chatty Brother" are both pull string talkers. Mint as possible; never played with. "Baby" is from 1962; "Brother" is from 1963. Mint - 70.00 each. Played with - $35.00 each. *Courtesy Chris Johnson.*

Fluff: 9" - $50.00 up.

Francie: 1966. (See photo in Series 8, pg. 265.) 11½" - $100.00 up. **Black:** 1967. $400.00 up. **Twist n' Turn:** 1967. $75.00. **Busy Hands:** 1972. $60.00. **Quick Curl:** 1973. $45.00. **Malibu:** 1978. $35.00. **Grow Pretty Hair:** $90.00. **Hair Happening:** $150.00.

Grandma Beans: 11" - $15.00, $8.00.

Gorgeous Creatures: 1979. Mae West style body with animal heads. Each - $30.00, $10.00.

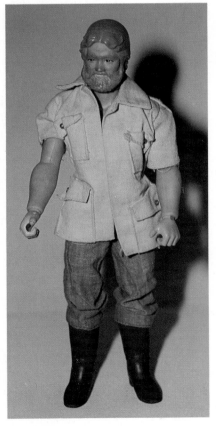

One of the "Perfume Kiddles" made in 1966. Every "Kiddle" is collectible and adorable. $25.00. *Courtesy Kathy Tvrdik.*

10" "Grizzly Adams" has molded hair and beard. Extra joints. Lever on back makes arm move. Marked "1971 Mattel Inc. U.S. & Foreign Patented/Hong Kong." $30.00. *Courtesy Don Tvrdik.*

Grizzly Adams: 1971. 10" - $30.00, $15.00.

Guardian Goddesses: 1979. Each: 11½" - $185.00 up.

Herman Munster: 16" - $40.00, $15.00.

Heros In Action: 1975. Set of 14. Marked "Mattel Hong Kong. Pat Pending." 3" - $30.00 each.

Hi Dottie: 1969. 17" - $30.00, $15.00.

Honey Hill Bunch: 1975. Set of six. 6" - $15.00, $3.00.

How West Was Won: 1971. 10" - $30.00. Indians: 10" - $35.00.

Hush Lil Baby: 15" - $15.00, $8.00.

Jamie, Walking: 1969. With dog. (See photo in Series 8, pg. 265.) 11½" - $250.00 up.

Jimmy Osmond: 1979. 10" - $18.00, $9.00.

Julia: 1969. Nurse from TV show by same name.11½" - $150.00 up. **Talking:** $175.00 up.

Lil Big Guy: 13" - $15.00, $8.00.
Kelly: 1973. Quick Curl: $95.00.
Yellowstone: 1974. $70.00.

Ken: Flocked hair: $125.00 up.
Molded hair: Non-bending knees.
$125.00 up. **Malibu:** $25.00 up. **Live
Action:** $50.00 up. **Mod hair:** $25.00
up. **Busy:** $50.00 up. **Talking:** $150.00
up. **Bend knees:** $325.00 up. **Hawaii:**
$50.00. **Talking:** 1970. $150.00.

Kiddles: 1966–on. **With cars:**
$50.00 up. **With planes:** $55.00 up. **In
ice cream cones:** $25.00 up. **In jew-
elry:** $35.00 up. **In perfume bottles:**
$20.00 up. **In bottles:** $35.00 up. **With
cup and saucer:** $100.00 up.
Storybooks: With accessories. $125.00.
Mint in box - $200.00 up. **Baby Biddle:**
In carriage. $175.00 up. **Peter Paniddle:**
Made one year. With accessories.
$150.00. Mint in box - $300.00. **Santa:**
Complete - $125.00 up. **Tinkerbelle:**
Mint - $80.00. Fair condition - $30.00.
Animals: $40.00 up. **Circus necklace:**
1968. $60.00 each.

Kitty O'Neill: 1978. (See photo
in Series 9, pg. 261.) 11½" - $25.00,
$9.00.

Midge: 1963. Freckles. 11½" -
$145.00 up. 1965: Bendable legs. $90.00
up.

Miss America: 1972. Walk Lively.
White gown. $245.00. 1974: Quick
Curl - $160.00.

Mother Goose: 20" - $40.00,
$15.00.

Mrs. Beasley: Talking. 16" -
$50.00, $20.00.

Peachy & Puppets: 1972. 17" -
$20.00, $8.00.

P.J.: 11½" - $50.00 up. **Talking:**
$85.00 up. **Live Action:** 1971. $65.00.
Gold Medal: 1975. $50.00. **Deluxe
Quick Curl:** 1976. $40.00. **Free Mov-
ing:** $45.00.

Randy Reader: 1967. 19" - $45.00,
$18.00.

Real Sister: 14" - $15.00, $8.00.

"Lazer Fire" is a "Brave Starr" character
made by Mattel. Marked "#3470A" on
foot and "1986 Filmation Associates" on
body. $12.00. *Courtesy Don Tvrdik.*

Ricky: 1965. Red hair and freckles. (See photo in Series 9, pg. 262.)
$95.00 up.

Rockflowers: 1970. 6½" - $20.00,
$10.00.

Rose Bud Babies: 6½" - $15.00
up, $10.00.

Saucy: 1972. 16" - $55.00. **Black:**
$75.00.

Scooby Doo: 1964. Vinyl and
cloth girl. 21" - $65.00, $25.00.

Shaun: 1979. 12" - $18.00, $9.00.

Shogun Warrior: 23½". All plastic. Battery operated. Each - $250.00 up.

Shrinking Violet: 1962. Pull string talker, features move. Cloth, yarn hair. (See photo in Series 7, pg. 265.) 15" - $50.00 up, $15.00.

Singing Chatty: 1964. Pull string. 17" - $30.00, $10.00.

Sister Belle: 1961. 17" - $35.00, $15.00.

Skediddles: 1966–on. (See photo in Series 9, pg. 264.) 4" - $40.00 up. **Disney:** $85.00 up. **Cherry Blossom:** 1967. $85.00. **Cartoon:** $60.00.

15" "Sheryl" made of plastic and vinyl with rooted hair, painted features, and pale pink lips. Original but has missing socks. Mint condition - $50.00.

Skipper: 1963. (See photo in Series 9, pg. 263.) $100.00 up. **Growing up:** 1976. $75.00 up. **Living:** $85.00. **Funtime:** 1967. Bend knees. $80.00. **Pose 'N Play:** 1970. $55.00; **Super Teen:** 1979. $35.00. **Western:** 1981. $30.00.

Skooter: 1964. Freckles. (See photo in Series 9, pg. 263.) $90.00 up.

Small Talk: 1967. Pull string. 11" - $20.00, $8.00. **Sister:** 1967. 10" - $20.00, $8.00. **Cinderella:** 1968. $25.00, $10.00.

Small Walk, Sister: 1967. 11½" - $25.00, $10.00.

Stacey: Talking: $165.00. **Twist 'N Turn:** 1968. $80.00.

Steffie: Busy or Talking: 1972. $150.00.

Swingy: 20" - $30.00, $10.00.

Tatters: 10" - $45.00, $20.00.

Teachy Keen: 1966. 17" - $30.00, $15.00.

Teeners: 4" - $40.00, $15.00.

Timey Tell: (Chatty Tell) 1964, watch attached to wrist. 17" - $35.00, $15.00.

Tinkerbelle: 19" - $35.00, $10.00.

Tippy Toes: 1967. 16" - $20.00, $9.00. Tricycle or horse: $20.00, $5.00.

Truly Scrumptious: Original. 11½" - $250.00 up. **Doll only:** $175.00 up. **Talking:** 1968. $200.00.

Tutti: 1965. 6" - $90.00 up. Packaged sets: $125.00 up.

Todd: 1965. 6" - $90.00 up.

Twiggy: 1967. 11½" - $225.00 up.

Upsy-Downsy: 1969. 3" - $25.00, $8.00.

Welcome Back Kotter: 1973. 9" figures - $12.00–20.00.

Zython: 1977. Has glow-in-dark head. Enemy in "Space 1999" series. $55.00, $15.00.

First prices are for mint condition dolls; second prices are for ones that are dirty or not original. For full Mego listing, see *Modern Collector Dolls*, Volume 4, page 172–177.

Action Jackson: 1971–1972. Beard and no beard. 8" - $150.00 up.

Batman: 1974. Action figure. 8" - $20.00, $8.00. Arch enemy set: Four figures in series. 8" - $25.00, $8.00.

Camelot: 1974. Five figures in series. 8" - $55.00, $15.00.

Captain & Tenille: 1977. 12" - $20.00, $9.00.

Cher: 12" - $20.00 up, $6.00. Dressed in Indian outfit: $25.00, $10.00.

CHIPs: Ponch and Jon, 1977. 8" - $15.00, $6.00.

Diana Ross: 12½" - $50.00 up, $20.00.

Dinah Mite: 1973. 7½" - $12.00, $5.00. **Black:** $15.00, $7.00.

Haddie Mod: 1971. Teen type, 11½" - $15.00, $6.00.

Happy Days Set: 1974. **Fonzie:** $15.00, $6.00. **Others:** $10.00, $3.00.

Jaclyn Smith: 1975. 12½" - $20.00, $9.00.

Joe Namath: 1971. 12" - $65.00, $25.00.

KISS: 1978. Four figures in series. 12½" - $50.00, $15.00.

Kojack: 1977–1978. 9" - $20.00, $9.00.

Lainie: 1973. Jointed waist. Battery operated. 19" - $40.00, $15.00.

Laverne & Shirley: 1977. 11½" - $20.00, $9.00. **Lenny & Squiggy:** 12" - $25.00, $10.00.

One Million BC: 1974–1975. Five figures in series. 8" - $15.00, $6.00.

Our Gang Set: 1975. Six figures in series. **Mickey:** 5" - $22.00, $10.00. **Others:** 5" - $12.00, $6.00.

8" *Star Trek* action figures made by Mego in 1975. Klingon "Kang" (Michael Ansara), "Scotty" (James Doohan), and "Dr. Leonard ('Bones') McCoy" (DeForest Kelley). All are marked "1974 Paramount/Pic Corp." on head and "MCMLXXI" on back. Each - $40.00.

Planet of Apes: 1974–1975. Five figures in series. 8" - $15.00, $7.00.

Pirates: 1971. Four figures in series. 8" - $60.00, $25.00.

Robin Hood Set: 1971. Four figures in series) 8" - $60.00, $25.00.

Soldiers: 8" - $25.00 up, $10.00.

Sonny: Smiling in 1977; not smiling in 1976. 12" - $20.00 up, $9.00.

Starsky or Hutch: 1975. 8" - $15.00, $6.00. **Captain or Huggy Bear:** $20.00, $8.00. **Chopper:** $22.00, $10.00.

Star Trek Set: 1974–1975. Six figures in series. (See photo in Series 8, pg. 269.) 8" - $40.00, $20.00.

Star Trek Aliens: 1974–1977. Mugatu, Romulan, Talos, Andorian, Cheron, The Gorn, The Keeper, and Neptunian. 8" - $25.00, $9.00.

Super Women: 1973. Four action figures in series. 8" - $15.00, $6.00.

Suzanne Somers: 1975. 12½" - $25.00, $10.00.

Waltons: 1975. Six figures in series. 8" - $15.00, $6.00.

Wild West Set: 1974. Six figures in series. 8" - $45.00, $15.00.

Wonder Woman: 1975. Lynda Carter. 12½" - $20.00, $9.00.

World's Greatest Super Heros: 1974–1975. Eight figures in series. (See photo in Series 9, pg. 267.) 8" - $20.00, $8.00. **Arch Enemy Set:** Eight figures in series. 8" - $20.00, $8.00.

World's Greatest Super Heros: 1975–1976. Second set with six figures in series.) **Isis:** 1977. 8" - $14.00. **Teen Titans:** 6" "Aqua Lad," "Kid Flash," "Wonder Girl," or "Speedy." Each - $12.00, $6.00.

Wizard of Oz: 1974. **Dorothy:** $25.00, $9.00. **Munchkins:** $15.00, $6.00. **Wizard:** $20.00, $8.00. **Others:** $10.00 - $4.00. **15" size:** Cloth/vinyl. Each: $100.00, $40.00.

12" "Sonny" and "Cher" by Mego. Both are action figures with extra joints. Original. "Sonny" - **$25.00;** "Cher" - **$20.00.** *Courtesy Kathy Tvrdik.*

Mollye Goldman of International Doll Company and Hollywood Cinema Fashions of Philadephia, PA made dolls from cloth, composition, hard plastic, and plastic/vinyl. Only the vinyl dolls will be marked with her name. The rest usually have paper wrist tag. Mollye purchased unmarked dolls from many other firms and dressed them to be sold under her name. She designed clothes for many other makers, including Eegee (Goldberger), Horsman, and Ideal.

First prices are for mint condition dolls; second prices are for crazed, cracked, dirty dolls or ones without original clothes.

Airline Doll: Hard plastic. 14" - $250.00 up, $100.00; 18" - $350.00 up, $125.00; 23" - $385.00 up, $100.00; 28" - $500.00 up, $250.00.

Babies, composition: 15" - $150.00, $65.00; 21" - $225.00, $95.00. **Composition/cloth:** 18" - $85.00, $35.00. **Toddler:** All composition. 15" - $175.00, $65.00; 21" - $250.00, $75.00.

Babies, hard plastic: 14" - $95.00, $65.00; 20" - $165.00, $90.00. **Hard plastic/cloth:** 17" - $95.00, $55.00; 23" - $165.00, $85.00.

Babies, vinyl: 8½" - $15.00, $7.00; 12" - $20.00, $8.00; 15" - $35.00, $12.00.

Cloth, children: 15" - $145.00, $65.00; 18" - $185.00, $75.00; 24" - $225.00, $80.00; 29" - $300.00, $100.00.

Cloth, young ladies: 16" - $195.00, $80.00; 21" - $285.00, $100.00.

Cloth, Internationals: 13" - $85.00, $40.00; 15" - $125.00 up, $50.00; 27" - $275.00 up, $85.00.

Composition, children: 15" - $150.00, $45.00; 18" - $185.00, $75.00.

7½" all hard plastic doll attached to 19" lamp with tin base. Doll is jointed at shoulders only. Dressed and marketed by Mollye International. Original. Made in 1954. (Doll was a "blank" purchased from Dutchess Dolls.) $35.00.

14" all cloth "Mollye International" dolls. Pressed face masks with oil-painted features. Yarn hair. Original. Each - $85.00.

Composition, young ladies: 16" - $365.00, $100.00; 21" - $525.00, $150.00.

Composition: Jeanette McDonald. 27" - $800.00 up, $250.00.

Composition: Thief of Bagdad Dolls: 14" - $300.00, $95.00; 19" - $475.00, $125.00. **Sultan:** 19" - $650.00, $200.00. **Sabu:** 15" - $600.00, $200.00.

Vinyl Children: 8" - $30.00, $10.00; 11" - $50.00, $20.00; 16" - $75.00, $25.00.

Hard Plastic, young ladies: 17" - $285.00 up, $95.00; 20" - $350.00 up, $100.00; 25" - $400.00, $125.00.

Little Women: Vinyl. 9" - $40.00, $15.00.

Lone Ranger or Tonto: Hard plastic/latex. 22" - $200.00, $75.00.

Raggedy Ann or Andy: See that section.

Beloved Belindy: See Raggedy Ann section.

18" "Debutante" made of all hard plastic with sleep eyes and saran wig. Glued-on earrings in center of ear. Strung and unmarked. All original. Dress tagged "Mollye." This is another example of a "blank" doll dressed by Mollye. (Nancy Ann Storybook was another buyer of 17–18" "blank" dolls.) $285.00 up. *Courtesy Kris Lundquist.*

21" beautiful "Monica" doll with painted features. All original with wrist tag. Has flower on top of head. Note human hair that is embedded in composition head. From late 1930s and early 1940s. 11" dolls: Mint - $275.00. Played with - $175.00. 15" dolls: Mint - $485.00. Played with - $385.00. 18" dolls: Mint - $700.00. Played with - $500.00. 21" dolls: Mint - $950.00. Played with - $600.00.

NABER KID

Three things stand out in a Naber Kid – humor, happiness, and a smile of tolerance. Even if that Naber Kid disagrees or looks different than his or her Naber, the smile shows that no intolerant words are spoken.

When you see a *character doll*, and you haven't met the artist, you often wonder what the artist was thinking when creating his/her dolls. As with most artists, character traits of the sculptor are within the finished item. Some doll artists may not realize just how much of themselves or someone close to them appear within their dolls.

For those who have not met Mr. Harold Nabers, he does not look like his Kids. (There was someone else in the wood pile.) But his Kids *do* have his personality and look as if they could have as much fun as he does. Mr. Nabers carves and designs to please himself first and the collector second. He has no real concerns with the secondary market. He has already sold that doll, and like Madame Alexander, he can just shake his head, smile, and be happy for the people that own them.

Naber began carving wooden figures of Eskimos while living and working mainly as a bush pilot for 22 years in Alaska. The early works of this very talented man are highly prized by those who own them. Many of his early carvings were done for his Indian friends and some were sold through stores.

"Jade," "Molli," and "Max" were his first production dolls to be introduced in 1984. As of January 1, 1994, production of Naber Kids ended. Naber will continue to make his Wild Wood Babies and in 1994, he will begin a new chapter in his doll career.

There is a newspaper called *Naber Kids News Report* put out by the company that can be ordered from *Naber Kids News Report* Subscription Service, 8915 S. Suncoast Blvd., Homosassa, FL 32646. Included in the newpaper are dolls for sale or trade, plus new information, list of dealers, and list of places Mr. Naber will be visiting.

17" "Paula" is a delightful little girl that retired 7-25-1993. Her large innocent eyes and her waist length ponytail make her a star. She wears the Pro-Life pacifier symbol made exclusively for Claudia's Collectibles. $275.00.

Retirement dates:

06-21-87:	Molli - $1,000.00 up.
01-16-88:	Jake - $1,300.00 up.
05-04-88:	Max - $1,100.00-1,500.00.
03-04-89:	Ashley - $750.00.
07-15-89:	Milli - $550.00.
09-28-90:	Maurice - $800.00 up.
03-04-90:	Maxine - $385.00 up.
19-28-90:	Sissi - $800.00.
11-30-90:	Frieda - $550.00.
12-17-90:	Walter - $425.00 up.
05-03-91:	Peter - $425.00.
05-03-91:	Pam - $425.00.
07-28-91:	Darina - $485.00.
03-09-92:	Henry * - $450.00 up.
	* as Pirate - $450.00 up.
	* as Diver (yellow) - $600.00 up.
	* as Diver (green) - $500.00 up.

This delightful child is "Eric" with his grin and missing tooth. He wears a tee shirt under his Eskimo outfit. Eric retired 11-13-1993. $250.00.

* as Diver (beige) - $650.00 up.
* as Farmer - $425.00 up.
* as Carpenter - $500.00 up.

04-13-92: Sami - $300.00.
04-13-92: Samantha - $350.00.
04-20-92: Freddi - $385.00.
06-28-92: Amy - $350.00.
12-08-92: Heide ** - $400.00.
    ** Without braces - $625.00 up.
05-27-93: Mishi - $300.00.
05-27-93: Hoey - $300.00.
07-25-93: Paula - $275.00.
11-07-93: Willi - $250.00.
11-13-93: Eric - $250.00.
11-21-93: Denise - $250.00.
03-24-94: Elsi - $250.00.
04-09-94: Benni - $250.00.
04-23-94: Posi - $250.00.

Dates unknown:
    Phil Racer - $500.00.
    Sarah and Benni Indians
    (20 sets made) - $500.00 up.

Early handcarved figures: Marked on head or foot. $900.00 up.

Later 1980s figures: Marked, plus tag. $250.00 up.

Specialty dressed: Alpine, Baker, Cheerleader, Detective, Doctor, Eskimo, Farmer, Gangster, Golfer, Indian, Nurse, Pilot, Waitress. Each - $200.00 up.

17" "Benni" dressed in an authentic chimmey sweep outfit. Includes top hat and ladder. He also wears the Pro-Life symbol for Claudia's Collectibles. Will retire 4-9-1994. $250.00.

17" "Henry Scuba Diver." Only 200 were made. It is such an adorable doll that prices on secondary market are high. Dressed in yellow - $600.00. Dressed in green - $500.00. Dressed in beige - $625.00. *Courtesy Don Meeker.*

The painted bisque Nancy Ann dolls will be marked "Storybook Doll U.S.A." and the hard plastic dolls marked "Storybook Doll U.S.A. Trademark Reg." The only identity as to who the doll represents is a paper tag around the wrist with the doll's name on it. The boxes are marked with the name, but many of these dolls are found in the wrong box. Dolls were made 1937–1948.

First prices are for mint condition dolls; second prices are for played with, dirty dolls.

Bisque: 5" - $50.00–75.00 up, $15.00; 7½–8" - $60.00 up, $15.00.

Jointed hips: 5" - $70.00 up, $18.00; 7½–8" - $75.00 up, $18.00. **Swivel neck:** 5" - $75.00 up, $20.00; 7½–8" - $80.00 up, $20.00. **Swivel neck, jointed hips:** 5" - $75.00, $20.00; 7½–8" - $85.00, $20.00. **Black:** 5" - $145.00 up, $50.00; 7½–8" - $175.00 up, $65.00. **White painted socks:** $160.00 up.

Plastic: 5" - $45.00 up, $10.00; 7½–8" - $50.00 up, $15.00. Black: $65.00, $20.00.

Bisque Bent Leg Baby: (See photo in Series 8, pg. 275.) 3½–4½" - $125.00 up, $35.00.

Plastic Bent Leg Baby: 3½–4½" - $85.00 up, $20.00.

Group of 5" to 7" painted bisque Nancy Ann Storybook dolls that may or may not be in correct boxes. Boxes have pale pink, dark pink, and blue polka dots. Each - $50.00–75.00.
Courtesy Turn of Century Antiques.

Judy Ann: Name incised on back. 5" - $325.00 up, $100.00.

Audrey Ann: Heavy doll with toddler legs. Marked "Nancy Ann Storybook 12." 6" - $1,000.00 up, $300.00.

Lori Ann: All vinyl. (See photo in Series 4, pg. 17.) 7½" - $165.00.

Margie Ann: Bisque. In school dress. 6" - $150.00 up, $45.00.

Debbie: Hard plastic in school dress. Name on wrist tag/box. $145.00 up, $40.00.

Debbie: Hard plastic, vinyl head. $90.00, $30.00.

Debbie: All hard plastic. In dressy Sunday dress. $165.00, $45.00. Same, vinyl head: $100.00, $20.00.

Teen Type (Margie Ann): All vinyl. Marked "Nancy Ann." 10½" - $90.00 up, $20.00.

Muffie: All hard plastic. **Walker:** $175.00 up. **Dress:** 8" - $250.00 up,

8" strung "Muffie" with no eyebrows. Dressed in outfit #704 from 1953. Marked "Storybook Dolls, California." $250.00 up. *Courtesy Nanette Ringer.*

8" "Muffie" as a Girl Scout. All hard plastic walker from 1956. $285.00 up. *Courtesy Maureen Fukushima.*

8" "Muffie" walker with no eyebrows. Dressed in outfit #903. Made in 1954. $250.00 up. *Courtesy Nanette Ringer.*

$85.00. **Ballgown:** $300.00 up, $95.00. **Riding Habit:** $225.00 up, $95.00. **Poodle:** Made by Steiff. (See photo in Series 9, pg. 273.) $80.00. In box - $100.00 up.

Muffie: Hard plastic. Reintroduced doll. 8" - $95.00 up, $25.00.

Nancy Ann Style Show Doll: All hard plastic. All dressed in ballgowns. Unmarked. (See photo in Series 8, pg. 273.) 17–18" - $500.00 up, $200.00.

Strung "Muffie" from the "Muffie Nursery Styles" series. Made in 1953. $300.00 up. *Courtesy Peggy Millhouse.*

NATURAL

18" cloth and vinyl "Baby Jasmine" with painted features. Frowning and wide open/closed mouth. Made by Natural Doll Co., ca. 1958. Most are marked "Natural" on head. Original - $45.00. *Courtesy Kathy Tvrdik.*

14½" plastic/vinyl "Dolly Ann" dolls by Natural Doll Co. Same mold as the "Linda Williams/Angela Cartwright" doll. Green sleep eyes and freckles. Painted smiles with teeth. Curly hair doll is redressed; doll with braids is original. Unmarked but removed "Linda Williams" mark is visible. Each - $30.00. *Courtesy Marie Ernst.*

Left: "Jill" made by Playmates Toys, Inc. from 1989–1991. Made of plastic and vinyl with rooted hair. Multi-jointed body. Record player in body. Mouth and eyes move as doll talks. Right is 2½ year old Bianca Pastermack. Doll - $185.00 up. Child - Not for sale! *Courtesy Theo Lindley.*

PRESS DOLLS

8" "Thailand" is one of the Disney Small World dolls. All vinyl with painted features and yarn hair. Marked "Press Doll/Walt Disney/Prod." $30.00.

Designed by Johnny B. Gruelle in 1915, these dolls are still being made. Early dolls will be marked "Patented Sept. 7, 1915." All cloth, brown yarn hair, tin or wooden button eyes, thin nose, painted lashes far below eyes and no white outline around eyes. Some are jointed by having knees or elbows sewn. Features of early dolls are painted on cloth.

First prices are for mint condition dolls; second prices are for played with, dirty, missing clothes or redressed dolls.

Marked with patent date: 15–16" - $1,700.00 up; 23–24" - $2,300.00 up; 30" - $2,800.00. Worn and dirty: 15–16" - $600.00; 23–24" - $900.00; 30" - $1,000.00.

Applause Dolls: Will have tag sewn in seam. 1981. 12" - $25.00; 17" - $40.00; 25" - $60.00; 36" - $100.00 up.

Averill, Georgene: Mid-1930s. Red yarn hair, painted features. Sewn cloth label in side seam of body. (See photo in Series 9, pg. 275.) 15" - $500.00, $125.00 up; 19" - $750.00; 22" - $900.00. **Asleep/Awake:** 13–14" - $450.00 up. Worn and dirty: $175.00

up. **1940s:** 18" - $350.00. **1950s:** 18" - $350.00. **1960–1963:** 15" - $95.00; 18" - $145.00.

Beloved Belindy: Black doll. **Knickerbocker:** 1965. (See photo in Series 7, pg. 276.) 15" - $600.00 up, $300.00. **Volland Co.:** Smile mouth, two rows of teeth, button eyes. Red/white legs, red feet. (See photo in Series 8, pg. 278.) 13" - $2,000.00, $600.00; 15" - $2,400.00, 800.00. **Averill:** (See photo in Series 8, pg. 276; Series 9, pg. 277.) 15" - $1,500.00 up.

Hasbro: 1983 to date. Under Playskool label. Still available.

Knickerbocker Toy Co.: 1963–1982. Printed features, red yarn hair. Will have tag sewn to seam. **1960s:** 12" - $145.00; 16" - $200.00; 23–24" - $300.00; 30–36" - $400.00–500.00. **1970s:** 12" - $45.00; 16" - $60.00; 23–24" - $100.00; 30–36" - $195.00–250.00. **1980s:** 16" - $25.00; 23–25" - $60.00; 30–36" - $85.00–125.00. **Talking:** 1974. 12" - $45.00. 1960s - $265.00.

Mollye Dolls: Red yarn hair and printed features. Heavy outlined nose. Lower lashes closer to eyes. Most will have multicolored socks and blue

13" "Asleep & Awake" Raggedy Ann made in the 1930s by Georgene Novelty Co. Original. $450.00 up. *Courtesy Ellen Dodge.*

15" "Huggable Nursery Pet" made by American Toy & Novelty Co. Oil cloth head with painted features. $165.00. *Courtesy Ellen Dodge.*

50" tall "Raggedy Ann" holds a pair of 16" Georgene Novelty Co. dolls. All are original. 50" - $545.00 up. 16" - $465.00 each. *Courtesy Greta Williams.*

19" "Raggedy Ann" and "Raggedy Andy" made by Georgene Novelty Co. in the 1930s. Really cute set. Both are original. Each - $350.00. *Courtesy Ellen Dodge.*

shoes. Will be marked in printed writing on front of torso "Raggedy Ann and Andy Doll/Manufactured by Mollye Doll Outfitters." First company to imprint solid red heart on chest. (See photo in Series 8, pg. 278; Series 9, pg. 275.) 15" - $900.00 up, $200.00; 22" - $1,100.00 up, $300.00.

Nasco/Hobbs-Merrill: 1973. Plastic/vinyl with rooted yarn hair. 24" - $165.00, $60.00.

Vinyl Dolls: 8½" - $12.00, $3.00; 12" - $18.00, $6.00; 16" - $22.00, $8.00; 20" - $28.00, $10.00.

Volland Co.: 1920–1934. Lashes low on cheeks. Feet turn outward. Can have brown yarn hair. Some have oversized hands with free-standing thumbs. Long thin nose, lines low under eyes. Different mouth appearances are:

(See photo in Series 8, pg. 277–278; Series 9, pg. 276.) 15" - $1,700.00 up; 18" - $1,850.00 up; 22" - $2,000.00 up; 24" - $2,300.00 up; 29" - $2,800.00 up.

Uncle Clem: Has center face seam, prominent nose. Red yarn hair and mustache. Red/white stripe socks and black shoes. Scots costume. 16–17" - $1,500.00.

18" "Raggedy Ann" pull string talker. Made by Knickerbocker in 1963. Original. "Raggedy Ann" book from 1961. Doll - $300.00; book - $75.00. *Courtesy Ellen Dodge.*

14" musical "Raggedy Andy" plays a lullaby. Key wound. Made by Knickerbocker in 1960. Original. Shown with hard to find "Raggedy Ann" book. Doll - $265.00; book - $90.00. *Courtesy Ellen Dodge.*

Three old Volland "Raggedy Ann" and "Raggedy Andy" dolls. The dolls (on left and in center) are 16" tall. "Andy" on right is 19" tall. "Ann" has unusual brown yarn hair. 16" - $1,700.00 up each; 19" - $1,900.00 up. *Courtesy Ellen Dodge.*

First prices are for mint condition dolls; second prices are for played with, dirty or not original dolls.

Addams Family: 5½" - $15.00, $8.00.

Baby Crawlalong: 1967. 20" - $20.00, $10.00.

Baby Grow A Tooth: 1969. 14" - $20.00, $10.00. **Black:** $30.00, $12.00.

Baby Know It All: 1969. 17" - $20.00, $10.00.

Baby Laugh A Lot: 1970. (See photo in Series 7, pg. 277.) 16" - $20.00, $7.00. **Black:** $30.00, $15.00.

Baby Sad or Glad: 1966. 14" - $25.00, $15.00.

Baby Stroll-A-Long: 1966. 15" - $20.00, $10.00.

Dave Clark 5: 1964. 4½" - $50.00, $20.00.

Heidi: 1965. (See photo in Series 9, pg. 279.) 5½" - $9.00, $3.00. **Herby:** 4½" - $12.00, $5.00. **Spunky:** Has glasses. 5½" - $14.00, $5.00. **Jan:** Oriental. 5½" - $14.00, $5.00.

Winking Heidi: 1968. $10.00, $4.00.

14" **"Baby Stroll Along"** is a battery-operated walker. Molded-on hat. Original. Marked **"Remco 1965." $20.00.** *Courtesy Kathy Tvrdik.*

Jeannie, I Dream Of: 6" - $20.00, $5.00.

Jumpsy: 1970. (See photo in Series 7, pg. 277.) 14" - $20.00, $8.00. **Black:** $22.00, $10.00.

Laura Partridge: 1973. 19" - $55.00, $25.00.

Lindalee: 1970. Cloth/vinyl. 10" - $20.00, $9.00.

L.B.J.: 1964. Portrait. 5½" - $30.00, $10.00.

Littlechap Family: 1963. Set of four. $300.00, $75.00. **Dr. John:** 14½" - $65.00, $20.00. **Lisa:** 13½" - $50.00, $15.00. **Libby:** 10½" - $45.00, $15.00. **Judy:** 12" - $45.00, $15.00.

4" **"Bottle Baby"** made by Remco in 1967. This one is #3272 and called **"Grandma." $16.00.** *Courtesy Kathy Tvrdik.*

Mimi: 1972–1973. Battery operated singer. (See photo in Series 9, pg. 279.) 19" - $45.00, $20.00. **Black:** $60.00, $20.00.

Orphan Annie: 1967. Plastic/vinyl. 15" - $30.00, $10.00.

Sweet April: 1971. All vinyl baby. 5½" - $10.00, $3.00. **Black:** 5½" - $15.00, $3.00.

Tippy Tumbles: 1966. 16" - $20.00, $8.00.

Tumbling Tomboy: 1969. 16" - $15.00, $8.00.

The 8" "Sandra Sue" doll has a slim body and limbs. She is a walker, but the head does not turn as she walks. The doll and her clothes are of excellent quality and she was first made in the late 1940s and into the 1950s. A large wardrobe of clothing was available for the doll along with accessories and scaled furniture of the finest quality. She is unmarked except for a number under an arm or leg.

Prices are for excellent condition dolls.

Nude: $95.00 up.

School/Street Dress: $150.00 up.

Dress, Coat & Hat: $165.00 up.

Ballgown: $200.00 up.

Sports Clothes: Cheerleader, baseball, etc. $185.00 up.

Beautiful group of all original "Sandra Sue" dolls. Many outfits were available for the doll. Each - $150.00–200.00. *Courtesy Peggy Millhouse.*

13" "Little Sweetheart of Alabama" made by Royal for Dolly Dears Shop in 1983. Limited edition of 250. Wears heart-shaped necklace with outline of Alabama and state flower. $200.00.

13" all vinyl Royal doll with sleep eyes and rooted hair. All original. Made exclusively for Dolly Dears Doll Shop of Birmingham, Alabama, in 1984. $325.00.

"Lonely Liza" with large painted eyes. Cloth body, vinyl hands. Wire posable arms and legs. Original outfit. $48.00. *Courtesy Gloria Anderson.*

Sasha dolls were manufactured by Trenton Toys, Ltd., Reddish, Stockport, England from 1965 to 1986, when they went out of business. The original designer of these dolls was Sasha Morgenthaler of Switzerland. The dolls are made of all rigid vinyl with painted features. The only marks will be a wrist tag. All dolls are 16" tall.

Boy or Girl in box: $225.00
Boy or Girl in cylinder: $350.00
Boy: "Gregor" - $200.00.
Girl: $200.00.
Black Boy: "Caleb" - $300.00.
Black Baby: $275.00
Cora: #119 (Black) - $300.00; #111 (White) - $250.00.

White Baby: $185.00
Sexed Baby: Pre-1979. $285.00
Early Dolls: Tube/sack packaging. Girl or boy. $350.00 each.
Limited Edition Dolls: Limited to 5,000. Incised #763. Dressed in navy velvet. **1981:** $300.00. **1982:** Pintucks dress. $350.00. **1983:** Kiltie Plaid. $375.00. **1985:** "Prince Gregor." $400.00. **1986:** "Princess." $1,800.00. **1986:** Dressed in sari from India. $1,400.00 up.
Pre-1965: Originals. **White:** 16–18" - $1,600.00 up. **Black:** $3,200.00 up. **Eskimo:** $4,900.00 up.

Two all original Sasha dolls. The girl is "Winter Sport" #13E, and the boy is "Sandy Hiker" (Gregor) #330E. Each - $300.00. *Courtesy Shirley Bertrand.*

First prices are for mint condition dolls; second prices are for played with, dirty, cracked or crazed or not original dolls. Allow extra for special outfits such as "Little Colonel," "Cowgirl," "Bluebird," etc. (Allow 25% to 50% more for mint in box dolls. Price depends upon clothes.)

All Composition: 11" - $725.00, $450.00. **Cowgirl:** $825.00, $500.00.

13" - $650.00, $400.00.

15–16" - $675.00, $425.00.

17–18" - $725.00, $500.00.

20" - $865.00, $500.00.

22" - $925.00, $550.00.

25" - $1,000.00, $600.00. **Cowgirl:** $1,200.00, $650.00.

27" - $1,000.00, $500.00. **Cowgirl:** $1,350.00, $675.00.

Vinyl of 1950s: Allow more for flirty eyes in 17" and 19" sizes.

12" in box - $200.00. Mint, not in box - $165.00. Played with, dirty - $40.00.

15" in box - $325.00. Mint, not in box - $265.00. Played with, dirty - $85.00.

17" in box - $400.00. Mint, not in box - $325.00. Played with, dirty - $95.00.

19" in box - $450.00. Mint, not in box - $400.00. Played with, dirty - $125.00.

36" in box. (See photo in Series 9, pg. 283.) $1,800.00. Mint, not in box - $1,500.00. Played with, dirty - $800.00.

1972: Reissue from Montgomery Ward. In box - $200.00; Mint, not in box - $165.00; Dirty - $45.00.

18" "Shirley Temple" wearing original American Legion coat and hat. All composition, very rare. With coat/hat - $900.00. Without coat/hat - $725.00. *Courtesy Martha Sweeney.*

17" "Shirley Temple" in original dress. From of 1950s. Marked "Ideal Doll/ ST-17-1." $95.00 up. *Courtesy Karen Geary.*

1973: Has box with many pictures of Shirley on it. Doll in red polka dot dress. 16" in box - $165.00. Mint, no box - $125.00. Played with, dirty - $45.00.

1982–1983: Plastic/vinyl. Made by Ideal. (See photo in Series 9, pg. 284.) 8" - $25.00, 12" - $30.00.

1984: Marked "Dolls, Dreams & Love." Henry Garfinkle Co. 36" - $275.00.

Shirley Display Stand: Mechanical doll. $2,500.00 up. **At organ:** $3,000.00.

"Hawaiian": Marked Shirley Temple, but not meant to be a Shirley Temple. (See photo in Series 6, pg. 291.) 18" - $950.00, $400.00.

Japan: **All bisque:** Painted. With molded hair. 6" - $225.00. **Composition:** 7–8" - $265.00.

German: 1936. All composition, sleep eyes, open mouth smile. Marked "GB42." 16" - $550.00 up.

Mold #480, 510X: Sleep, flirty eyes. Open mouth. 13" - $425.00 up.

Babies: Open mouth with upper and lower teeth. Flirty, sleep eyes. Marked on head. 16" - $900.00, $565.00; 18" - $950.00, $650.00; 22" - $1,300.00, $650.00; 25" - $1,500.00, $800.00; 27" - $1,800.00, $900.00.

Look-Alike Dolls: Composition, with dimples. 16" - $200.00; 20" - $350.00; 27" - $600.00. **Vinyl:** 36" - $800.00.

Shirley Temple Accessories:

Script Name Pin: $20.00–35.00.

Pin Button: Old 1930s doll pin. $90.00. Others - $15.00.

Boxed outfits: 1950s: $40.00 up. 1970s: $30.00 up.

Tagged 1930s dress: $145.00 up.

Purse with name: $15.00–25.00.

Buggy: Made of wood. (See photo in Series 7, pg. 283.) 20" - $550.00; 26" - $400.00 up; 32" - $450.00 up; 34" - $500.00 up. Wicker: 26" - $500.00 up.

Large 27" "Shirley Baby" with molded, painted hair. Open smile mouth with cheek dimples. Cloth body with composition head, shoulder plate, and limbs. All original. She also has baby bonnet. Mint - $1,800.00; played with - $900.00. *Courtesy Martha Sweeney.*

36" "Shirley Temple" made by "Dolls, Dreams & Love," a company owned and operated by Henry Garfinkle. Vinyl and plastic with rooted hair and sleep eyes. Uses the 1960 36" "Shirley" body. Vinyl is rather orange and high colored. Marked "1984/Mrs. Shirley Temple Black/Dolls, Dreams & Love" on head. $275.00. *Courtesy Helen Weeks.*

Trunk: $145.00 up. **Gift set:** Doll and clothes. **1950s:** $450.00 up. **1930s:** $175.00.

Statuette: Chalk in dancing dress. 7–8" - $265.00; 4½" - $185.00.

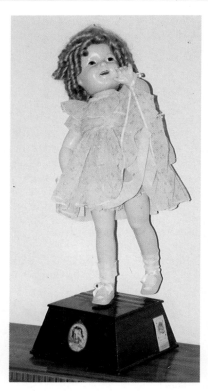

Large Shirley Temple in wooden case that had 10¢ slot on side (been replaced with on/off switch.) Legs, arms, and head move. At right is doll removed from case. She is standing on small mechanical works. **$2,500.00 up.** *Courtesy Roger Jones and Lorraine.*

TERRI LEE

First prices are for mint condition dolls, which could be higher due to the outfit on the doll. Second prices are for soiled, poor wig or not original.

Terri Lee: Composition: $350.00, $100.00. **Hard plastic:** Marked "Pat. Pend." $325.00 up, $100.00. **Majorette, Cowgirl, etc:** $500.00 up. **In original box:** $500.00 up. **Others:** $285.00 up, $100.00. **Vinyl:** $200.00, $75.00. **Talking:** $500.00, $185.00. Mint in box: $500.00 up.

Jerri Lee: Hard plastic. Caracul wig. 16" - $300.00, $185.00. Mint in box: $500.00 up.

Tiny Terri Lee: 10" - $165.00, $80.00.

Tiny Jerri Lee: 10" - $185.00, $80.00.

Patti Jo: Black doll. (See photo in Series 8, pg. 285.) $550.00 up, $250.00.

Benjamin: Black doll. (See photo in Series 8, pg. 285.) $600.00, $250.00.

Connie Lynn: 19" - $400.00 up, $150.00.

Gene Autry: 16" - $1,800.00 up, $700.00.

Linda Baby: (Linda Lee) 10–12" - $200.00 up, $95.00.

So Sleepy: 9½" - $300.00 up, $100.00.

Clothes: Ballgown: $100.00 up. **Riding Habit:** $100.00 up. **Skater:** $100.00 up. **School Dresses:** $50.00 up. **Coats:** $35.00 up. **Brownie Uniform:** $40.00 up.

Clothes for Jerri Lee: Two-piece pants suit: $100.00 up. **Short pants suits:** $100.00 up. **Western shirt/jeans:** $70.00 up.

Mary Jane: Plastic walker. Teri Lee look-alike with long molded eyelids. (See photo in Series 9, pg. 285.) 16" - $285.00 up.

"Jerri Lee" and "Terri Lee" are both in mint condition and all original. He has a caracul wig. She has her original box. "Jerri Lee" - $450.00 up. "Terri Lee" - $500.00 up. *Courtesy Susan Girardot.*

Front row: All original "Terri Lee" and "Jerri Lee" dolls. Also shown is original "Terri Lee" monkey, "Zip." Back row: "Sweet Sue" by American Character, "Honey" by Effanbee, "Toni" by Ideal, "Sweet Sue" by American Character, and "Jeannie Walker" by Madame Alexander. All dolls are hard plastic except "Jeannie" which is made of composition. All dolls mint and original. "Terri Lee" - $285.00–350.00. "Jerri Lee" - $350.00. "Honey" - $350.00 up. "Toni" - $325.00 up. "Sweet Sue" - $325.00 up. "Jeannie Walker" - $600.00 up. *Courtesy Patricia Wood.*

TERRI LEE

Auburn haired "Terri Lee" in shadow print organdy dress. All original. Has her original box. $500.00 up. *Courtesy Susan Girardot.*

16½" "Mary Jane" walker with flirty, sleep eyes and long molded lashes. All hard plastic. Head turns as she walks. $285.00 up. *Courtesy Margaret Biggers.*

TOMY

11" "Dream Dancers." Ballerina has large lavender eyes and serious facial expression. Non-removable ballet slippers. Skater has blue eyes and smile. Wearing non-removable skates. Battery operated. Their arms and legs move as they twirl on platform stage. Both dolls came in box marked "Tomy 1984." Dolls marked on lower back "Tomy/China." In box - $65.00. Doll alone, each - $15.00.

17" "Kimberly" as "Little Bo Peep." Full closed mouth. Wears beautiful pink gown. Holds staff and fleece/wool lamb. $75.00. (Black - $90.00.)

17" "Kimberly Ballerina" in blue tutu. Full closed mouth. Also came in pink and yellow. $50.00. (Black - $60.00.)

17" smiling version of "Kimberly." Plastic and vinyl with painted eyes. All original. Marked "Tomy" on small of back. $45.00 up.

TROLLS

Trolls: 2½–3" - $15.00 up; 5" - $20.00–25.00; 7" - $30.00–40.00; 10" - $50.00; 12" - $60.00; 15" - $80.00 up.

Troll animals: Cow - $65.00; Donkey - $80.00; Ape - $80.00; Turtle - $55.00; Giraffe - $70.00.

4" **"Clown Troll"** with inset eyes. All original. Marked **"Dam"** on back. **$25.00.**
Courtesy Gloria Anderson.

UNEEDA

First prices are for mint condition dolls; second prices are for soiled, dirty or not original dolls.

Baby Dollikins: 1958. 21" - $35.00, $18.00.

Baby Trix: 1964. 16" - $25.00, $10.00.

Ballerina: Vinyl. 14" - $20.00, $7.00.

Blabby: 1962. $28.00, $12.00.

Bare Bottom Baby: (See photo in Series 7, pg. 289.) 12" - $20.00, $12.00.

Bob: 1963. 10½" - $20.00, $10.00.

Coquette: 1963. 16" - $25.00, $10.00.

Dollikins: 1957. 8" - $30.00, $8.00; 11" - $35.00, $10.00; 19" - $60.00, $20.00.

Fairy Princess: 32" - $90.00, $40.00.

Freckles: 1960. 32" - $90.00, $45.00.

Freckles Marionette: 30" - $65.00, $30.00.

Grannykins: 1974. Painted-on half-glasses. 6" - $10.00, $4.00.

Lucky Lindy: (Charles Lindbergh) Composition. 14" - $400.00, $235.00.

Magic Meg: 1971. Grow hair. 16" - $20.00, $9.00.

Pollyanna: 1960. 10½" - $30.00, $9.00; 17" - $45.00, $15.00; 31" - $100.00, $50.00.

Pri-Thilla: 1958. 12" - $18.00, $8.00.

Purty: 1961. Press stomach to make eyes squint. (See photo in Series 7, pg. 289.) 15" - $25.00, $15.00.

Rita Hayworth: 1948. Composition. 14" - $400.00, $185.00.

Serenade: 1962. Battery-operated singer. 21" - $50.00, $15.00.

Suzette: 1959–1960, 1962. 10½" - $50.00, $25.00; 11½" - $50.00, $25.00. Sleep eyes: 11½" - $75.00, $40.00.

Tiny Teens: 1957. 5" - $12.00.

8" "Rosanna" of the "Little Sophisticate" set. There are six dolls in set. Eyes painted closed. Long rooted lashes. Marked "Uneeda Doll Co/1967/Made in Japan." Each - $15.00. *Courtesy Kathy Tvrdik.*

11" "Elf" made by Uneeda. Foam body and gauntlet vinyl hands. Molded hair and painted features. Very posable. Marked "Uneeda Doll Co./11." $25.00. *Courtesy Kathy Tvrdik.*

19" "Baby Glee" with cloth body and vinyl limbs. Sleep eyes and lashes. Open/closed mouth and dimples. Painted hair. From 1978. Marked "28/82079/Uneeda Doll Co." $55.00. *Courtesy Kathy Tvrdik.*

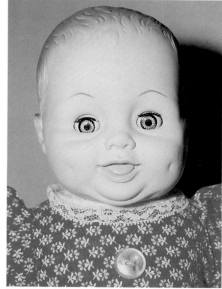

VIRGA

Virga Dolls were made 1949–1952. On left is "Old Woman Who Lives In A Shoe" and on right is "Simple Simon." Both have painted features and mohair wigs. Jointed at shoulders only. All hard plastic and original. Note wide stare eyes and formation of hands. In box, each - $60.00. Doll only, each - $35.00. *Courtesy Sharon Hamilton.*

VOGUE DOLLS, INC.

The last year Ginny dolls were made in America was 1969. Tonka purchased the Vogue name in 1973 and continued to make dolls. The dolls and clothes did not sell well though, due greatly to inferior designs and materials and poor manufacturing. In 1977, Tonka sold the Vogue rights to Lesney of England which made a tall slender Sasson Ginny for three years. During the first two production years, the Sasson Ginny had sleep eyes. The last issue had painted eyes. Although the Sasson Ginny did not look like the earlier Ginny versions, she was dressed and made better.

In 1983, Lesney sold its rights to the Meritus Corporation. With much work, Walter Reiling, owner of Meritus, made a public impact once more with Ginny. In 1986, Dakin purchased the Vogue rights and are the current manufacturer of Ginnys. Dolls manufactured now closely resemble the original 1950s rigid vinyl dolls. One person responsible for the "Ginny Renewal" through her wonderful clothes designs and calendars is Sue Nettlingham Roberts.

First prices are for mint condition dolls; second prices are for played with, dirty, crazed, messed up wig or not original.

Baby Dear: 1960–1961. 12" - $60.00, $20.00; 17" - $95.00, $40.00. 1964: 12" - $50.00, $20.00. **Newborn:** 1960. Sleep eyes. $75.00.

Baby Dear One: 25" - $165.00, $85.00.

Baby Dear Two: 27" - $165.00, $85.00.

Baby Wide Eyes: 1976. Very large brown sleep eyes. All vinyl. 16" - $40.00, $12.00.

Brickette: 1960. 22" - $65.00, $25.00. **Reissued:** 1979–1980. 18" - $40.00.

Ginny: 1948–1949. Composition "Toddles." $450.00 up, $90.00.

Ginny: 1950–1953. 8" hard plastic, strung, painted eyes. $450.00 up, $100.00.

Ginny: 8" hard plastic, sleep eyes, painted lashes and strung. $400.00 up, $100.00.

Ginny: Caracul (lamb's wool) wig. Child, not baby. $400.00 up, $200.00.

Ginny: 1954. Painted lashes, sleep eyes, hard plastic walker. $300.00 up, $100.00.

Ginny: 1954–1957. Hard plastic molded lash walker. $300.00 up, $100.00.

Ginny: 1957–1962. Hard plastic, jointed knee, molded lash walker. $175.00 up, $70.00.

Ginny Hawaiian: 8" brown/black doll. $725.00 up, $365.00.

Ginny Queen: $1,600.00 up, $600.00.

Ginny Crib Crowd: Bent leg baby with caracul (lamb's wool) wig. $650.00 up, $300.00.

Crib Crowd Easter Bunny: $1,400.00 up, $600.00.

Ginny: 1977. All vinyl Internationals. $50.00 up. Other: $35.00 up.

Ginny Exclusives: 1986–1991.

Shirley's Doll House: Ginny Goes Country (1985) - $90.00. Ginny Goes To Country Fair (1986) - $90.00; Black Ginny in swimsuit (1987) - $95.00; Santa/Mrs. Claus (1988) - $80.00; Babysitter: $65.00; Sunday Best (1989). Black boy or girl - $60.00.

Gigi and Sherry: Gigi's Favorite - $80.00. Fairy Godmother (1986) -

16" "Ginny Baby" that is a toddler made of vinyl and plastic. Original, 1960s. Marked "Ginny Baby/Vogue Doll, Inc." **$40.00.** *Courtesy Kathy Tvrdik.*

$165.00. Cinderella and Prince Charming (1987) - $175.00. Clown (1988) - $80.00. Cowgirl (1989) - $80.00. Storytime Ginny (1992), limited - $100.00. Sweet Violet Ginny (1993), limited - $150.00.

Little Friends: Alaska (1991) - $60.00.

Toy Village: Lansing, Michigan. Ashley Rose - $60.00.

Enchanted Doll House: Enchanted Ginny (1988) - $135.00.

Beautiful face of 8" Ginny from 1953. This one is "Angela" of Debutante Series. Made of all hard plastic. $450.00. *Courtesy Peggy Millhouse.*

Different versions of "Jill" doll. Left to right: 1957 - #7406 (replaced shoes), 1958 - #3313 (replaced shoes), 1957 - #7409, 1957 - #7414, 1957 - #7417 (missing satin stole and necklace), 1957 - #7402 (replaced shoes). Each - $175.00–300.00. *Courtesy Peggy Millhouse.*

Modern Doll Conventions: Rose Queen (1986) - $250.00. Ginny At Seashore (1987) - $85.00. Ginny's Claim (1988) - $80.00. Ginny in Nashville (1989) - $125.00. Ginny in Orlando (1990) - $80.00.

U.F.D.C.: Miss Unity (1987) - $175.00. Luncheon Ginny (1988) - $145.00.

Vogue Review Luncheon: 1989 - $150.00. 1990 - $85.00. 1991 - $70.00.

Vogue Doll Club: Member Special, 1990 - $95.00.

Ginny Accessories: Ginny Gym: $275.00 up. **Ginny Pup:** Steiff. $165.00 up. **Luggage Set:** $100.00 up. **Shoes/ Shoe Bag:** $35.00 up. **Furniture:** Chair, bed, dresser, wardrobe, rocking chair. $60.00 each. **Name Pin:** $55.00.

15" "Miss Ginny" with sleep eyes and rooted hair. Made of plastic and vinyl. Original. Head marked "Vogue Dolls/ 1974." Dress tagged "Vogue Dolls/Made in U.S.A." Box marked "Vogue Dolls, Inc. Sub. of Lesney Products Corp. 1977." **$60.00 up.** *Courtesy Marie Ernst.*

Left: "Jeff" wearing extremely rare "Phantom Skater" outfit. (Mask missing.) Doll made of plastic and vinyl. Right: "Jill" is ready for skating, too. She is all hard plastic with jointed knees. "Jeff" in skater outfit - **$200.00 up; "Jeff" alone - $85.00 up; "Jill" - $165.00 up.** *Courtesy Sandy Johnson Barts.*

Book: *Ginny's First Secret* - $135.00. **Parasol:** $15.00. **School Bag:** $70.00.

Hug A Bye Baby: 1975. 16" - $30.00, $15.00. **Black:** $35.00, $15.00.

Jan: 1957. 12" - $135.00, $50.00.

Jeff: 1957. 10" - $85.00 up, $35.00.

Jill: 1957. 10" - $165.00, $55.00. In box/ballgown: $300.00 up.

Lil Imp: 11" - $45.00, $20.00.

Love Me Linda: 15" - $35.00, $10.00.

Miss Ginny: 1967–1970s. Young lady type. 11–12" - $30.00, $15.00; 15" - $60.00, $25.00.

Star Bright: 1966. 18" - $125.00, $40.00. **Baby:** 18" - $75.00, $25.00.

Welcome Home or Welcome Home Baby Turns Two: 20–24" - $90.00, $45.00.

Wee Imp: 8", red wig. $500.00 up, $100.00.

The dolls designed and made by the Robin Woods Company over the years have been some of the finest quality dolls available in their price range. These dolls stand out in a crowd because Robin Woods used imagination and creative talent that bears her signature. The dolls are beginning to show up on the secondary market and more will appear as time goes on. The last "pure" Robin Woods doll appeared on the market during 1991. In 1992, Robin Woods became the creative designer for the Alexander Doll Company and will be designing dolls under the name of "Alice Darling."

The following are a few of the dolls that can be found on the secondary market.

1987: Cathryn: 15" - $425.00 up. **Christmas Dolls:** 14", each - $325.00.

1988: Merry Carol: 14" - $300.00 up. **Scarlett Christmas:** 14" - $250.00 up.

1989: Hope: $265.00. **Lorna Doone:** $225.00. **Heidi:** $225.00. **William Noel:** $185.00. **Elizabeth St. John:** $200.00. **Dickens' Boy:** $200.00 up. **Mary of Secret Garden:** 14" - $225.00 up.

1990: "Camelot Series." Kyliegh Christmas: $225.00; **Melanie Phebe:** $200.00; **Tess Circus:** $200.00; **Bobbi:** $225.00; **Marjorie:** $195.00; **Meaghan:** $275.00; **Tess of the D'urbervilles:** $275.00.

15" "Chrissie" was made for 30 doll dealers, Christmas 1988. Holds basket with gift and toy angel. Has painted features. $800.00 up. *Courtesy Shirley Bertrand.*

1991: Laurel, Lily, Bouquet, Rosemary, Rose, Violet: 14". Each - $200.00. **Delores:** $225.00. **Victoria:** $185.00. **Miss Muffet:** $160.00. **Sleeping Beauty:** Set - $385.00. **Pumpkin Eaters:** 8" - $1,100.00. **Eliza Doolittle:** $200.00. **Mistress Mary:** 8" - $125.00. **Bette Jack:** $300.00. **Alena:** $275.00. **Tennison:** $300.00.

Robin Woods Limited Editions:
Merri: 1991 Doll Convention, Disney World. Limited edition. 14" - $450.00 up.

Mindy: Made for Disney's "Robin Woods Day." Limited to 300. 14" - $300.00 up.

Rainey: 1991 Robin Woods Club doll. Limited to 300. 14" - $250.00 up.

Angelina: 1990 Christmas angel for J.C. Penney's. Limited edition. 14" - $550.00.

14" "Peter Pan" from 1990. Has green painted eyes. All original. $325.00.
Courtesy Shirley Bertrand.

14" "Samatha" from the Poetry of Childhood collection. All vinyl and beautifully designed clothes. $285.00 up. *Courtesy Robin Woods 1991 catalog.*

Noelle: Limited edition Christmas angel for J.C. Penney's 14" - $250.00 up.

Julianna: Little girl shopping for holidays. 1991 J.C. Penney's limited edition. 14" - $300.00.

Robin Woods Specials:
Gina, The Earthquake Doll: For Ann's of Burlingame, CA. $650.00.

Camelot Castle Collection: 1989 – 1990: 14" dolls. Each - $250.00. **1991:** 8" dolls. Each - $100.00 – 130.00.

Christmas Tree Doll: Doll becomes the tree. For Disney. $675.00.

14" "Dimitri Gypsy" with pointed face and painted features. All original, 1991. $225.00. *Courtesy Shirley Bertrand.*

Colorful 14" "Miri Gypsy" with painted features. All original, 1991. $225.00. *Courtesy Shirley Bertrand.*

INDEX

INDEX

T

NUMBERS

LETTERS AND SYMBOLS

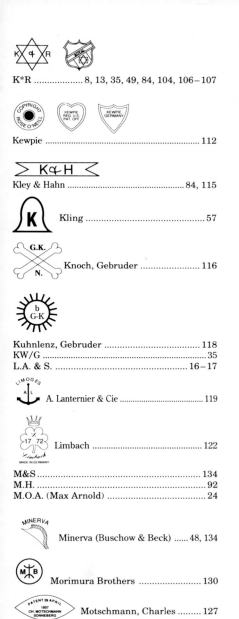

Schroeder's
ANTIQUES
Price Guide
... is the #1 best-selling antiques & collectibles value guide on the market today, and here's why . . .

Schroeder's
ANTIQUES
Price Guide

OUR
1
BEST
SELLER!

Identification & Values Of Over 50,000 Antiques & Collectibles

8½ X 11 • 608 Pgs. • PB • $12.95

• *More than 300 advisors, well-known dealers, and top-notch collectors work together with our editors to bring you accurate information regarding pricing and identification.*

• *More than 45,000 items in almost 500 categories are listed along with hundreds of sharp original photos that illustrate not only the rare and unusual, but the common, popular collectibles as well.*

• *Each large close-up shot shows important details clearly. Every subject is represented with histories and background information, a feature not found in any of our competitors' publications.*

• *Our editors keep abreast of newly-developing trends, often adding several new categories a year as the need arises.*

If it merits the interest of today's collector, you'll find it in *Schroeder's*. And you can feel confident that the information we publish is up to date and accurate. Our advisors thoroughly check each category to spot inconsistencies, listings that may not be entirely reflective of market dealings, and lines too vague to be of merit. Only the best of the lot remains for publication.

Without doubt, you'll find
**SCHROEDER'S ANTIQUES
PRICE GUIDE**
the only one to buy for
reliable information and values.

COLLECTOR BOOKS
A Division of Schroeder Publishing Co., Inc.